Entangled Narratives

Explorations in Narrative Psychology

Mark Freeman
Series Editor

Books in the Series

Speaking of Violence
Sara Cobb

Narrative Imagination and Everyday Life
Molly Andrews

Narratives of Positive Aging: Seaside Stories
Amia Lieblich

Beyond the Archive: Memory, Narrative, and the Autobiographical Process
Jens Brockmeier

The Narrative Complexity of Ordinary Life: Tales from the Coffee Shop
William L. Randall

Rethinking Thought: Inside the Minds of Creative Scientists and Artists
Laura Otis

Life and Narrative: The Risks and Responsibilities of Storying Experience
Edited by Brian Schiff, A. Elizabeth McKim, and Sylvie Patron

Not in My Family: German Memory and Responsibility After the Holocaust
Roger Frie

A New Narrative for Psychology
Brian Schiff

Decolonizing Psychology: Globalization, Social Justice,
and Indian Youth Identities
Sunil Bhatia

Entangled Narratives: Collaborative Storytelling and
the Re-Imagining of Dementia
Lars-Christer Hydén

ENTANGLED NARRATIVES
Collaborative Storytelling and the Re-Imagining of Dementia

Lars-Christer Hydén

OXFORD
UNIVERSITY PRESS

OXFORD
UNIVERSITY PRESS

Oxford University Press is a department of the University of Oxford. It furthers the University's objective of excellence in research, scholarship, and education by publishing worldwide. Oxford is a registered trade mark of Oxford University Press in the UK and certain other countries.

Published in the United States of America by Oxford University Press
198 Madison Avenue, New York, NY 10016, United States of America.

Library of Congress Cataloging-in-Publication Data
Names: Hydén, Lars-Christer, 1954– author.
Title: Entangled narratives : collaborative storytelling and the re-imagining of dementia / Lars-Christer Hydén.
Description: New York, NY : Oxford University Press, [2018] |
Series: Explorations in narrative psychology | Includes bibliographical references.
Identifiers: LCCN 2017020879 | ISBN 9780199391578 (hardback : alk. paper)
Subjects: LCSH: Dementia. | Discourse analysis, Narrative.
Classification: LCC RC521 .H93 2018 | DDC 616.8/31—dc23
LC record available at https://lccn.loc.gov/2017020879

9 8 7 6 5 4 3 2 1

Printed by Sheridan Books, Inc., United States of America

CONTENTS

Acknowledgments   *vii*

1. Personhood Regained   *1*
2. Dementia, Selves, and Stories   *29*
3. Dementia: Living with a Changing Brain   *53*
4. Stories: Making Worlds and Selves   *87*
5. Collaborative Compensation: Scaffolding   *115*
6. Embodied Memories   *143*
7. Selves and Interdependent Identities   *171*
8. Listening with a Third Ear   *195*

References   *207*
Index   *221*

ACKNOWLEDGMENTS

Not only humans have biographies, as we all know. Books also have biographies, and their own life stories. The book *Entangled Narratives* is the result of almost 15 years of attempts to understand stories told by persons with dementia. I became interested in storytelling and narratives in the early 1990s as a result of my interest in how people use language in social interaction. Like many other researchers, I quickly discovered that all conversation and small talk was full of stories—no matter who told the stories, or where they were told. I was incredibly lucky to get an opportunity to learn about storytelling and narratives from two masters, Professor Elliot Mishler and Professor Catherine Riessman. Their comments and discussion are still, many years later, part of my internal conversations—and will continue to be so.

Being a psychologist, I was also interested in the connections between stories, identity, and sense of self. The general idea from the 1990s onward was that there is a strong connection between narrative and identity. For me the obvious question then became: If persons cannot tell stories, do they lack an identity? Having worked with people with dementia as a student and young psychologist, I remembered all the stories and fragmented stories I had listened to during the days and nights at the big mental hospital's geriatric wards, where I worked in the 1970s. Even as a young person, I was intrigued by the fragmented and entangled stories I heard, and some 30 years later I decided to return to these stories.

In the late 1990s I applied for and received a grant for exploring storytelling and identity among persons with dementia from the Swedish Council for Social Research. This work resulted in a number of publications together with my (then) doctoral student Linda Örulv, now an Assistant Professor and colleague. We mainly studied storytelling at a nursing home for persons with dementia. This theme was further pursued when we received another grant—also from the Swedish Council for Social

Research—to look at storytelling involving couples with dementia in home environments. Together with another doctoral student, Eleonor Antelius, now Assistant Professor, who did research on storytelling among younger persons with acquired brain injuries, the inquiry became wider and also included other diagnostic groups.

In 2010, together with a number of colleagues, I was fortunate to be awarded a major program grant from the Swedish Riksbankens Jubileumsfond. Together we created The Center for Dementia Research (CEDER) and embarked on a joint mission to study and understand how people lived with dementia. One of the topics we pursued was storytelling in couples with dementia. We also decided to compare this with storytelling among couples with aphasia—a theme I have pursued together with Professor Christina Samuelsson.

During the years, as I have pursued this theme, I have been able to present findings and papers at a number of universities and conferences. Many thanks to Professor John Keady and his colleagues for inviting me to Manchester University, United Kingdom, and to Professor Renata Kokanovic for inviting me to Monash University, Melbourne, Australia. Thanks also to Professor Andrew Balfour at Tavistock Clinic in London for inviting me to a wonderfully stimulating seminar, and to Professors Molly Andrews and Corinne Squire for inviting me to take part in their important narrative seminars at East London University over the years. In the very cold winter of 2014, I was invited by Professor Maria Medved to the Department of Psychology, University of Manitoba, Canada. I then went west to the Centre for Research on Personhood in Dementia at the University of British Columbia in Vancouver—many thanks to Professors Deborah O'Connor, Jeff Small, Alison Phinney, Habib Chaudhury, and Barbara Purves. Over the years I have made many presentations at Professor Srikant Sarangi's COMET conferences; many thanks for these stimulating discussions, always leading to new insights.

For the past 15 years or so, Professor Jens Brockmeier has visited Linköping University regularly. Numerous are the walks and talks we have had. He has not only influenced my thinking about narrative, but has also got me listening to Hans Werner Henze's music. It was through Jens that I met Professor Maria Medved, who shared her neuropsychological experience, ideas, and research.

For the past six years, I have had the privilege of working together with gifted, spirited, and lively colleagues at CEDER. Every Tuesday afternoon at one o'clock we have gathered for our weekly two-hour seminar, come rain or shine. The discussions at the seminar, as well as after the seminars, have given birth to so many ideas and articles, collaborations, insights, and revisions, that I sometimes have had problems keeping up. Many thanks to all of you, as you have influenced my writing and thinking in fundamental ways: Linda Örulv, Eleonor Antelius, Charlotta Plejert, Christina Samuelsson, Anna Ekström, Ali Rheza Majlesi, Ingrid Hellström, Lisa Käll, Ann-Charlotte Nedlund, Agneta Kullberg, Marie Jansson, Parvin Pooremamali, and the late Jan Anward. Then there are all the doctoral students: Johannes Österholm, Jonas Nordh, Mahin Kiwi, Elzana Odzakovic, and Therese Bielsten. The first year, Professor Per Linell and Professor Lennart Nordenfeldt both shared their wisdom with the seminar.

A deeply felt thanks to Riksbankens Jubileumsfond, whose grant gave me and my colleagues the possibility to embark on an extremely fruitful research endeavor.

Some chapters contain material that has been published in journals over the years. And some of these articles were written together with colleagues, in particular Linda Örulv, Eleonor Antelius, Charlotta Pleijert, and Christina Samuelsson.

Many thanks to my language editor, Margot Lundquist, who has turned my Swenglish into a more readable English. Unfortunately she did not live to see this book in print.

Finally, many thanks to my wife Margareta. Most—if not all—of this book's life stories have been told, retold, and commented upon during dinners and walks with you. Without your listening and comments it would have been an entirely different book—if indeed it had been written at all.

ENTANGLE /ɪnˈtaŋg(ə)l,, ɛn-/

▶ *verb* [with *obj.*] cause to become twisted together with or caught in: *fish attempt to swim through the mesh and become entangled.*

■ involve (someone) in difficulties or complicated circumstances from which it is difficult to escape: *they were suspicious of becoming entangled in a civil war.*

Oxford Dictionary of English (third edition)

Full Definition of ENTANGLE
transitive verb
1
a: to wrap or twist together: interweave
b: ensnare
2
a: to involve in a perplexing or troublesome situation <became *entangled* in a lawsuit>
b: to make complicated <the story is *entangled* with legends>
Merriam-Webster

Entangled Narratives

CHAPTER 1
Personhood Regained

My husband has ceased beginning discussions with the words, "Do you remember . . . ," and now talks to me about the experience we had shared as though advising me for the first time. Indeed, sometimes his reminiscences were lost from my memory. Other times, however, his words would spark a memory still alive and retrievable within my brain, giving me a chance to expand, "Yes, and that was also when. . . . " It was a kind way of determining whether I had recall of that particular occurrence, without humiliation. Asking if I could remember a particular event was demeaning, regardless of whether I could remember it or not. I felt much more comfortable when he simply recounted an event, as it left the door open for me to either listen to this "new" old memory or to join in his remembrance.[1]

At the age of 45, Diana Friel McGowin started to have memory problems. Later, she was diagnosed with Alzheimer's disease. In her book *Living in the Labyrinth*, she writes about her struggle with her memory problems and how she found new ways of living with her disease. In the preceding quotation, it is obvious that dementia "is an illness that reveals the impossibility of telling one's story alone," as dementia researcher Alison Phinney writes.[2] Losing memories makes it difficult to tell stories and engage in reminiscing with others. Diana Friel McGowin's husband, like many relatives, tried to invent ways to be supportive—sometimes successful, other times less so.

The quotation from McGowin's book is a reminder that storytelling is an important activity in most human contexts; by telling stories, shared experiences are brought forward and become a topic to jointly think about, evaluate, and set up as a mirror to gauge the current relation. These jointly remembered events and stories are part of the couple's shared identity, their sense of belonging together in a "we."

Losing shared memories means that the couples' and families' shared world and identities will begin to change. A loss due to an illness is always painful. It means a change of selves that no one asked for. Bodily change forces itself not only on the person with the disease, but also on spouses, family, friends, and work colleagues. Most persons at first attempt to "counteract" and resist these changes by continuing life as it was. The spouse without dementia often tries to help the person with dementia to "remember"—as Diana Friel McGowin's husband did. Over time, many couples will find new ways to live *with* dementia—rather than counteracting it. To most persons, this implies finding new ways of reminiscing together by retelling old stories and inventing new ones. Storytelling and reminiscing become possible if the healthy family members—as McGowin's husband did—"[leave] the door open for me to either listen to this 'new' old memory or to join in his remembrance."

The effects of the dementia challenge many everyday chores and activities for individuals and family members. But the ability to remember and to tell stories—about the distant past, the recent past, and the immediate future—is one of the most difficult challenges. Storytelling goes to the heart of individuals', couples' and families' lives, to their identities and their senses of self and family. This is one of the main reasons that this book focuses on storytelling and dementia. It is a book about people with dementia telling stories—together with their spouses, with other persons with dementia, and with other caregivers. It is about what happens with identities and selves when the ability to tell stories and to listen to stories becomes challenged by dementia. It is also about the—often very creative—ways in which persons with dementia, along their spouses and their caregivers, continue to tell stories and remain participants in storytelling. It is a book less about loss, and more about possibilities and the often ingenious approaches to storytelling that are found when listening—and looking—carefully at persons with dementia and their significant others engaging in storytelling.

This chapter introduces the basic question examined by this book: Do persons with dementia still have identities, and can they tell autobiographical stories even though their memories are challenged? First, this question will be expanded and explained in terms of the relation between stories, identity, and dementia.

STORIES, IDENTITY, AND DEMENTIA

There are countless forms of narrative in the world. First of all, there is a prodigious variety of genres, each of which branches out into a variety of media, as if all substances could be relied upon to accommodate man's stories. [. . .] Moreover, in this infinite variety of forms, it is present at all times, in all places, in all societies; indeed narrative starts with the very history of mankind; there is not, there has never been anywhere, any people without narrative; all classes, all human groups, have their stories, and very often those stories are enjoyed by men of different and even opposite cultural backgrounds: narrative remains largely unconcerned with good or bad literature. Like life itself, it is there, international, transhistorical, transcultural.[3]

The French literary scholar and critic Roland Barthes gives narrative a universal human value, as stories are ubiquitous to human life. Everyone tells stories everywhere, and they have always done so. As stories have always been around, they have evolved into a number of different forms, expressed in various media. Where there are humans there are stories, Roland Barthes seems to be saying. A similar idea is reflected in the suggestion by literary scholar Barbara Hardy when she writes that

> narrative, like lyric or dance, is not to be regarded as an aesthetic invention used by artists to control, manipulate, or order experience, but as a primary act of mind transferred to art from life. [. . .] For we dream in narrative, daydream in narrative, remember, anticipate, hope, despair, believe, doubt, plan, revise, criticize, construct, gossip, learn, hate, and love by narrative.[4]

Stories are present everywhere, and one reason for this, Barbara Hardy suggests, is that stories are the basic form for human experiences, from dreams to love. In her view, narrative is a natural form for human expression and thus is primordial. Humans later learn to transform these narratives into various forms of art, from novels to movies.

Implicit in both Barthes's and Hardy's arguments is also the observation that stories are one of the most powerful instruments that exist for *communicating* and *sharing* human experiences and knowledge. Stories are a special way of letting others "see" and experience the world through the "eyes" of other persons. Stories are therefore important tools for an invitation to share something "seen" by an individual—thus establishing, confirming, and negotiating common experiences.

It comes as no surprise, then, that many researchers have suggested that the study of stories and storytelling can be of interest in understanding both human lives and individual persons. Beginning in the 1980s, the interest in narratives and the study of narratives has spread from the human and social sciences into the medical and other fields.[5] A number of researchers have suggested that collecting and listening to stories could bring new knowledge into the fields of aging studies and dementia studies.[6]

Collecting and analyzing stories and storytelling episodes that involve persons with dementia are considered to be a way to understand and describe experiences, and above all to contextualize these experiences politically and culturally. Stories and storytelling are also conceived as tools in care contexts by using what has been called "life story work."[7]

A growing number of researchers have argued that both identity and self are narrative: a person's identity develops and changes through a constant narrative elaboration and revision.[8] The stories that form and define identities also function as guidelines for action and, as psychologist Jerome Bruner writes, "in the end, we become the autobiographical narratives by which we 'tell about' our lives."[9] The process of growing old tends to be connected to a *rewriting*[10] or a *restorying*[11] of the life story. This implies going back over old memories and stories, identifying elements that have been lost and forgotten, or that never received attention, and re-evaluating these. As a result, it is assumed that the individual's life story will include new elements and connections, but also more coherence, "depth," and wisdom.[12]

Dementia conditions like Alzheimer's disease, as well as many other brain disorders, challenge the deep connection between human identity and stories. The reason for this is that brain disorders like dementia change not only the story, but also the storyteller. When pathological processes affect the brain, the kind of stories persons tell generally tend to deviate from most of the implicit cultural narrative norms and expectations. The stories told by persons with acquired brain injuries or dementia are often characterized, at best, as *broken stories*. The stories are perceived to be broken and fail because in contrast to other stories they are fragmented, partial, jumbled, and repetitive; they lack temporal and thematic coherence, and shift between characters, places, and times without any notice. At other times, these broken stories are full of unspoken memories that are never translated into audible words.[13] The stories, the storyteller, and the listeners become *entangled* in broken stories; beginnings and endings are twisted together, interwoven with repetitions of the same event, resulting in shared states of narrative perplexity. Ultimately, the person with dementia will lose the ability to tell stories in conversational interaction, no longer giving voice to or authoring those stories in which he or she features as a main character, and thus it is left to others to continue the telling.

A reason for the broken and entangled stories told by persons with dementia, many psychological researchers argue, is the fact that persons with dementia progressively lose most of their memories as a consequence of the neurodegenerative processes at the center of dementia. In particular, memories of events in the past and in the present will be lost, or at least will be difficult, if not impossible, to "retrieve." Many psychological researchers have argued that a substantial part of the lost memories can be defined as autobiographical memories, that is, memories of unique personal events and experiences. A consequence of these losses will be a loss of the persons' life histories.

The loss of autobiographical memories has led many narratively inclined researchers to argue that a person with dementia actually cannot have a self or an identity, as he or she cannot remember and tell autobiographical stories. So, for instance, says psychologist Jerome Bruner in his book *Making Stories*, where he argues that it

> is through narrative that we create and re-create selfhood, that self is a product of our telling and not some essence to be delved for in the recesses of subjectivity. There is now evidence that if we lacked the capacity to make stories about ourselves, there would be no such thing as selfhood.[14]

Bruner is defending a very common idea: *identity* and a sense of *self* are connected with *stories*, which in turn are connected with *memories*—and if persons cannot remember, they cannot tell autobiographical stories, and as a consequence they will lose their identities. This notion has also been very influential among researchers who are interested in dementia, as pointed out by Alison Phinney:

> The ability to narrate is presumed to be contingent on memory, language, and awareness. Therefore, it is little surprise that illness narratives in dementia have been mostly overlooked or discounted, for such stories would indeed be difficult to tell and understand.[15]

The dementias are thus a group of diseases that seem to challenge the connection between memory, narrative, and self, as "memory is essential for at least a sense of self."[16] The question that Alzheimer's disease and other brain disorders raises is whether it is possible for a person to have an identity and a self without being able to remember and tell stories about what he or she has done and experienced in the past. Are people with dementia to be excluded from those humans who "dream in narrative, daydream in narrative, remember, anticipate, hope, despair, believe, doubt, plan, revise, criticize, construct, gossip, learn, hate, and love by narrative"? Are they persons without "such a thing as selfhood"?

The basic premise of this book is that this assumption is very problematic and needs to be qualified. The argument in this book is that storytelling is still a relevant activity for the person with dementia at all the different stages of the disease process for the simple reason that both the person with dementia and other family members have much of their identity invested in everyday stories, and they all continue to tell stories, even when the person with dementia has severe problems with animating the stories. As the dementia progresses, there are changes in patterns of engagement of the person with dementia in the storytelling activity. Typically for storytelling involving persons with dementia, the storyteller as storyteller is affected by the disease. Some persons with dementia can tell autobiographical stories on their own, while others can do it with support, especially from their spouses. Some persons with dementia tell autobiographical stories that leave the listener with a sense of confusion, as their stories can be fragmented and repetitive; others repeat the same story over and over again, or never find the words and abandon the story. In the last stage of the disease process, many persons living with dementia no longer have access to linguistic resources or higher cognitive functions; participation in storytelling at this stage is often reduced to touch, gaze, head direction, while the responsibility for the telling has been taken over by others.

The rest of this chapter presents some of the central arguments around storytelling in dementia and the connection between identity and storytelling, along with some of the central concepts and ideas that will be used in this volume. The first step is to argue that persons with dementia actually are persons and have a voice. The concept of personhood is thus established as fundamental, although it is also pointed out that persons with dementia are bounded as storytellers. Persons have identities, and a central question is how to understand what an identity is. A classical argument is to connect identity with memory, while the argument presented here is that a person's identity is not only based on self-reflection, but also can be based on shared stories told together with other persons, as well as on embodied experiences. Thus, the joint activity of telling stories becomes central to understand how persons with dementia co-construct identities.

PERSONHOOD REGAINED

Doris is 76 years old. She has been living with a dementia diagnosis for many years, but she is still socially active in her local community. In a research interview about her everyday life with dementia, she expressed strong opinions on how other people view her:

> I think there is need to talk about this illness so people know what it
>   is about.

Just because you have this illness it does not mean that you are
   dangerous.
You are not dangerous to your neighbors or others in the community.
I do not walk around hitting others.
It is just that sometimes you do not remember what you talked about.
Or it can be hard to find your way around when you are going
   somewhere.

Doris clearly expresses the problem quite a few persons living with dementia encounter: they are seen as being dangerous or transformed into a different kind of being. In the same vein, to many writers about dementia, identity, and storytelling, the person with dementia is often assumed to be identical with the person in the late stage of the disease process, almost living beyond words. A problem with this idea is that it disregards the fact that most persons with dementia live with their diagnosis for many years, most often at home in the family, and can engage with others and are able to take part in storytelling events. The stereotypical social representations of people with dementia have been challenged by much of the research about people with dementia, dating before the 1990s. Central to this research has been the restoration of people with dementia as persons with identities, feelings, and social relations. This makes it possible to reconceptualize identity, stories, memories, and their relationships as being part of the relations between several persons—storytellers and story listeners—rather than something that is "stored" inside the individual's "skull" and then recalled or retrieved.

In an article published in 1993, researchers Victoria Cotrell and Richard Schultz argued that

> In the majority of research on AD [Alzheimer's disease], the afflicted person is viewed as a disease entity to be studied rather than someone who can directly contribute to our understanding of the illness and its course.[17]

They suggest instead that researchers should involve persons with dementia in their research and above all, talk *with*—rather than *to*—persons with dementia about their illness and its consequences. In the following, five central issues in relation to seeing persons with dementia as *persons* will be discussed.

A first implication of listening to persons with dementia and taking their experiences and stories seriously was expressed by psychologist and dementia researcher Tom Kitwood in his concept of personhood. Kitwood argued that personhood is "a standing or status that is bestowed upon one human being by others in the context of particular social relationships and institutional arrangements."[18] Not engaging with persons with dementia would be to deny their personhood and result in "malignant social psychology," in turn exacerbating the symptoms of dementia.[19]

Second, neither Kitwood nor other researchers and clinicians who have attempted to re-evaluate the status of the person with dementia denied that dementia is a disease that affects the brain of the person with dementia. What they did deny, however, was that the changes in the brain's function could be automatically translated into specific symptoms manifested in the person's action. Rather, they argued, persons with dementia are challenged by the fact that fewer cognitive and semiotic resources are available to them, and thus they must solve everyday tasks, like interacting with other persons, by using their remaining resources. This re-evaluation of the person in the disease implies that dementia is not only a medical and social phenomenon, but also a subjective experience, a specific type of being-in-the world. Rather than focusing exclusively on the persons diagnosed with dementia as isolated patients, as targets of care, it became crucial to see the persons as agents of their own lives, and hence as agents of care, even under what are sometimes extremely difficult conditions.

A third implication of the re-evaluation of persons with dementia is that personhood is not dichotomous; someone either is or is not a person. Philosopher Eric Matthews argues that the personhood concept allows for "levels of individuality";[20] that is, as individuals develop from infancy, they over time develop both specific habits and ways of interacting with other persons, as well as reflections on their own lives. The argument of Jerome Bruner and others against counting individuals with dementia as persons hinges on the concept of defining people through their self-reflection (i.e., autobiographical storytelling). Matthews points out that a person is more than self-reflection; that is, individuals are defined not only by their abilities to tell autobiographical stories. A person is also defined through habits, ways of approaching various everyday situations, even patterns of intonation. It is thus up to others to be able to see and appreciate the various aspects of personhood that a specific individual presents.

The fourth important implication of this approach is that personhood must be seen in relational terms, as Kitwood pointed out; an individual is not a person on his or her own, but only in relation to and with others. A relational view of personhood implies that others can support the personhood of individuals with dementia by supplying some of those cognitive and semiotic resources that the dementia lack. Other persons can even "carry" the personhood of other, as has been suggested by the philosopher Hilde Lindemann.[21]

A fifth implication is that, similarly, personhood is not dichotomous, nor is autobiographical storytelling; that is, people do not either have or not have the ability to tell autobiographical stories. Rather, individuals can construct, tell, and understand stories in many different ways. Some are closer to the taken-for-granted everyday narrative norms, while others are further away. The understanding of entangled stories—that is, stories that involve the teller and listeners in "complicated circumstances"—need cooperation in order to untangle the stories and establish a joint meaning, or some meaning.

In conclusion, given this re-evaluation of the person with dementia, the concept that persons with dementia do not have memories and cannot tell stories, and thereby develop a self and an identity, must be qualified. The argument against persons with dementia being able to tell stories and thus express and negotiate a sense of self and identity seems to be based on older conceptions of dementia and identity, rather than on active listening to and engagement with persons with dementia as storytellers. At the same time, it is also obvious that persons with dementia gradually will change their patterns of participation in storytelling, eventually becoming bodily present but making few, if any, verbal contributions to the story. One way to think about persons with dementia as storytellers would be to conceptualize them as increasingly *bounded* storytellers; that is, storytellers who tell stories using semiotic and cognitive resources that are limited, compared to their possibilities before the onset of the disease.

JOHN LOCKE, IDENTITY, AND DEMENTIA

One central aspect of personhood is identity, that is, how individuals themselves as well as others present who they are in various contexts. As has been suggested in the preceding, many researchers have argued that identity and a sense of self are connected with stories. Stories are in turn connected with memories as people remember events and experiences, turn these into a story, and thus become the person presented in the story. This relationship between identity and story is challenged when dementia severs the links between self, memory, and stories.

The tight connection between the individual and his or her memories in fact goes back to British philosopher John Locke. In his work *Essay on Human Understanding* (1690), he defines personal identity thus:

> to find wherein personal identity consists, we must consider what person stands for;—which, I think, is a thinking intelligent being, that has reason and

reflection, and can consider itself as itself, the same thinking thing, in different times and places; [. . .] it being impossible for anyone to perceive without perceiving that he does perceive. [. . .] in this alone consists personal identity, i.e. the sameness of a rational being: and as far as this consciousness can be extended backwards to any past action or thought, so far reaches the identity of that person; it is the same self now it was then; and it is by the same self with this present one that now reflects on it, that that action was done. [. . .] as far as any intelligent being can repeat the idea of any past action with the same consciousness it had of it at first, and with the same consciousness it has of any present action; so far it is the same personal self.[22]

In this quotation, John Locke connects identity with memories; a person is the same self because he or she can remember his or her past experiences. The modern addition to John Locke's idea is that the remembered past experiences are expressed in a story. Thus these concepts are tightly interconnected and form a triangle (Figure 1.1).

As already pointed out, a consequence of this idea is that if a person cannot tell stories or does not remember, his or her identity will be lost (see Figure 1.1). People with dementia will slowly lose some of the cognitive and linguistic (or wider semiotic) resources needed for storytelling—but does that imply that a person also loses his or her self and identity?

One way to pursue this question would be to explore persons with dementia as storytellers, and in particular to see how storytelling can be used to present and negotiate both identities and a sense of self. This would involve an attempt to challenge the traditional connection between the concepts of story, identity, and memory that tend to exclude persons with dementia or other brain disorders. The way to do this is by questioning the concepts of memory, story, identity, and self, showing how persons with dementia are quite skillful in using their remaining abilities to tell stories, create shared meaning, and thus project themselves both *in* and *through* their stories.

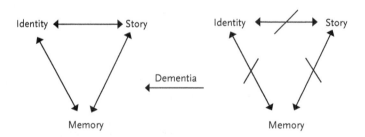

Figure 1.1. The relationship between memory, identity, and story.

In this book a *social and relational approach* to the dementia field, in particular to the field of stories and storytelling, is suggested. It is *social and relational* because it is an approach that stresses the importance of relations and interactions, that is, what takes place between people when they do something together. It is also *psychological* in contrast to being sociological or anthropological, something that would imply much more interest in the societal and cultural context of dementia, and thus have less interest in the individuals and their interaction.[23] This approach is an alternative to the more traditional psychological approach with its focus on the individual, his or her behavior, and "inner" cognitive processes. Much of the psychological research about persons with dementia, and their identities and storytelling abilities, has traditionally been focused on the individual's inner cognitive processes and the consequences of cognitive loss. As a result, not much effort has been spent on understanding how persons with dementia actually engage with other persons in their lives and how doing things together can help persons with dementia to accomplish things they could not do on their own.

This social and relational approach has much in common with Kitwood's emphasis on relations in understanding dementia. In one of his texts about personhood in dementia, Kitwood wrote:

> To see personhood in relational terms is, I suggest, essential if we are to understand dementia. Even when cognitive impairment is very severe, an I-Thou form of meeting and relating is often possible. [. . .] Social life can be considered to consist of a series of episodes, each with certain overriding characteristics (buying a potted plant, sharing a meal, and so on). In each episode the participants make their "definitions of the situation," usually at a level just below conscious awareness, and then bring more or less ready-made action schemata into play. Interaction occurs as each interprets the meaning of the other's actions.[24]

A consequence of this emphasis on relations makes it a necessity to develop a theoretical approach that will allow a description and an understanding of how the "episodes" of social life, the "overriding characteristics" of activities, and the mutual interpretation of actions actually are organized in storytelling activities involving persons with dementia. Steps in this direction have already been taken by a number of researchers on dementia, from sociologist Jaber Gubrium's early groundbreaking work in the 1980s, to Heidi Hamilton's and Vaidehi Ramanathan's studies of dementia, language, and interaction in the 1990s, to the more recent work of Steven Sabat and others, in the field of dementia studies as well as in clinical work with people with dementia.[25] Such a theoretical approach is also important because it would help in understanding broken and entangled stories and in finding meaning, and thus will create possibilities for a shared appreciation of and emotional response to these stories. Finding meaning in stories is one of many ways to sustain personhood—to validate someone as a unique individual with experiences and stories that define him or her.

In order to pursue a new look at the relationship between identity and storytelling in dementia, a number of partially intersecting traditions in psychology, philosophy, and general social science are relevant. Many of these traditions have been interested in understanding how stories are related to both selves and illnesses, as well as how persons engage in joint actions such as storytelling. There are at least three such traditions that could add arguments and concepts to the understanding of storytelling, dementia, and identity. These include theories about narrative and identity, illness narratives, and sociocultural aspects of development.

SELF AND IDENTITY

The concepts of "self" and "identity" have recently become quite popular, especially in the field of dementia studies. As with all concepts that are being used by authors with quite varied academic backgrounds, the concepts of "self" and "identity" are defined and used in different ways. This variety of conceptual definitions and meanings can be challenging and confusing. A number of early narrative researchers like psychoanalyst Roy Schafer and social psychologist Elliot Mishler suggested that the concepts should be treated as members of a large family of concepts that strive to represent various aspects of persons.[26] "Identity" and "self" would thus belong together with concepts like "personality," "ego," and "individuality." They suggested that neither the concept of "self" nor that of "identity" refers to entities found "inside" a person. Rather, both concepts are used as resources for describing and discussing various aspects of persons. Both "identity" and "self" are thus concepts that are central to the "construction" of selves and persons.

The concept of "self" goes back to American philosophers William James and George Herbert Mead and to sociologist Erving Goffman. They all regarded "the self" as including all the properties and aspects of a person that can be noticed, observed, and discussed by all persons who engage with each other. The "self" defined in this way includes bodily as well as behavioral aspects of the person. The common denominator of these aspects is their relevance for the participants in engaging with each other. In his first book, *The Presentation of Self in Everyday Life*, Erving Goffman wrote,

When an individual enters the presence of others, they commonly seek to acquire information about him [*sic*] or to bring into play information about him already possessed. [. . .] Information about the individual helps to define the situation, enabling others to know in advance what he will expect of them and what they may expect of him. Informed in these ways, the others will know how best to act in order to call forth a desired response from him. [. . .] Regardless of the particular objective which the individual has in mind and of his motive for having this objective, it will be in his interests to control the conduct of the others, especially their responsive treatment of him.[27]

What Goffman suggests is that "the self" is important in interactions between people because the situation and the interaction are seen in relation to the participating individuals' selves. What the participants "see"—what Goffman calls "the information"—of each other helps them to understand not only what is happening in the situation, but also how to understand the meaning of an individual's actions and verbal utterances. Diseases in general tend to challenge a person's "self." For the individual, self-presentations often become problematic because the disease may imply a stigma, that is, a risk of being perceived as a "flawed" person by others. This is especially true of Alzheimer's disease, as well as other dementias, as these diseases often seem to imply a challenge of a person's status as a participant in ongoing activities.

Historically the concept of "identity" has often been used to discuss the sameness of a person—that is, a person's continuity in time and space. Since the 1950s, the concept has been used more often to stress cultural and social belonging, membership, or roles.[28] From a social and relational perspective, the concept of "identity" is often used to refer to a person's own presentation of him- or herself as belonging to a certain kind of category, for example, social roles such as being a husband or wife, father, mother, or child, or being a person with dementia, a healthy person, and so on; that is, the identity concept has to do with belonging to various social groups (like a family or a couple) or to some kind of community. Another very important aspect of identity has to do with temporal continuity, that is, being the same person as before. To many persons with dementia, the progressive disease will alter basic aspects of their existence and thus disrupt their sense of continuity and of being the same person as before the onset of the illness.

Both "identities" and "selves" could thus be understood to be what George Herbert Mead called "social objects"; that is, they are the kind of objects that are constructed in the interaction between people and can be used by them in referring to and discussing them. "Identity" and "self" are thus not only theoretical concepts but also "objects" that are of concern in everyday situations and discussions. In most everyday interactions, persons introduce an "identity" or a "self" that is relevant in the specific situation. "Identities" or "selves" are rarely self-evident or given in situations, but a person needs to present what kind of person he or she is at that moment. This is all the more important, as all individuals can be many things at the same time: mother, daughter, grandmother, professor, employee, sick, and so on. Although a person wants to pursue a certain identity, it is important that other participants understand and accept this identity. Thus, "identities" and "selves" are often negotiated. Furthermore, both "identities" and "selves" can be challenged by other persons as well as by life circumstances, as when someone is diagnosed with a progressive brain disease like Alzheimer's.

Identity and Narrative

A number of social scientists and philosophers have argued that identities and selves have a strong connection to stories and storytelling. Many have argued that it is by turning lived experiences into events in a story that both identities and selves emerge. Philosopher Paul Kerby writes, "It is [. . .] the narrated past that best generates our sense of personal identity [. . .] . Narration into some form of story gives both a structure and a degree of understanding to the ongoing content of our lives."[29]

The autobiographical story not only connects events with each other, but also configures these events in relation to a central theme or plot. Through the plot, a direction is introduced, and the life acquires a higher order of meaning, as particular events and happenings become part of a larger movement. When memories become stories, the person can start to "read" these stories and interpret them; that is, he or she can revise the meanings of experiences or even give events in the past a totally new meaning.[30] It is through this "reading" or reflection on the stories told by others, as well as on the person's own memories and stories, that the person can construct a self and an identity. In that sense, identity is not only "a construction, but a reflexive construction," as Jens Brockmeier, psychologist and narrative researcher, points out:

> it means interpreting and reconstructing these [life] events along the lines of genres or other narrative conventions provided by culture. In this view, then, the discourse genre of autobiographical narrative is the central place where personal experiences and their evaluations come to be interwoven with the threads of a life history.[31]

Through this process, the life story becomes enmeshed in cultural concepts about what a person is as well as preferences for certain values; in the modern world, this often means that an individual is exposed to a number of not only different, but also often conflicting, norms and values.

These autobiographical life stories can be used in several ways in order to tell or show something about who the teller is and what kind of person he or she has been, presently is, and intends to be in the future. One obvious possibility inherent in narratives is to connect the past with the present by telling stories about how events in the past have led to the situation at the time of telling the story. The life story can stress the sameness of the person by stressing continuity in life over time, as well as pointing to a fundamental disruption and change in life, through events that have been halting or changing the course of the life process, and thus to tell a story that includes turning points.[32] In focusing on either continuity or change, it is primarily the *discursive organization* of the autobiographical narrative that is in focus, especially the narrative's temporal and *referential* aspects and its *validity*; that is, the focus is on ordering events in a temporally progressing manner that is coherent and that roughly corresponds to the individual's actual life *history* and experiences.

Autobiographical stories are often thought of as individual stories, reflecting the individual's personal experience. But families share stories, and children growing up are enmeshed in these stories, and learn to tell them and use them in order to express their identities and selves. Thus the boundary between individual and family or other groups becomes quite porous.[33] When stories are told in families, or in other groups, the traditional roles of story author and teller are also challenged, as the stories told may be co-constructed and thus have several authors as well as tellers. Furthermore, stories in these contexts are negotiated as the tellers attempt to construct joint meaning.[34] Autobiographical stories are thus often part of storytelling activities involving at least two persons, forming a joint activity.

In fact, identity and self thus do not refer to something that is found "inside" the individual, as for instance some kind of cognitive structure holding knowledge about the self. Rather, identity and self, following the proposed social and relational approach, are to be conceived of as "social objects," that is, various primarily discursive formulations of the person. As social objects, identities and selves can also be presented by a person, as well as be ascribed to a person; in both cases, identity and selves can be negotiated. As a consequence of this approach, it would not be meaningful to say that identities or selves *are* narrative, as this would be to again reduce identity to something outside itself, a story or self-knowledge. The argument is rather that stories can be used by persons in order to construct identities and selves; that is, they can be used as a tool for persons to present and negotiate who they are in specific situations. This argument is in line with Matthew's argument discussed earlier, namely that persons are more than self-reflections. Identities and selves can be expressed in many different ways—as narratives, but also in embodied ways of engaging with the world beyond the use of discursive means.

It is also clear that as the person living with dementia enters the last phase of the disease, his or her use of verbal storytelling will decrease. As Matthews argued, in this situation other kinds of communicative means will be central in providing a sense of identity: embodied patterns of being-in-the-world will be at the center: certain idiosyncratic body or hand movements, a specific gaze, will communicate the sameness of the individual. Further, as the disease progresses, the narrative identity of the person with dementia will increasingly be presented and told by others, and the person with dementia will be present as a character in these other persons' autobiographical stories.

STORIES AND ILLNESS NARRATIVES

The idea of a close connection between narrative and identity is, as already mentioned, challenged by illnesses that disrupt the orderly sequence of events constituting everyday life, and hence also the narrative constructions of this life. Sociologist Gareth Williams writes that

> [t]he routine narrative expressing the concerns of the practical consciousness as it attends to the mundane details of daily life is pitched into disarray: a death in the family, serious illness, an unexpected redundancy and so forth. From such a situation narrative may have to be given some radical surgery and reconstructed so as to account for present disruptions.[35]

Williams, like most other social scientists, argues that identity, self, and narrative are connected through the orderly representations of events. The ideal is to be able to represent events as temporally progressing and to tell a coherent narrative. Illnesses tend to disrupt this smooth flow of events and demand "surgery," so that a new order of events is reconstructed out of the temporary chaos. A new autobiographical story, covering the events resulting in a chronic illness and revising both the past and the future, becomes a necessity.

The fact that any illness constitutes a disruption, a discontinuance of an ongoing life, led many researchers in the late 1980s and early 1990s to examine the concept of narrative. The reason was that stories offer an opportunity to knit together the ends of time split by disease, by constructing a new context and fitting the illness disruption into an ordered temporal framework. Narratives can provide a context that encompasses both the illness event and the surrounding life events, thereby recreating a state of interrelatedness. Depicting illness in the form of narratives is a way of contextualizing illness events and illness symptoms by bringing them together within a biographical context. Further, to narrativize illness enables other people to comment on the narrative and to offer new interpretations and suggestions. Thus, narratives serve as arenas or forums for presenting, discussing, and negotiating illness and how we relate to illness.

One of the first books to discuss such narratives was *Illness Narratives*, written by psychiatrist and medical anthropologist Arthur Kleinman, published in 1988. In this book he gave the narrative concept a broader definition and a clinical foundation. For Kleinman, patients shape and give voice to their suffering in the form of a narrative. To him, the illness narrative depicts events that have been experienced personally and that pose problems for the individual in one way or another; the narrative is at the same time a way of integrating or solving the problems that confront the sick person:

> The illness narrative is a story the patient tells, and significant others retell, to give coherence to the distinctive events and long-term course of suffering [. . .] . The personal narrative does not merely reflect illness experience, but rather it contributes to the experience of symptoms and suffering.[36]

To Kleinman, the illness narrative makes it possible to integrate the symptoms and the consequences of the illness into a new whole. This whole becomes part of a new social reality, a new world of illness.

In a work published in 1995, *The Wounded Storyteller*, sociologist Arthur Frank focuses on stories told by people afflicted with what he terms "deep illness," that is, chronic or life-threatening illness.[37] He suggests that the emerging interest in illness stories has to do with sick persons in late modernity wanting to have their own suffering recognized in its individual particularity. Patients' illness narratives capture the individual's suffering in an everyday context, in contrast to the medical narratives that reflect the needs of the medical professions and institutions. Frank suggests that being ill initiates a journey toward a new identity, and as witnesses to their own transformation, the individuals believe they have learned something valuable that they can bring back and pass along to others, particularly to other sufferers from pain and illness.

In conclusion, it could be suggested that the stories told by persons with dementia are a bit different from many other illness stories. The story is no longer a story *about* illness; it is rather *part* of the illness and disorder. In this way, the relationship between story and illness is no longer external. It is not a person telling *about* an illness, but rather a disorder that interrupts and at least in part reconstitutes both the storyteller and the story. Furthermore, insisting on the idea that narratives must be coherent and organized methodically in order to express a person's identity introduces the risk of excluding certain persons. A case in point is persons with dementia. Their unique voices are often excluded not only from research, but also from both everyday and clinical interactions, because their stories are considered to be incoherent and disorganized.

JOINT ACTIVITY AND THE SOCIOCULTURAL TRADITION

Telling stories in families and telling illness stories are examples of joint activities, of people doing things together. This implies a focus on the joint activity, its organization and performance, rather than on the individuals and their behavior. From a collaborative perspective, individuals and their behavior and acts are seen as part of the joint activity. As a consequence, in these traditions the individual is primarily seen as emerging from joint activities and not as an entity that exists either before or outside joint activities. Individuals bring their abilities and experiences to and into a joint activity, but these are then transformed through the organization of the activity.

The tradition stemming from Russian psychologist Lev Vygotsky, often called the sociocultural tradition, has always argued that the interaction between persons is the basis of the child's (and adult's) cognitive, linguistic, and social development.[38] A similar position has been taken by researchers engaged in evolutionary research, suggesting that not only humans but also primates develop through social interaction with others.[39] In research on language use and the micro-organization of interaction and language use, the interaction between persons, as well as between persons and artifacts, has also been the theoretical foundation.[40]

Taking interaction, cooperation, and joint action as the starting point could most certainly be beneficial for studies of the persons with dementia in interaction with other persons, and especially how they jointly deal with the consequences of cognitive and linguistic loss. This means that it is not the individual with dementia who is the prime focus of studies, but rather the interactions involving persons in the everyday network and the way these persons jointly take on the problems caused by the progressing disease.

This approach has often been used to study developmental processes, but it is suggested in this book that it is also a framework that can be used to study the way persons deal collaboratively with problems and changes caused by a progressive disease like Alzheimer's disease. From a historical perspective, this is what Russian neuropsychologist Aleksander Luria did in his classical studies of brain trauma; more recently, a number of interactionist studies have examined how persons with brain traumas creatively and in collaboration with others sustain their personhoods and identities.[41]

The benefit of this theoretical approach is then that it will allow us to better conceptualize storytelling and stories as part of everyday interaction in everyday contexts, irrespective of whether this everyday context consists of couples living independently or persons with dementia living in some kind of care facility.

There are three key concepts that are especially central. The first is storytelling as a *joint activity* and collaboration—that is, a conception of persons telling stories together, rather than of individuals telling stories on their own. Stressing joint activity implies a move away from psychology's traditional focus on individuals, their behavior, and cognitive abilities. A turn to joint activities means that it is rather individuals in collaboration that are of interest. A reason for focusing on individuals doing things together is, of course, that much of everyday life consists of interaction involving other persons. There is also strong evidence that the human brain in the evolutionary process has developed in order to work together with other "brains," that is, other persons, as well as with both the natural and the manmade environment.[42] In this perspective, the socially decontextualized individual is rather more a special case than the paradigmatic case.

Second is the *organization* of storytelling as a joint activity. Joint activities are achieved through individual contributions to the joint activities. These contributions are *coordinated* so that each new contribution is related to the previous one and aims at bringing the activity ahead. Thus, in most joint activities some kind of division of actions is to be found between the participants. One group of people tells stories together, and each participant is expected to make a new contribution to the story. If one participant echoes what another already has said, this is often an indication of something being very funny or noteworthy. This "micro-expectation" about new contributions in, for instance, conversations can be quite problematic for persons with brain injuries or dementias, as they might have difficulties finding words quickly and thus may just "echo" the previous speaker. And, as always, not living up to social expectations often leads others to search for an explanation, with the risk of withdrawal from interaction.

The interactional division is also reflected in a division of *interactional roles*; when one participant speaks, the other listens, and then they shift roles. Making contributions to a joint activity implies that the participants have some kind of *joint goals* or *intentions*; that is, the participants are engaged in the same activity and are pursuing two parallel but uncoordinated individual projects. Joint goals or intentions are not primarily something internal to the participants, that is, to be found "inside" the head of each participant. Rather, joint goals or intentions are displayed in the activities, in the orientation, and in embodied doings—but often also in comments and sometimes discussion about what to do and how to do it.[43]

In order to fit a new contribution to the ongoing activity, the participants need to *monitor* each other and themselves. If two persons perform a piece of music together, they not only have to play the same music, but must start at the same time, use the same key and rhythm, and so on. They must monitor each other during the performance in order to coordinate their individual performances.

Being part of joint activities is not only about coordination of actions, but also about the participants' *social statuses*, their identities, and senses of themselves. Having difficulties with making contributions—not finding words and thus missing a slot for a new contribution—implies that the social status of the person with dementia is at risk, even more so if the difficulties of finding words and missing slots are repeated and become a pattern. Then the social status of the person with dementia might change from that of being a person at the center of the conversation to a more peripheral position, as other participants start to fill in the missing contributions by taking over the story or not talking about certain topics, as Diana Friel McGowin's husband is reported to have done in the quotation at the beginning of this chapter. This movement from center to periphery often has consequences for identities, as the person with dementia no longer can "be" the person he or she was before the onset of the disease.

Third, taking part in joint activities like storytelling makes it necessary to use a number of different *resources*, cognitive as well as linguistic and pragmatic. In traditional psychological theory, cognitive and linguistic resources are considered to be the property of the individual mind, situated inside the individual's skull. Furthermore, these functions are based on rational rules and calculations. So are abilities like that of telling stories thought to be linked to retrieval of past events stored in the mind; the retrieved events are then fitted into a story grammar and into linguistic structures and finally are told in a process in which phonological rules are applied.[44] What happens with persons with dementia, according to this view, is that cognitive and linguistic functions stop working as the disease progresses, and thus these functions are lost.

An alternative view would be to think of cognitive and linguistic—or better, semiotic—resources as being distributed. Of course the individual has cognitive and semiotic functions, but these are developed to work together with resources external to the individual. Mathematical calculations can be done "in one's head," but most people would use paper and pen or the calculators built into their iPhones; that is, in making mathematical calculations, some of the calculations are taken over by the artifacts (whether paper and pen or calculator), while the person organizes and is in control of the process. When two persons who have known each other for a long time are reminiscing about past events, they can supply each other with names and places that the other has forgotten or cannot remember. Thus, these two individuals function together as a sort of memory system.

Viewing cognitive and semiotic resources as distributed is in line with the idea mentioned earlier, that the human brain has evolved in order to function together with other persons and their brains, as well as with tools (i.e., artifacts).[45] As a consequence, cognitive functions may be viewed as systems involving other persons as well as artifacts, which are coordinated to function together. Furthermore, it supports the concept that the cognitive and semiotic functions are better seen as embodied than as abstract and rational operations.

Thus, people telling stories make up such a system; they can make use of each other's memories and semiotic abilities, and they may also use photographs or videos as external memory and communicative resources. Seeing cognitive and semiotic resources as socially distributed implies that when one person for some reason has difficulties in remembering events, that person can be supported by someone else who is better at remembering. Thus the system of persons and artifacts can compensate for individual difficulties and thereby support persons with dementia in continuing to participate in joint activities.

AN ALTERNATIVE MODEL

It was argued earlier that the theoretical concept of dementia as disrupting the relationship between self, memory, and story might risk ending up in denying persons with dementia the possibility to sustain an identity and sense of self (see Figure 1.1). Alternative conceptions of the relationship

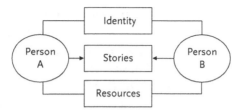

Figure 1.2. New model.

between stories and illness that don't view the storyteller as outside the story were introduced, but rather as part of the storytelling situation. Storytelling was suggested to be seen best as a joint activity engaging several persons who support each other and share cognitive and semiotic resources. Finally, it was suggested that identity is less something that individuals harbor "inside," but is instead a way to create, negotiate, sustain, and change social relations involving other persons.

As a consequence, much more emphasis is put on what goes on between persons and what they can do together, rather than what goes on "inside" individuals. A way to summarize this idea can be found in Figure 1.2.

This model has its emphasis on storytelling as a joint activity resulting in stories that are co-produced rather than the product of an individual and his or her "inner" workings. The model will serve as a tentative start for an inquiry into how persons with dementia actually tell—or could tell—stories together with others as a way to sustain both their identity and sense of self.

INQUIRY-GUIDED APPROACH

The suggested theoretical framework in many ways marks this book as being *inquiry-guided*; it relies on the "dialectical" interplay of questions, theory, methods, and findings, which is a feature that marks its "departure from the dominant model of hypothesis-testing experimentation," as social psychologist Elliot Mishler writes.[46] This book is based on empirical research, and the theoretical framework has informed the collection of various data material, as well as the analysis of these in order to enrich and further develop the theoretical concepts. This also means that a very pragmatic approach toward theories and concepts is favored. Concepts are developed in order to solve analytical problems and help to understand experiences and empirical data.

The inquiry-guided approach also means favoring examples about *possibilities*, such as what persons with dementia actually can do, rather than using examples illustrating the loss of abilities, or for that matter, describing hindrances. This has several consequences. First, the focus in this book is on stories told in conversations involving persons with dementia. Studies about how either relatives or professionals tell stories about persons with dementia are not discussed, as they are stories *about* persons with dementia, rather than stories told by these persons themselves.[47] Nor are autobiographical texts and books about the dementia experience discussed.[48] Written autobiographical texts are often produced as a way for the author, the person with dementia, to both document and comment upon the progression of the disease, as well as to serve as a site for extended biographical self-reflection.[49] As such, they are very valuable, but in relation to this book, these texts are often edited in order to comply with the norms of written stories, and thus reflect a different set of narrative norms and practices from those stories told in conversations.

Second, the book is not so much about the actual stories told by persons with dementia. Rather, the book is about *how* people with dementia together with other persons (with or without dementia) go about telling a story—how they organize their interaction, help each other find words and memories, and use their bodies, their embodied abilities, and their creativity. The reason for this is that the book is about what can be learned from understanding the ways in which people in everyday settings deal with problems that emerge as a consequence of dementias, and how this knowledge may be put to use by relatives as well as by professionals.

Third, this is a book about how persons with dementia are involved, and can become even more actively involved, in their own lives. This means that the book is based on "good examples" in order to explore the possibilities for developing interaction and storytelling involving persons with dementia. "Good examples" are interesting, as they imply that it is possible for people to learn to do what others already can do. Thus, finding "building blocks" that work and that are teachable is important.

Finally, some caveats. First, although the term "dementia" is used in the book without many qualifications, this book is primarily about persons with early to mid-phase Alzheimer's disease. This means that they still live at home (early to early mid-phase dementia) or have moved into residential care (late mid-phase dementia). It also implies that most persons can still use language and engage in storytelling, although they may face many challenges. Storytelling involving persons with dementia in the late stage is outside the scope of this book, not for any reasons of principle, but for more practical ones, as it is a huge endeavor involving new challenges.

Second, this book is based on research on dementia in the Western industrial world. Furthermore, the persons appearing in the book are white and heterosexual, at least as far as indicated in interviews and observations, and have working-class or middle-class backgrounds. This means that vast areas of experiences are not covered in this book, from living with dementia in non-industrial countries to living in "white" countries with a different skin color.

THE STORYTELLERS

In this book, storytelling involving a number of persons with dementia, their spouses, and sometimes professional caregivers makes up the empirical research basis for most of the claims made about dementia, stories, and storytelling. Most voices belong to persons who have been part of the research conducted by the research group around "life with dementia" at Linköping University in Sweden. Some of the persons with dementia are living in residential care homes for persons with dementia; others are living in their homes with their spouses and sometimes other family members. All of these people have let us listen to them, videotape them, and ask questions, often repeatedly over many years. Some are still with us, others have died. Hopefully their voices—although anonymous in the book—can carry forth their creativity and their will to be persons.

THE ORGANIZATION OF THE BOOK

This book is basically an interdisciplinary endeavor striving to combine knowledge and theories from academic areas that usually are kept apart: in this case, knowledge about dementia from academic research as well as from clinical experience, and from narrative research, especially autobiographical stories and storytelling. This means that this book has several audiences. Some of the readers will have a background in nursing, psychology, occupational therapy, physiotherapy, gerontology, dementia studies, or some related areas, that is, readers with a background, knowledge, experience, and interest in dementia, particularly in persons living with dementia. To them, this book hopefully can make a contribution around how to think about people living with dementia in narrative terms. Other readers will mainly come from narrative studies and will be most interested in learning aboutthe use of narrative theory in the medical field, in this case, dementia.

The aim of the book is to make a contribution to the dialogue between these groups of readers so that readers with a background in clinical dementia work can learn more about narrative theory, and readers from the narrative field can learn about how diseases affecting the brain affect the person's narrative possibilities.

An implication for the composition of the book is that in some chapters, issues primarily having to do with how to understand people living with dementia (e.g., Chapters 2, 3, 5, and 7) are foregrounded, while narrative theory is placed in the background; other chapters foreground narrative theory (e.g., Chapters 4 and 6) and put dementia in the background. Although readers could skip certain chapters, I think that in order to engage in a dialogue between different knowledge areas, learning about fields that are seemingly apart often will promote this dialogue.

As argued earlier, there are especially four concepts that are claimed to be in need of reconsideration: dementia, story, memory, and self and identity. These concepts are discussed in the various chapters, without reserving specific chapters for specific concepts. The first chapters in the book (Chapters 2–4) pay more attention to presenting a general context for the interest in dementia and storytelling by providing a historical background as well as an overview of previous research.

Chapter 2, "Dementia, Stories, and Selves," gives some of the historical background to the notion of dementia, with a special emphasis on the work of Alois Alzheimer and the disease named after him. Tracing this disease through the last century, it is argued that the question about personhood is central and thus about issues related to identity and self. The concept of broken narratives is used to introduce an overview of research on illness stories, specifically storytelling in persons with both psychiatric and other neurological diseases and dementia. Concerning the entangled stories told by persons with dementia, it is suggested that meaning-making—in particular joint meaning-making—is a central problem.

Chapter 3, about living with a changing brain, starts with a critical look at the medical conception of dementia. It is argued that the traditional view of brain degeneration resulting in specific symptoms is quite problematic, as it does not account for the ways in which persons with dementia relate to themselves—that is, how they compensate for functional impairments. It is argued that the brain has developed specifically to enhance collaboration and has a functional organization. This organization allows for still-functioning networks in the brain to be used. This approach is also used to argue that storytelling is based on a complex relationship between cognitive and semiotic resources. Dementia is thus introduced as a social and relational, rather than medical, concept.

Chapter 4, "Stories: Making Worlds and Selves," introduces some basic narrative concepts and notions and a discussion about narrative norms. Special emphasis is on autobiographical storytelling in everyday conversational settings. It is argued that much narrative research on autobiographical storytelling is based on textual, narrative norms. These norms often exclude the kind of stories that are told by persons with dementia and ignore the efforts of significant others to support their storytelling. Ideas about how autobiographical storytelling is used in order to present and negotiate selves and identities are discussed with special reference to persons with dementia. In this chapter a more open story concept is introduced that is better suited for understanding storytelling involving persons with dementia.

In Chapter 5, "Collaborative Compensation: Scaffolding," the concepts of collaboration, compensation, and above all, that of scaffolding are introduced. The concept of scaffolding has been used by developmental psychologists and educational researchers in order to show how "experts" support "novices" to perform actions on their own. It is argued that spouses without dementia often—quite successfully—scaffold the spouse with dementia in storytelling situations. It is further argued that scaffolding is actually a practice that involves work by both spouses; they have to collaborate in order to create shared meaning and to sustain their joint activity. A basic argument in this chapter is hence that in order to understand persons with dementia as storytellers, it is important to include the other participants in the storytelling activity and thus see storytelling as a collaborative activity.

Chapter 6 has a focus on embodiment and is an attempt to reconsider the idea of memory and autobiographical memory. The cognitivist model of memory conceptualizing memory in terms of an "archive" of amodal representations is discussed critically.[50] It is shown that memories are often modal, that is, connected to certain perceptual and motor modes (seeing, hearing, moving). By using the approach introduced in Chapter 3, it is argued that these "memories" must be constructed and above all transformed to fit linguistic structures in order to be told. It is also argued in this chapter that most autobiographical stories are told by being based on previous tellings; that is, the important "memories" used are less a set of original experiences, but rather, are composed of prior tellings of the story. Thus the concept of memory is given a slightly different meaning from what is generally the case.

Chapter 7 is about the notion of identity. An old idea in the Western tradition is that an individual's identity is based on remembering experiences and thus on the possession of memories. One aspect of this conception is that it is based on individuals. Most people live with other people or at least engage with other people. People living together tend to identify and recognize things they have done together and often refer to these moments by saying "we did . . . ," "we went. . . . " They establish a joint identity that is dependent on their mutual recognition of this identity. This is what is called "interdependent identity"—a notion that is explored in relation to couples living with dementia.

The final chapter returns to Chapter 1 and the challenge from Jerome Bruner about the possibilities for people with dementia to have an identity and a self. There is also a brief discussion about the possibilities of alternate ways of meaning-making in storytelling activities with people with dementia. Finally, the limits of storytelling are discussed, especially the risks involved in attempts to avoid including the present situation of the person with dementia in conversations and storytelling.

NOTES

1. Diana Friel McGowin, 1994, p. 98.
2. Phinney, 2002, p. 338.
3. Roland Barthes, 1975, pp. 237–272.
4. Barbara Hardy, 1968, p. 5.
5. A good introduction to recent views on narrative and narrative research is found in the book *Doing Narrative Research*, edited by Molly Andrews, Corinne Squire, and Maria Tamboukou (2014).
6. See Phoenix, Smith, & Sparkes, 2010; Randall & McKim, 2008.
7. Keady, Ashcroft-Simpson, Halligan, & Williams, 2007; McKeown, Clark, & Repper, 2006.
8. Brockmeier & Carbaugh, 2001; Brockmeier, 2015; Bruner, 2001; Freeman, 1993.
9. Bruner, 1987, p. 15.
10. Freeman, 1993.
11. Randall & McKim, 2008.
12. Freeman, 2010.
13. For the concept of broken stories, see Hydén & Brockmeier, 2008.
14. Bruner, 2002, pp. 85–86.
15. Phinney, 2002, p. 331.
16. Randall & McKim, 2008, p. 143.
17. Cotrell and Schultz, 1993, p. 205.
18. Kitwood, 1997, p. 7.
19. Kitwood, 1990.
20. Matthews, 2006, p. 173.
21. Lindemann, 2014b.
22. John Locke, *Essay Concerning Human Understanding* (1690), Book II, Chapter 27.
23. Readers interested in an anthropological approach to dementia are referred to Margaret Lock's *The Alzheimer Conundrum* (2013) or Lawrence Cohen's *No Aging in India* (1998); readers with an interest in sociology would find Anthea Innes's *Dementia Studies* (2009) or Ruth Bartlett and Deborah O'Connor's *Broadening the Dementia Debate* (2010) rewarding.

24. Kitwood, 1997, pp. 12, 15.
25. Gubrium, 1986; Ramanthan, 1997, Hamilton, 1994; Sabat, 2001; Keady & Nolan, 1994.
26. See Roy Schafer's *Retelling a Life* (1992) and Elliot Mishler's *Storylines: Crafts Artists' Narratives of Identity* (1999).
27. Goffman, 1959, Introduction.
28. For a history of the identity concept, see Philip Gleason's article "Identifying Identity: A Semantic History" (1983).
29. Paul Kerby, 1991, p. 33.
30. Randall & McKim, 2008; Freeman, 1993, 2010.
31. Brockmeier, 2000, p. 53.
32. McAdams, 2006; McAdams, Josselson, & Lieblich, 2001.
33. Fivush, 2007; Kellas, 2005.
34. Ochs & Capps, 2001.
35. Williams, 1984, p. 178.
36. Kleinman, 1988, p. 49.
37. Frank, 1995/2014.
38. Bruner, 1985; Lave & Wenger, 1991; Rogoff, 1998.
39. Tomasello et al., 2005; Enfield & Levinson, 2006.
40. Clark, 1996; Goffman, 1967; Goodwin, 1981; Hutchins, 1995; Müller & Mok, 2013.
41. In particular, see the seminal work of Charles Goodwin, 2003.
42. Tomasello, 2014.
43. About shared goals and intentions, see the helpful discussion about shared mental states in Susswein and Racine (2008). Also see, Barnier, Sutton, Harris, & Wilson, 2008.
44. For a classical expression of this view, see the article by Kintsch and van Dijk: "Toward a Model of Text Comprehension and Production" (1978).
45. See the works by Michael Tomasello cited earlier.
46. The concept of inquiry-guided research was developed by Elliot Mishler, 1990.
47. Gubrium, 1988; Holst, Edberg, & Hallberg, 1999.
48. See, for instance, the books by DeBaggio, 2003, 2007, and Lee, 2003.
49. Ramanathan, 2009.
50. The archive metaphor has been introduced by Jens Brockmeier, 2010 and 2015.

CHAPTER 2

Dementia, Selves, and Stories

Tuesday, November 26, 1901, Royal Psychiatric Clinic, Munich
(She sits on the bed, wearing a helpless expression.)

ALOIS ALZHEIMER: What is your name?
AUGUSTE DETER: Auguste.
AA: Family name?
AD: Auguste.
AA: What is your husband's name?
AD: I believe Auguste.
AA: Your husband?
AD: Oh, my husband . . .
(She looks as if she didn't understand the question.)
AA: Are you married?
AD: To Auguste.
AA: Mrs. D?
AD: Yes, yes, Auguste D.
AA: How long have you been here?
(She seems to be trying to remember.)
AD: Three weeks.
AA: What do I have in my hand?
AD: A cigar.
AA: Right. And what is this? (I show her a pencil.)
AD: A pencil.
(A purse and key, diary, cigar are identified correctly.)
On Friday of the same week Doctor Alois Alzheimer requests his patient to write
her name. In the medical journal he notes:

> when she has to write Mrs. Auguste D, she writes Mrs. and we must repeat the
> other words because she forgets them. The patient is not able to progress in
> writing and repeats, "I have lost myself."

Later the same Friday Doctor Alois Alzheimer notes in the medical journal:

> The reactions of the pupils to light and accommodation are instantaneous.
> Tongue has normal mobility, dry, yellow-red-brown. No disturbance in speech
> articulation. She frequently interrupts herself in the articulation of words
> during the interview (as if she did not know whether she had said something

correctly or not). She has dentures. No facial nerve differences. Muscular strength: at the left side considerably reduced compared with the right side. Patellar reflex normal. Radial reflex is lightly (but not relevantly) rigid. Cardiac ictus is not felt. Cardiac obtusity not enlarged. The second pulmonary and aortic tones are not accentuated.[1]

All the questions were there—the questions about her name, how long she had been at the clinic. Could she recognize and name a pencil? A cigar? The questions all had a focus on *cognitive* issues: recognizing things, naming things, remembering names and places, and being oriented in time, place, and person. Alois Alzheimer is searching for what Auguste Deter cannot do, her *cognitive loss*. Few, if any, of Alois Alzheimer's questions dealt with emotions or feelings, identity, or sense of self, although Auguste Deter stated that she had lost herself.

Auguste Deter, who at this time was aged 51 and a half years, could in this conversation say her first name but not her last, nor could she say the name of her husband or recognize him as her husband. The medical examination did not find any obvious signs of neurological disease—with the possible exception of decreased muscular strength on her left side.

The doctor interviewing Auguste Deter was Alois Alzheimer, a German medical doctor and researcher who, after Deter's death, would perform an autopsy on her brain and identify something that looked like tangles. He would connect this discovery with his previous clinical observations and publish a small paper in a German medical journal. German psychiatrist Emil Kraepelin read the paper and incorporated Alzheimer's findings in the eighth edition of his extremely influential book *Psychiatry*, and called the "new" disease *Alzheimer's disease*.

At the end of the nineteenth century, the term *dementia* "was used to name any state of psychological dilapidation associated with chronic brain disease. [. . .] When dementia states occurred in the elderly they were called 'senile dementia,'" writes German Berrios, historian of psychiatry.[2] There were at that time no necessary connections between dementia and old age; "senile dementia" was just one of many cases of "dementia"; thus, for instance, the term "dementia praecox" invoked dementia at a young age (what today is called "schizophrenia"). Nor was there any consensus connecting memory problems with "senile dementia," as some physicians argued that it was "confusion" that characterized "senile dementia," rather than specific cognitive impairments. All this was to change, partly as a consequence of Alois Alzheimer's discoveries.

From a historical point of view, Alois Alzheimer was just one among several researchers simultaneously working on the same kind of problem, and thus it was not by chance that Alzheimer was interested in making a connection between the results of his histological analysis of Auguste Deter's brain and his clinical observations. Alzheimer's findings contributed to the fact that the connection between aging and "dementia" began to be established. This, together with an increase in the number of elderly patients at psychiatric hospitals and mental institutions, cemented a clear connection between old age (senility), pathological changes in the brain, and symptoms of cognitive impairment (dementia) during the early twentieth century. This matrix was probably further supported by cultural stereotypes of senility.

This chapter will provide some general background for the social and cultural context of dementia from the early twentieth century into the early twenty-first century. The chapter will present an overview of the discussions about dementia, self, and identity, with a particular emphasis on research on narrative and dementia.

FROM DEMENTIA TO NEUROCOGNITIVE DISORDER

Although the new medical research at first seemed very successful, defining mental diseases including dementia in terms of changes in the brain, in the long run few convincing results were presented. For the next decades, 1930–1950, it was rather psychodynamic theories that became influential, especially in American psychiatry, but also in Europe, while biological theories receded. It was not until the 1960s that medical researchers again started to search for the neurological mechanisms of Alzheimer's disease. In his book *Self, Senility, and Alzheimer's Disease in Modern America*, historian Jesse Ballenger shows how researchers in the early 1960s started to propose that "deterioration and disability in old age were the result not of age but of disease." This idea was supported with the help of "more rigorous correlations of brain pathology and clinical dementia, electron microscopic studies of the senile plaques and neurofibrillary tangles, and the measurements of neurotransmitter levels in the diseased brain."[3]

This idea questioned the previous strong connection between the aging process and the progressive loss of memory and other cognitive and linguistic functions as a "natural" process. Rather, Alzheimer's disease started to be identified as a specific disease, not to be identified with "normal" aging. Thus the connection between "senile" and "dementia" was severed, and "dementia" became a neurological disease.

During this period, the 1960s and onward, not only was the connection between dementia and aging questioned, but the term "dementia" itself became more precisely defined and increasingly referred to a whole group of symptomatically related diseases, including the neurodegenerative diseases (e.g., Alzheimer's disease, frontotemporal dementia), vascular dementia, and dementia as the result of other neurodegenerative diseases (e.g., Parkinson's and Huntington's diseases) or viruses (e.g., Creutzfeldt-Jakob disease). This development continues; in the recent version of the *Diagnostic and Statistical Manual of Mental Disorders* (DSM-5, published in 2013), it is suggested that the term "dementia" should be dropped altogether in favor of the umbrella term *neurocognitive disorders*. It is even argued that "the term *dementia* is retained in DSM-5 for continuity and may be used in settings where physicians and patients are accustomed to this term."

The views in DSM-5 seem to finally disentangle dementia and old age; dementia has become a species of the neurocognitive disorders group.[4] At the same time, a number of researchers have started to show that the generally assumed relationship between old age and declining cognitive powers also does not hold up in the face of modern psychological research; "normal," healthy aging does not automatically imply declining memory or learning abilities. Rather, older people are even better at solving certain problems compared to younger persons, although they generally use other cognitive strategies.[5]

PUBLIC HEALTH ISSUES AND NATIONAL POLICIES

As dementia during the 1960s and 1970s slowly turned into a defined and recognized group of diseases, it also became a public health issue, and governments in the United States and Western Europe started to formulate policies on how to deal with dementia. A number of studies tried to estimate the number of persons with dementia and the expected increase in the number of persons diagnosed with dementia. The World Health Organization (WHO) began to construct and collect statistics worldwide in order to provide a global perspective of the development and expected increase in the number of persons with dementia.

In a WHO report published in 2013, the total number of persons worldwide with dementia was estimated to have been 35.6 million in 2010. With an increase of 7.7 million persons with dementia every year, the number will almost double every 20 years. This will result in a total of approximately 65.7 million persons with dementia worldwide in 2030 and 115.4 million in 2050. The increase is predicted to be much higher in what are called low- and middle-income countries and to be less steep in high-income counties like the United States and the United Kingdom. As a result of this development, 63% of all persons with dementia are expected to live in low- and middle-income countries by 2030, and 70% in 2050.[6]

Most of these estimations are based on today's views on the proportions of persons with dementia in specific age groups. Some concern has started to arise over whether this assumption is correct. For instance, a large Danish study based on two cohorts born 10 years apart found that persons born in 1915 performed significantly better on measures of cognitive functions and daily living as compared to the cohort born in 1905. This indicates that these persons are less likely to develop cognitive impairment and thus dementia until they are significantly older. In a British population-based study, researchers found a decrease in the number of persons with dementia in the population older than 65 years. Over a period of 20 years, the decrease was about 24%. These studies and several other smaller ones indicate that it might not be correct to assume that the percentage of persons with dementia will stay constant over time. Rather, better education, food, and work and living conditions may change patterns of dementia in relation to age and thus flatten the expected steep increase.[7]

In 2010 the global societal costs of dementia were estimated at US\$ 604 billion, corresponding to between 0.6% and 1% of the aggregated worldwide gross domestic product (GDP). Furthermore, the "total cost as a proportion of GDP varied from 0.24% in low-income countries to 1.24% in high-income countries, with the highest proportions in North America (1.30%) and Western Europe (1.29%)."[8] In high-income countries, the medical costs were 15% of the total cost for persons with dementia, while informal care costs were about 45% and formal care costs 40%. In low- and middle-income countries, the cost of informal care is much higher, while the costs for medical and formal care are significantly lower due to less-developed medical and social welfare systems and institutions.

In terms of etiology of dementia, there is strong evidence indicating that genetic factors are associated with risk for Alzheimer's disease. Diseases and conditions like "diabetes, elevated blood cholesterol level in midlife, and depression have been positively associated with increased risk for Alzheimer's disease," as well as dietary and lifestyle factors and medications (for instance, high saturated fat consumption, low fruit and vegetable consumption, not using statins, moderate to high alcohol consumption, low educational levels, low cognitive engagement, low participation in physical activities, current smoking, never having been married, and having low social support are factors that increase the likelihood of dementia).[9]

Thus, although age-related dementia may have a strong connection to hereditary factors, it is obvious that demographic, social, and economic circumstances also play an important role in the actual number of persons diagnosed with dementia, as well in the ways they will be cared for and encountered.

DEMENTIA AND THE SELF

Although Alzheimer's disease today is recognized as a disease by many persons, especially in the Western world, it is at the same time a disease that stirs existential anxiety, not only because it is associated with death, but also because it seems to rob us of something that is very close to our core existence: the self and personal memories, as well as the means of engaging with other people through language. Comments on this theme can be found in Alois Alzheimer's clinical notes. When Auguste Deter had been at the hospital a couple of weeks, Alzheimer one day entered her room and asked if she knew where she was. Deter answered:

I don't know myself.
I don't know at all.
Oh, goodness gracious.
What is it all.[10]

Auguste Deter did not seem to recognize herself; she had become a stranger to herself. Her words, as well as those of others, have often been interpreted as indicating that something has been lost.

The notion of *loss* has been used in quite a number of articles and books about the consequences of dementia. A number of different "things" can be lost following this line of thinking: cognitive and linguistic functions can be lost, including memories and especially autobiographical memories; personalities, selves, and identities also can be lost. All the "things" that are lost are, according to this way of thinking, found "inside" the individual's head. Through the disease process, the "inner" functions are lost, as well as the inner "thing" these authors consider the "self" and "identity" to be. Actually, researchers and clinicians who talk about "loss" are actually using a metaphor; when a person loses a thing, the thing is lost—until it in some cases it is found again; following this metaphor, it is possible to lose "everything," as when a person goes into bankruptcy and loses all money and belongings. When a person with dementia loses both cognitive functions and self, this will result in what has been called an "inner void," that is, an "inner" emptiness, when nothing is left of the previous person.

In a much-discussed article published in 1989, two American sociologists, Andrea Fontana and Ronald Smith, argued that in people with Alzheimer's disease,

> the self has slowly unraveled and "unbecome" a self, but the caregivers take the role of the other and assume that there is a person behind the largely unwitting presentation of self of its victims, albeit in reality there is less and less, until where once there was a unique individual there is but emptiness.[11]

A problem with using this metaphor for dementia is that functions are rarely lost in the sense of "being lost and never found again." The various forms of dementia are often *changing* basic functions in the brain, rather than obliterating these functions; it means that persons with dementia have some aspect of their original functionality, but must learn how to use their changed brains—a theme that will be discussed in the next chapter. A further problem is the idea that the self and the identity are "inner" entities that can be lost. If persons are seen in a relational perspective, then self and identity are to be found instead in relationships between persons.

As already mentioned, Fontana and Smith's article was very much discussed, and in a sense it opened a new discussion; from the 1990s, researchers and philosophers challenged the notion that a person with Alzheimer's disease had lost his or her self. In a sense, *a struggle over the self* began as American anthropologist Elizabeth Herskovits succinctly puts it: "what seems to be at stake on a deeper level in the struggle over the self in Alzheimer's is our very notion of what comprises the 'self' and what constitutes subjective experience."[12]

Since the 1990s, an increasing number of researchers and clinicians have begun to argue that Alzheimer's disease does not rob a person of self and identity, nor does it turn persons into non-persons. This has resulted in debates about various ideas and conceptions of personhood as well as selfhood and the ways diseases like Alzheimer's affect persons and their selves. These discussions involve both theoretical issues, like what a person is, as well as the clinical and practical consequences of viewing people with dementia as persons with selves. The struggle around personhood and selfhood in dementia has to do with the fact that if someone is defined as a person, this has certain moral obligations; persons have certain rights, and others have obligations toward persons.[13]

UK psychologist Tom Kitwood was one of the first to voice a criticism of what he called "the standard paradigm of dementia," namely the idea that dementia could be seen as a direct expression of neuropathic changes in the brain. Kitwood claimed that this "paradigm" faced at least three severe problems. First, there is a weak correlation between "measures of dementia and indices of the extent of neuropathology." Second, it can be observed that persons with dementia deteriorate functionally much faster under certain conditions than the degeneration of the nervous tissue in their brains. Third, under certain conditions there is a virtual arrest of functional deterioration of persons with dementia, even sometimes a partial recovery of certain functions.[14]

To Kitwood these problems indicated both the need for and possibility of a social psychological theory of dementia. He argued that dementia could be seen as caused by five interacting factors: the *personality* of the person, his or her *biography*, the physical *health*, the neurological *impairment*, and finally, the *social psychology*. Of these factors, especially the general physical health and the social psychology were open to positive change. Kitwood was especially interested in the social psychological factors that either contributed to the progression of dementia (what he called "malignant social psychology") or could help slow down or even reverse this process (what he called "a culture of care/dementia"). In other words, Kitwood argued that the process of dementia was *mediated* by social factors, and especially by the way social interaction with persons with dementia was organized.

Central to Kitwood's credo for a new view of dementia and a more humane care was his belief in what he called "the personhood" of persons with dementia. He defined personhood in social psychological terms as "the status bestowed upon one human being, by others, in the context of social relationship and social being. It implies recognition, respect and trust."[15] To him, a person with dementia had to be treated as if he or she were a person, with respect and dignity; otherwise the person with dementia would be turned into an object or "vegetable." Kitwood's concept of personhood quickly became central to many of the philosophical and empirical discussions about dementia.[16]

The strengths of Kitwood's work have to do with his introduction of a relational view of dementia. To him, the central question was not whether the brain changed as a result of a disease or not, but rather how people dealt with this change *relationally*. For Kitwood, relations mainly had to do with how healthy persons—relatives and professional caregivers—treated the person with dementia. If persons with dementia were treated and respected as persons, this would help them stay active as real participants in their own and other's lives. This is of course a very important idea; nevertheless, though it presented a relational perspective, it was still moored to a focus on individuals and what they do *to* each other, rather than what they do *together* and what they *share*. Further, Kitwood did not discuss how the personhood and the self were actually produced in relational interactions. Instead he assumed personhood to result from a positive relational interaction.[17]

How the selves of persons with dementia were produced and affected was the focus of the work of psychologist Steven Sabat and philosopher Rom Harré. Taking a constructionist and discursive perspective, they argued in an article published in 1992 that a person with dementia still had a self, contrary to many of the ideas at the time. One of the central tenets of their article was

> that (1) there is a self, a personal singularity, that remains intact despite the debilitating effects of the disorder, and (2) there are other aspects of the person, the selves that are socially and publicly presented that can be lost, but only indirectly as a result of the disease. In the second case, the loss of self is directly related to nothing more than the ways in which others view and treat the A.D. sufferer.[18]

The idea of a "malignant social psychology" and its consequences for "the social self" was taken over from Kitwood. The idea that people with dementia still had "a self" that was unaffected by the disease was a radical position. They further argued that selfhood is *discursively* produced and presented publicly, expressing the experience of one's personal identity.

Sabat and Harré argued that persons have what they called a "primary self." This self is the individual singularity, a formal, philosophical notion, indicating that persons are able to identify themselves as specific points in time and space. Thus this kind of self is independent of "content," for instance specific memories. It has rather to do with the ability to actually refer to oneself in everyday talk by using pronouns like "I," "me," and "self." The "social self," on the other hand, can be expressed as many different selves or personae. These social selves are all the different selves a person presents in everyday interaction with others, for instance as characters in autobiographical stories. In later writings, Sabat made a further distinction of the social self. Here he argued that there is one social self that consists of all the "mental and physical attributes" and "the beliefs about those attributes" that a person has assembled during a lifetime, as well as another social self, consisting of those aspects that a person displays in public.[19]

In their original 1992 article, Sabat and Harré argued that persons with dementia are able to keep their former selves, and by using a number of examples they were able to show that persons with fairly advanced dementia actually still refer to themselves as an "I." What may happen, though, is that persons with dementia may "lose" their social selves because other people do not support these personae. On the other hand, they also show that the social self can be upheld in many situations with the support of relatives and care providers. They concluded that

> it is clear that the thesis that the self of personal identity remains intact even in the face of quite severe deterioration in other cognitive and motor functions is well supported [. . .] . If there is a loss of self as a result of AD, that loss is not in the management of the organising powers of the indexical creation of self, until the time when virtually no behaviour of any consequence occurs. [. . .] It is also clear that the repertoire of selves, the personae that are socially and publicly presented and which require the cooperation of others in the social sphere in order to come into being, can indeed be manifested even in the later stages of the disease.[20]

One problem with their argumentation is that they are still focusing on individuals with dementia and the properties of these individuals in terms of having a self (or identity) or not. Furthermore, they focus on language use, the discursive production of self and identity, while leaving aside other ways of showing or expressing self and identity. A number of researchers coming from a phenomenological background have argued that self (identity and subjectivity) is not something inner that then is expressed openly. Instead of just investigating the use of discursive tools for expressing subjectivity, personhood, identity, and self, they argued that philosopher Maurice Merleau-Ponty's concept of embodiment is important to understanding persons with dementia as a special way of being-in-the-world.

As noted in Chapter 1 of this book, philosopher Eric Matthews has argued that persons are more than can be expressed discursively. He writes that subjectivity exists "in speech, in gesture, in behaviour, in interactions with [. . .] environment, both human and natural."[21] Subjectivity, like identity and self, is embodied, that is, found in all the different ways in which persons engage with the world: how they talk, move around in a room, and their preferences and dislikes.

Also referring to Merleau-Ponty and the embodiment concept, anthropologist Pia Kontos suggested that the notion of "embodied selfhood" can be seen as "a complex interrelationship between primordial and sociocultural characteristics of the body, all of which reside below the threshold of cognition, grounded in the pre-reflective level of experience, existing primarily in corporeal ways."[22] Both Matthews and Kontos argue that the person is a "body-subject," rather than an "inner" cognitive self. To Matthews, this also allows for a dynamic view of selfhood and what he calls "levels of individuality." Although persons with dementia eventually lose some of the individuality they had as "mature" adults, there

> survives something of their adult individuality in habits of behaviour in which it has become "sedimented" in the course of their development to adulthood and beyond. These characteristic gestures and ways of doing things are what keep alive the sense of the individual that once was, even if the more sophisticated levels of that individuality have been removed.[23]

Thus, following the phenomenological approach, a person with dementia is not in a position to either have or not have a self. Persons with dementia instead express their subjectivity in different embodied ways. The ability to use language and to tell stories is thus less important following the phenomenological perspective.

Whether language is important or not for establishing and communicating subjectivity, personhood, self, and identity, has partly to do with the duration of the dementia. Kontos and Matthews both take their examples from persons who have lived a very long time with dementia and thus have severe problems using language. To them, other non-discursive communicative means, such as gestures or various bodily habits, are much more important. Kitwood, Sabat, and Harré all write about persons with dementia in an early stage and thus are much more concerned with spoken language.

Although persons with dementia in later stages are challenged in their use of spoken language, they have not lost their ability to use language; instead, as will be argued later, their abilities to use language are restructured and reorganized. Furthermore, these persons are still part of language-using communities; that is, they engage with people who use spoken language as their main semiotic tool for communication. The personal histories of persons with dementia are still shaped by language use, and they have lived in a world of language users, based on language use. Thus it is important to think about language in relation to persons with dementia, even in late stages of dementia, and even if spoken language is not their primary communicative, semiotic tool at this point in time.

A possible conclusion is that persons with dementia use different communicative tools to establish and negotiate their identities and selves in different contexts. As the disease progresses, the number of communicative resources available for persons with dementia decreases, but the persons with dementia are still meaning-constructing persons, even very late in the dementia process.

As Roland Barthes has argued, stories and storytelling are ubiquitous in all cultures and societies. Barbara Hardy has argued further that narrative is a basic form for all kinds of human expression. Although stories can be told using many different media besides spoken language, from picture and film to ballet and sculpture, most everyday autobiographical stories are told by using spoken language. As already noted, even though the linguistic abilities are challenged for persons with dementia in later stages, they still are part of social worlds where stories and storytelling are important. Persons with dementia have told numerous autobiographical stories during their lives and have figured in at least as many. For them over time, as well as for most people, the stories told about important events become more important than the events themselves. In a sense, it is the stories that define persons. In line with this, many clinical researchers have argued that life stories and life history work are very important for establishing persons with dementia as persons in relation to staff. Learning the stories and autobiographical contexts that are important to people with dementia is a prerequisite for learning to know the person beyond the diagnosis.[24]

A number of researchers writing about self and identity have argued that both self and identity are constituted by and consist of *narratives*. Human lives, argue narrative gerontologists William Randall and Elizabeth McKim, consist of a constant flow of events, and some of these events will be noted by the person and turned into memories, in most cases as stories: "the various events that constitute our lives, or at least those to which we attend, get perceived and evaluated, edited and articulated, and refashioned as memories: that is, as anecdotes, episodes, stories."[25]

It is by turning these lived experiences and memories into events in a story that persons' lives acquire meaning. The story not only connects events with each other, but also configures these events in relation to a plot. Through the plot, a direction is introduced, and the life acquires a higher order of meaning, allowing particular events and happenings to become part of a larger movement. In this way, every individual will be in possession of an ever-expanding number of small stories, corresponding to what we often refer to as memories. Through the development and elaboration of these stories, a life story emerges together with the individual self and identity.[26]

An implicit assumption of much of the theorizing about narratives, selves, and identities is that the storyteller is healthy, or at least can be considered to be cognitively healthy. Randall and McKim argue, for instance, that "memory is essential for at least a sense of self."[27] But memories of events, as well as of stories, can be at peril for some persons. Obviously there are connections between brain functions, traumas, and pathologies, and both the way people tell stories and the stories they tell. This has been suggested by a number of neurologists from Kurt Goldstein and Aleksander Luria to Oliver Sacks.[28] For instance, neurologist Oliver Sacks describes the case of a patient who had developed a Korsakow syndrome as a result of brain injury and thereby lost the ability to formulate narratives. Instead, he was forced to constantly invent new stories in an attempt to create a context for his actions and self.[29] This is an example, not of narrative *about* an illness, but of narrative *as* illness.[30]

Similarly, psychoanalyst Roy Schafer points to the same phenomenon as he defines the central problem of neurotic people to be their struggle to understand their lives through narratives that exclude central events in their lives.[31] They may be events from early childhood (abuse, for example), or an inability to understand actual events and experiences (such as phobias), or an overpowering sense of one's future as being totally bereft of possibilities and choices (as in depressive states). In each case, the person's narratives are inadequate to articulate events and experiences, and it is this lack that is the basis for the suffering. Psychiatrists Robert Shay and Judith Herman advanced similar ideas in their interpretation of psychological trauma, as did Lisa Capps and Elinor Ochs in their analysis of agoraphobia.[32]

More recently, psychologist Paul Lysaker and philosopher John Lysaker have argued that "[s]chizophrenia is often characterized by profound diminishments in the ability to experience and represent one's life as an evolving story." They developed a typology in order to include at least the three most central forms of "narrative impoverishment": the barren, monological, and cacophonous narratives.[33] In *barren narratives* the person with schizophrenia basically keeps to a small number of inflexible self-positions, resulting in almost no story at all. In the second type, *the monological story*, the person uses the same story for all kinds of situations, trying to fit everything into the same patterns and self-positions. Finally, the *cacophonous story* lacks all structure and internal organization with "a dizzying array of self-positions."

Literary theorist Kay Young and neurologist Jeffrey Saver have developed a typology of four different types of "dysnarration" due to neurological problems.[34] Their idea is to identify specific narrative problems and relate these to neurological pathologies. The first type of dysnarration is what they call *arrested narration*, which is an inability to create new narrative due to a general amnesia; after trauma, the person is unable to form new memories or to tell stories about recent events. Persons with lesions on their frontal lobe structures exhibit what Young and Saver call *uncontrolled narration*; that is, they have no ability to self-monitor and as a result tell stories unconstrained by memories of actual events, often thought of as confabulatory. Individuals with damage to their bilateral ventromedial frontal lobe have access to their autobiographic memories but have problems with inhibiting their immediate responses, for instance to requests. This means that they cognitively fail to set up several possible answers with different consequences and thereby don't make a choice between several possible narratives, but instead choose as their first response something that results in *undernarration*. Finally, individuals with lesions to their dorsolateral frontal cortices have problems constructing and organizing meaning in ongoing activities. This means that they are basically unable to construct narratives about their experiences—a sort of *denarration*.

In many ways, these different typologies are related to medical sociologist Arthur Frank's more general typology of illness narratives. Arthur Frank proposes three storylines specifying relations between patients' selves, bodies, and illnesses and their expectations for the future. He calls them *restitution, chaos*, and *quest* narratives. These three different storylines can all be found in patients' illness narratives to varying degrees and in various relationships with one another. The storyline of the restitution narrative positions the illness as a temporary and limited time of bodily impairment or affliction. The afflicted persons remain the same persons as before the illness, and when it passes or they are in remission they expect to be restored to their former levels of functioning. Essentially, being ill does not change the identity of the sick person. By contrast, the chaos storyline depicts life as radically disrupted; the self is submerged in the illness, chaos reigns, the severity of symptoms is unpredictable, and the future is uncertain. The final storyline, the quest narrative, expresses a sense of self that has been changed by the illness.

Thus a number of authors argue that neurological impairments—in some cases some kind of psychological problem—restrict the narrative resources available to the person. As a result, the organization of the story becomes problematic, and may in the extreme result in cacophonous, chaotic stories, or no story at all. From a more psychological point of view, the restricted resources make a limited number of self-positions possible. Common to these self-positions is a *diminished sense of agency*. It is important to note that the self as agent generally is present in the stories; that is, the presence of a self as agent is rarely the problem. Instead, the self as agent is fragmented and has few possibilities to handle the challenges brought about by the disease.

Although all these different classifications capture various aspects of broken stories, they give very limited insight into the processes through which these stories are produced. The stories are often seen as products, while the interactional processes through which they were produced is often out of sight. The classificatory schemas primarily classify the types of stories or the neurological pathologies and their perceived narrative consequences, but include very little of the social contexts, especially interactional relations. Thus the value of the classifications becomes quite limited, as they do not help in understanding what kinds of interactional contexts facilitate the emergence of certain types of stories. Furthermore, with classificatory schemas it always becomes a problem what to do with stories that do not fit into the established patterns. In the case of persons with dementia, this quickly comes to the fore, as the pathological processes in, for instance, Alzheimer's disease are very individualized. A better knowledge of the social processes through which stories are produced would thus be more helpful than a general classificatory schema in this case.

STORIES AND DEMENTIA

In the field of dementia studies, much of the early research that took an interest in narratives in relation to persons with dementia grew out of research on persons with aphasia. The focus was on the linguistic abilities of persons with dementia, as the disease is assumed to particularly affect these abilities. It was argued that stories introduce a particular problem, specifically how a longer stretch of talk or text is constructed from utterances or sentences, and how persons with dementia deal with this specific task. Furthermore, linguist Michael Perkins pointed out that "[c]linical research on discourse has tended to focus on genres like narrative and picture description primarily because they exclude interlocutors and therefore supposedly provide a clearer account of individual ability."[35]

In other words, the study of narrative abilities would be especially suited for experimental research that *excludes* interlocutors. As a consequence of this approach, investigating the communicative and collaborative aspects of storytelling was ruled out by definition.

It was found that Alzheimer's disease in particular progressively affects first word finding, then word meaning, and later syntactic and phonological aspects of language, and finally pragmatic functions.[36] Furthermore, a review of the research on problems in conversations and storytelling involving persons with Alzheimer's indicates a number of problems that are frequently identified.[37] It has been found that persons with dementia

- beginning in the early stage of dementia, cannot find a word, use strange words or neologisms, or pronounce words in a strange way;

- have increasing difficulties in identifying references to past events, persons, or places;
- may have difficulties managing discourse topics and will as a result make sudden topical shifts without notifying the listener about the upcoming shift or giving a reason for introducing a new topic;
- often repeat things already said, or events or stories already told.

In order to understand how the impairments of the low-level linguistic abilities affect the way sentences are connected into larger discursive units, researchers began to take an interest in the way discourse is affected in dementia. In typical experimental studies, patients had a story read aloud to them, or were given one picture depicting an event, or a number of pictures depicting the progression of an event. The patient was then asked to retell the story, or was asked a number of questions pertaining to the story. The retold story was then coded on a number of aspects, for instance number of words used, coherence, cohesion, ordering of events, and details of events. The implicit evaluative norm was that stories should be repeated, with all events mentioned in a full verbal discourse.

In a review of this kind of research, speech pathologist Jonathan Ehrlich writes,

> The discourse abilities in DAT [Dementia of Alzheimer Type] adults deteriorate in a characteristic way [. . .] and may be marked by fewer substantives, more circumlocutions and digressions from topic. This profile of "empty" speech in discourse is also characteristically egocentric and concrete with ideational preservations, and either excessive speech or little or no speech in the late stages.[38]

The discourse changes start with a mild word-finding difficulty together with "elaborate speech and occasional repetition of ideas" in the early phase of Alzheimer's disease. In the middle stage of the disorder a "more frequent repetition and revision of ideas" are found, together with "a decrease in the amount of information relative to the amount of talk." In the later stages, the language of persons with Alzheimer's disease becomes "cluttered with repetitions, revisions, and intrusions" and becomes increasingly empty of content.[39] The concept of incoherent stories is further found in a review of research on language and dementia from a neuropsychological perspective by two authors, Daniel Kempler and Mira Goral:

> Patients with DAT [Dementia of Alzheimer Type] are known to have difficulty constructing an informative and coherent narrative. Their narratives are often

repetitive with topic changes, unclear references (e.g., "he," "there"), and lack of coherence and informativeness.[40]

This quotation captures in a nice way a view of persons with dementia that has also been prevalent in the field of narrative: stories told by persons with dementia have primarily been characterized as being fragmented, confused, or even confabulatory. A further—probably unintentional—consequence of this idea is that a person with dementia appears to be what literary scholar Wayne Booth once called an "unreliable narrator." In his book *The Rhetoric of Fiction* he wrote, "For lack of better terms, I have called a narrator *reliable* when he speaks for or acts in accordance with the norms of the work [. . .], *unreliable* when he does not."[41]

Booth's idea was that the narrator—that is, not the author, but the figure who tells the story in the narrative—could adhere to those social and cultural norms presented in the narrative, thus being a "reliable narrator." On the other hand, if the narrator diverted from these norms, he must be judged to be an "unreliable narrator": one who lies, does not know what he is talking about, and so on. If the concept of the unreliable narrator is widened to include how *actual, physical tellers* in conversational storytelling are judged by other participants (and by caregivers, health professionals, and researchers), it is obvious that persons with dementia are examples of *unreliable storytellers* because they tend to deviate from most of the implicit cultural *narrative norms* and expectations.

The research discussed by Jonathan Ehrlich and others was mainly based on experimental studies measuring linguistic performance of storytelling and comparing the mean values between different groups of subjects (typically groups consisting of persons with dementia, persons with aphasia and older, healthy persons). As a consequence of this design, very little is known about how the persons with dementia actually produced the stories, or about the structure of these stories. Above all, nothing is known about interaction in the situation (if indeed there was any at all, as researchers involved are prompted not to interact).

None of this was known until the two linguists Heidi Hamilton and Vai Ramanathan presented their studies in the 1990s of how persons with dementia used language in conversations, and especially how they constructed their identities in conversations. Their studies were based on detailed analysis of how both the stories and the telling actually were accomplished, including an analysis of the interaction between the person with dementia and other participants in the storytelling situation.

Hamilton conducted an interview study with a woman called Elsie, who at the start of the study was 82 years old, and had medium severe dementia.[42] She was an active conversational partner at the beginning of study, with problems finding words, and over the four and a half years of study her communicative challenges increased. Previous to Hamilton's study, very few studies existed that tracked the changes of conversational language for people with dementia. In her study Hamilton could show in detail how Elsie's problems with participating in conversations went from word-finding problems, to becoming less active in producing questions, but also less aware of her own communicative needs and those of others. In a third phase, Elsie increasingly used invented words (neologisms), empty words, and unrelated words, and also repeated single words. Finally, in a fourth phase, Elsie basically produced no lexical items (i.e., words), but mainly used expressions like "uhhuh" and "mm," although she still could request repetition of her conversational partners' utterances.

In further analysis of her data, Hamilton focused on identity construction and how conversational partners can contribute in ongoing talk to the construction of a patient's identity. She was particularly interested in how what she called "relative dependence and independence are negotiated in talk."[43] Hamilton showed how her partners in conversations actively shifted between establishing Elsie as independent and dependent, and how similar positions could also be found in conversations over the following years.

Ramanathan studied autobiographical storytelling by a person with Alzheimer's disease.[44] In her study she interviewed a woman, Tina, repeatedly and in various settings (at home and at a day care center). She also recorded storytelling situations involving Tina and her husband. At the time of the interviews, Tina was 65 years old and diagnosed with mild to moderate Alzheimer's disease. She had been a teacher of math and English but decided to quit her job when she was diagnosed with dementia. The focus of Ramanathan's study was on the relationship between the well-formed qualities of the story and the organization of the interaction in storytelling, both in terms of who participated and where the conversation took place. Narrative well-formedness was assessed in relation to what degree Tina was able to tell a story that could be parsed into smaller parts. In her conclusions Ramanathan points out that

[w]hile one cannot draw any firm conclusions from the above study, it is evident that there is much variability involved in interactions and contexts, and AD patients—like those of us who are "normal"—are sensitive to contextual phenomena. It is crucial, then, that notions of interactions and settings be factored in when making assessments about the linguistic skills of these patients.[45]

She thus points out that it matters both where—that is, in what social context—the storytelling takes place, as well as who is involved in the conversation. In her study, Ramanathan introduces a new conception of what kind of story ought to be studied. Her argument is that *autobiographical stories*, in contrast with the kind of generic stories that had been solicited in the experimental studies, are inherently both much more interesting and relevant for the person with dementia, and it could be expected that these stories better reflect his or her narrative competence. Furthermore, she makes it clear that any analysis of storytelling involving persons with dementia needs to include an analysis of the interaction involved.

AUTOBIOGRAPHICAL STORIES

Many other researchers have continued the work on autobiographical stories, and in particular the connection between these stories and the individual's identity. It was found that despite the fact that persons with dementia may have severe problems in connection with their autobiographical memories and stories, they are still able to sustain their identities through the use of autobiographical stories. In her study of psychotherapeutic group activities with people with dementia, psychotherapist Marie Mills notes that "stories, which provided identity, gradually faded as memories succumbed to the inexorable destruction caused by illness."[46]

In spite of this, Mills found that storytelling was important for upholding an identity. When she analyzed the group conversations she found that

> as informants became more cognitively impaired by their disease there was an awareness, on the part of the interviewer, that they had bequeathed their narrative to another. It is argued that the sharing of such a narrative, within dementia care, reinforces carer attitudes of respect, understanding, and acceptance. In this sense, therefore, the personal narrative of dementia sufferers is never lost. It continues its existence in the form of a valuable resource which can be returned to them, either verbally or non-verbally, during subsequent interactions.[47]

Mills points out that other persons in the group took over some of the lost memories and stories that the person with a failing memory had previously told. This implies that persons with dementia may enhance both their memories and storytelling through interaction with others, and especially through interaction that supports the person with dementia.

Richard Cheston developed psychotherapy groups in the United Kingdom involving persons with dementia. The aim was to stimulate autobiographical storytelling in order to challenge the dominant perspective of persons with dementia as having lost their memories and being unable to tell stories that are of any interest. Cheston found that persons with dementia were quite good at telling stories, although these stories fairly often could be seen as metaphorical or even fragmented. This, in turn, demanded that we as listeners can "allow ourselves to listen to the poetical, the metaphorical aspects of language," rather than language's "truthfulness." Basically, he argued, reminiscence in group contexts helped persons to develop a social identity through their storytelling as participants.[48]

Kevin Buchanan and David Middleton pursued a similar theme in a study of the discursive interaction in reminiscence groups. By analyzing the interaction, they showed that reminiscing may have many functions, and reminding the participants about the past is just one of them. They argued that the participants use autobiographical storytelling in order to establish and negotiate their individual identity in the group; memories of the past were connected to the present and hence displayed several dimensions of the participants' identities. The group members also pursued a kind of collective identity and group membership by describing and discussing typical practices of the past.[49]

The connections between identity, self, and autobiographical stories have been used in interventions and research around life stories for people with dementia. In a review, Jane McKeown and Amanda Clarke define the field of life-story work (LSW) as

> a form of intervention carried out in health or social care practice, and is an umbrella term, encompassing a range of terms/interventions, for example biography, life history, life stories. It is usually undertaken to elicit an account of some aspect of a person's life or personal history that goes beyond a routine health assessment undertaken to plan care and treatment, and aims to have an impact on the care the person receives. LSW implies collaboration with another/others to gather and record information, and it usually results in a "product," for example a story-book, collage, notice board, life history/biography summary, or tape recording. It is an ongoing, dynamic process rather than a task to be completed and is usually planned and purposeful, although it does not need to be carried out systematically.[50]

Although the idea of a story is used quite generally, it is about enhancing and restoring what William Randall called the "narrative environment." By sharing biographical knowledge about one person in particular, staff is supposed to be more familiar with the living *person* with dementia, not just the patient. When biographical knowledge is used in caregiving, the person with dementia is also reminded of his or her life history and hence identity. This will help to enhance the sense of self. Typically, staff collects biographical information about a person with dementia living at a nursing home by inviting family members to tell stories about the person with dementia. This information is collected and structured in some kind of life story-book. It is basically a way to personalize resident care.[51]

ENTANGLED STORIES AND MEANING-MAKING

The review of research on storytelling and dementia presented in this chapter can be summarized in a number of issues that will be central to the rest of the book.

First, the research discussed clearly supports the idea that persons with dementia both can and actually do engage in storytelling. Especially compelling evidence comes from the various studies of support groups for people with dementia, clearly demonstrating that persons even in the middle phase of dementia could participate in these groups and tell stories, although with support. Several researchers, among them Richard Cheston, argued that persons with dementia can be good at telling stories, although these stories quite often could be seen as metaphorical or even fragmented. Alison Phinney proposed a similar idea in her study about people's awareness of their dementia disorder. She argued that the Alzheimer's symptom story is "inherently and fundamentally unknowable and untellable" and that "meaning is in the telling itself"; listeners are called to bear witness to the suffering when meanings cannot be told.[52]

Second, both Cheston and Phinney highlight a problem that is central in studying storytelling in dementia, namely that the stories told by persons with dementia are *entangled stories*; that is, they are stories that involve both the teller and the listener in—to quote the Oxford Dictionary of English— "difficulties or complicated circumstances from which it is difficult to escape"; they are stories that put heavy demands on all participants in finding shared meaning. The only possible "escape" would be to abandon the joint effort to understand, to withdraw from engagement with others. The endeavor to find a shared meaning in stories is at the heart of *all* storytelling. It becomes especially important in storytelling involving persons with dementia due to the fact that the progression of the dementia implies that the resources available for meaning-making become challenged for the individual with dementia.

Third, this review also shows that the story concept has been used differently. Researchers in the experimental tradition have viewed stories primarily as examples of discourse, while researchers interested in issues around interaction and identity have focused on autobiographical storytelling. The experimental research on storytelling is mainly interested in the losses of the person with dementia, especially the linguistic losses. Few, if any, of the researchers have investigated various compensatory strategies used by persons with dementia in storytelling. In contrast, researchers interested in identity and stories have stressed the ways in which interaction between participants in the storytelling situation actually can benefit the person with dementia. Researchers in this tradition in many ways accepted the idea of loss, although they stressed compensatory actions. Some of the researchers who engaged in the identity function of stories acknowledged that it is important to develop a different notion of what a story is, and especially how to listen to stories told by persons with dementia. Pursuing this line of research is important and central to the ambition of understanding the relation between autobiographical storytelling and identity in dementia.

Fourth, in particular those researchers engaged in the study of either spontaneous storytelling involving persons with dementia, as in support groups, or storytelling in interviews, clearly show that storytelling is much more than an individual act. Telling stories involves other persons, not just as listeners, but also as co-tellers. Being a co-teller might imply co-producing the stories either because both participants shared an experience of the events in the story, or they had been part of previous tellings of the story. It might also imply supporting the primary storyteller by helping to find words or names, or identifying a specific event. These findings support the idea that stories must be seen as part of storytelling activities, and that these activities have certain properties that are especially beneficial for people with dementia—the sharing of cognitive and semiotic resources.

A general conclusion from this chapter is that although persons with dementia over time will become increasingly challenged as storytellers, they are still active meaning-makers. They are obviously still engaged in the never-ending activity of making sense of their social as well as physical world—events and happenings in the world, as well as what people are saying and doing. Telling stories is central to this endeavor that entails "world-making" as well as "self-making" through constructing, presenting, and negotiating a sense of self and identity.

NOTES

1. The conversations quoted here are taken from Alois Alzheimer's notes in Auguste Deter's medical journal. Parts of this journal have been published in Maurer, Volk, & Gerbaldo, 1997. For a biography of Alzheimer, see Maurer &

Maurer, 2003. Some biographical information about Auguste Deter can be found in Page & Fletcher, 2006, as well as in the Alzheimer biography.

2. Berrios, 1990, p. 356.
3. Ballenger, 2006, pp. 81–82. Also see *Concepts of Alzheimer's Disease* (edited by Peter Whitehouse, Konrad Maurer, & Jesse Ballenger, 2000) for further historical aspects of dementia.
4. For a critical analysis of this development, see Margaret Lock's *The Alzheimer Conundrum* (2013), as well as *Thinking about Dementia* (edited by Annette Liebing & Lawrence Cohen, 2006).
5. For a review of recent research, see Greenwood & Parasuraman, 2012.
6. WHO, 2013, p. 13.
7. Christensen et al., 2013; Matthews et al., 2013;. Also see a number of smaller studies that have identified a similar pattern: Lobo et al., 2007; Qiu et al., 2013; Schrijvers et al., 2012.
8. WHO, 2013, p. 25.
9. Barnes & Yaffe, 2011; Daviglus et al., 2010, p. 177; Daviglus et al., 2011; Valenzuela & Sachdev, 2006.
10. Maurer, Volk, & Gerbaldo, 1997.
11. Fontana & Smith, "Alzheimer's Disease Victims: The 'Unbecoming' of Self and the Normalization of Competence" (1989), p. 45.
12. Herskovits, 1995, p. 148.
13. See Lindemann, 2014a.
14. These arguments are found in a book chapter—"A Dialectical Framework for Dementia"—published in 1996. This and other writings by Tom Kitwood are collected in the volume *Dementia Reconsidered: The Person Comes First* (1997).
15. Kitwood, 1997, p. 8.
16. See, for instance, Downs, 1997; Hughes et al., 2006; O'Connor et al., 2007.
17. For further critical views of Kitwood's work, see the volume *Tom Kitwood on Dementia: A Reader and Critical Commentary* (2007), edited by Clive Baldwin & Andrea Capstick.
18. Sabat & Harré, 1992. This article was lfollowed by a further article in 1994.
19. See Sabat's *Experience of Alzheimer's Disease: Life Through a Tangled Veil* (2001).
20. Sabat & Harré, 1992, p. 459. For research based on Sabat and Harré's work, see, for instance, Cohen-Mansfield et al., 2000; Hedman et al., 2013, 2014; Small et al., 1998.
21. Eric Matthews, 2006, p. 173.
22. Pia Kontos, 2005, p. 559.
23. Matthews, 2006, p. 176.
24. See, for instance, the article by Keady et al., 2007.
25. Randall & McKim, 2004, p. 241.
26. Brockmeier & Carbaugh, 2001; Bruner, 2001; Freeman, 1993.
27. Randall & McKim, 2008, p. 143.
28. See Goldstein, 1948; Luria, 1973; Sacks, 1985.
29. Sacks, 1985.
30. An argument for this notion is to be found in my article "Illness and Narrative" (1997).
31. Schafer, 1983, 1992.
32. Capps & Ochs, 1995; Herman, 1992; Shay, 1995.
33. Lysaker & Lysaker, 2006. Also see their *Schizophrenia and the Fate of the Self* (2008).

34. Young & Saver, 2001.
35. Perkins, 2007, p. 136.
36. Obler & Gjerlow, 1999.
37. Bohling, 1991; Hamilton, 1994; Perkins et al., 1998; Ramanathan, 1997; Watson et al., 1999.
38. Ehrlich, 1994, p. 151.
39. Ibid.
40. Kempler & Goral, 2008, p. 76. Also see Usita, Hyman & Herman, 1998.
41. Booth, 1983, p. 158.
42. Hamilton, 1994. Also see Hamilton, 1996, 2008.
43. Hamilton, 1996, p. 70.
44. Ramanathan, 1995, 1997. Also see her comments on these studies 30 years later, in Ramanathan, 2009.
45. Ramanathan, 1995, p. 24.
46. Mills, 1997, p. 695.
47. Ibid.
48. Cheston, 1996.
49. Buchanan & Middleton, 1995.
50. McKeown, Clark, & Repper, 2006, pp. 238–239.
51. For a review, see Kindell et al., 2014. Also see Caron et al., 1999; Hepurn et al., 1997; Angus & Bowen, 2011.
52. Phinney, 2002, p. 340.

CHAPTER 3

Dementia

Living with a Changing Brain

Suddenly I am surrounded by clutter. I look around my room. To the right of the computer is my desk. Floating on the desk are deep piles of paper, scattered envelopes, hastily scribbled notes. File folders full of papers almost cover the telephone, the two answering machines, and the fax. [. . .] There is more of this mess than needs to be cataloged. This is a tragedy for a man who was once tidy but it is a snapshot of a room that mirrors my brain, a jumble of words awaiting order with nowhere to go. Meaning is lost in a hurried moment, a word lost in confusion is never recovered. So it is that Alzheimer's begins its conquest.[1]

Thomas DeBaggio had his own garden shop. He started it and developed it into a successful business. In his mid-fifties he started to suffer from memory lapses and eventually contacted his doctors for an examination. That was the start of a journey that resulted in a diagnosis of Alzheimer's disease. The diagnosis was of course a shock, but Thomas DeBaggio decided to continue his life and to write about his life—including his life with Alzheimer's disease. He published two volumes of memories before his death in 2011, at the age of 67.

In the preceding quotation, Thomas DeBaggio writes that the jumble in his room mirrors the jumble of his brain. Although this might be conceived as a metaphorical expression, his brain is in fact injured, and in a state of disorder. Alzheimer's disease and many other dementias have one thing in common: they progressively injure the brain in such a way that the brain eventually cannot function as a life-supporting and action-coordinating organ. From a medical perspective, the injuries to the brain caused by the disorder are often translated into more or less specific psychological injuries, like memory problems, lack of social control, or a disappearing self. Many of these psychological dysfunctions can often be established and assessed through the use of various kinds of neuropsychological tests. The results of the tests, in combination with medical tests, are of course important in establishing a diagnosis of, for instance, Alzheimer's disease. The problem is that these tests and what they tell about the individual have limited validity outside the clinical test situation, as has been pointed out by Steven Sabat.[2] Often individuals are able to perform better outside the test situation, in settings that are familiar, and together with persons they know. As was shown in the previous chapter, persons with Alzheimer's disease are generally fairly poor storytellers in a test situation or in an experimental setup where they are asked to either recollect a story or tell personal memories. When they tell stories together with others, they are much more competent storytellers. These facts raise issues about the limits of the clinical—both medical and psychological—understanding of the functioning of the brain with a disease like Alzheimer's, and indicate that the clinical conception of dementia is not sufficient if we want to understand how people with dementia live outside the clinical situation.

In more general terms, progressive brain disorders like Alzheimer's disease raise questions about the relationship between the brain, its structure and functions, and the activity and life of the person who lives with the (diseased) brain. Questions are also raised about what it is like to live with a brain that is not only injured, but also continues to change as the pathological processes progress, in an everyday context, beyond the clinical setting, and of course, how storytelling is possible with a brain that gradually loses much of its former functionality.

In order to better understand what persons with changing brains can do as storytellers together with other persons, it is necessary to add a social psychological perspective to more traditional psychological knowledge, which often is centered on a decontextualized individual and that person's diseased brain. In the following, this will be done in three steps.

First comes a discussion of function of the brain as an organ specialized for coordinating and regulating human relations and ultimately life in a society. The aim is to point out that the brain is evolutionary, designed for dealing with human relations and the human world. Then the question is how various injuries to the brain change the functionality of the brain as a specialized organ developed to deal with human relations and to remember and tell stories.

Second comes a discussion about the brain's part in storytelling. Storytelling is a ubiquitous and important everyday activity, but also a very complex social activity taking many different resources into account; cognitive as well as semiotic resources are used, together with a host of emotional resources, to regulate social interaction.

Finally comes a discussion about living with a changing brain. The focus here is on the limitations of the clinical understanding and descriptions of the effects of brain injuries, and the theoretical concepts that are needed in order to understand how the brains of persons with dementia are affected. Central to the argument is to learn *how individuals live with a changing brain*, how they deal with the challenges that the brain presents to them, and how they compensate for lost resources.

THE BRAIN ORGAN: A FUNCTIONAL PERSPECTIVE

The human brain evolved as an organ to help the human organism engage not only with the *physical world*, but also with the *social world*—or perhaps for dealing with the physical world in a social context. Furthermore, the human brain has developed in order to function in a *cultural world*, that is, in a world full of conventions, tools, and institutions that are not transferred through genes but through socialization and enculturation.[3]

It seems that at least three aspects can be detailed in this evolution. First, in humans (and other higher organisms), the brain is an organ that has evolved to enhance and allow *cooperation* with other persons. Cooperation entails that the individual participants can make use of the other participants' abilities (for instance, their knowledge, experience, or point of view), as well as those created jointly between them. All this is according to the principle that two persons can accomplish more than one. The brains of higher mammals have developed areas that are specialized in recognizing and responding to other animals (including people) and their actions, so-called mirror neurons. The brain has further evolved systems that facilitate attachment and other emotional aspects that are extremely important in coordinating actions and activities, as well as handling conflicts and threats coming both from outside the group as well as from inside the group.[4]

Second, the brain has evolved as an organ for the *manipulation* and use of *tools*, together with others. The brain has evolved as an ecological control system that opportunistically assembles resources in the brain and the body in order to solve specific problems in the interaction between organism(s) and the world, as well as using and changing things so that they enhance actions (using a stone as an ax and then chiseling the stone into a better ax). Furthermore, the brain has developed systems that allow the use of very complicated semiotic resources like spoken sounds, thus allowing coordinated meaning-making. The implication is that the brain has developed in order to function together with artifacts of various kinds, from things, to language, and other codified practices.[5]

Third, the brain has developed systems involving many different areas in the brain that make it possible to engage in a world that is not present, through modeling and *imagination* as in storytelling and planning, but also in imagining new possible devices or solutions to problems. By combining the development of imagination with complex sign use and later written language, storytelling became possible and thus made more complex meaning-making possible. Several authors have even argued that the development of storytelling helped develop more complex cognitive functions, as well as more complex linguistic functions. Central to these functions is the ability to "decenter" cognition, that is, to imagine worlds that are not present, as in storytelling, as well as the possible perspectives of others, that is, understanding what others might have experienced in a story world. Imagination in this sense is deeply connected to thinking about possibilities.[6]

In order to accomplish these functions, the brain as an organ has developed a special kind of organization during the evolutionary process, built on the intertwining of cultural, social, and biological processes. The brain consists of highly specialized areas, as well as areas specialized in integrating information from these areas; all specialized areas are interconnected and are thus parts of networks that are connected to subcortical structures (emotional networks, for instance). Information that enters the brain is not analyzed in a linear fashion, but information is recycled and fed back to previous areas in the brain, but now as part of larger cortical networks that include new areas. These new relationships between specialized centers are possible because of the use of language and other semiotic signs—"external" aids or tools. Language is a system that both presupposes complex relations between various brain centers as well as helps to establish these connections. Russian neuropsychologist Aleksander Luria described these intertwined processes in the following way:

> [. . .] these external aids or historically formed devices are *essential elements in the establishment of functional connections between individual parts of the brain*, and that by their aid, areas of the brain which previously were independent *become components of a single functional system*. [. . .] It is this principle of construction of functional systems of the human brain that Vygotsky called the

principle of "extra-cortical organization of complex mental functions," implying by this somewhat unusual term that all types of human conscious activity are always formed with support of external auxiliary tools or aids.[7]

Luria points out that human activities are based on what he calls *functional systems*. This concept—as Luria uses it—indicates that the various (specialized) parts of the brain are connected in a way that is determined by which parts are needed in order to solve a problem or perform a specific task. It also indicates that functional systems involve "external tools" like language in the system. As Luria points out, this implies that the very functional organization of the brain builds on cultural practices.

What Luria calls "external aids" and "historically formed devices" consists of culturally evolved procedures and "tools." As we grow up, we learn a number of ways of doing things, such as how to set up numbers in order to calculate additions, how to hold and use a fork when eating, how to drive a car—that is, how to handle, manipulate, and change something in the surrounding world as part of acting in the world. All these procedures consist of schemas for the ordered sequential organization of actions. Although these schemas often are the objects of conscious awareness during the learning process, once established they function outside awareness—that is, until they fail. Failing brings the schema back to attention and often leads to deliberation in order to repair actions or to find another solution, and thus to be able to continue with life.

These "devices" or procedures involve cognitive processes like perception, various kinds of memory processes, often together with certain physical objects, such as a pen or a coffee brewer. Other "external aides" primarily aim "to alter one's own or someone else's relation to the world."[8] Every culture, for instance, has developed a number of categorizations of things in the world as well as of humans and events, from simple distinctions between living and inanimate objects, to family relations and other social roles, to more complex relations where categories are related to multiple, sequential event schemas having to do with how certain things are done (funerals, weddings). Besides categories and event schemas, speech acts are also institutionalized ways of doing things with words (asking questions, requesting, etc.). They also include narratives and metaphors, as narratologist David Herman has pointed out.[9]

All these external aids and devices are part of cultural institutions that are learned by developing and shaping the brain's "internal" functional systems to work together with "external" tools. This means, as Luria points out, that the brain can basically be thought of in terms of networks and functional systems that involve not only the brain but also external tools, "a network of complex dynamic structures or combination centers, consisting of mosaics of distant points of the nervous system, united in a common task."[10]

This implies that everyday actions and interactions always involve various specialized parts of the brain connected to various kinds of functional systems, as well as various "tools" from linguistic and cognitive categories and their relations and potential cultural meanings, to artifacts like computers, and to other persons. In other words, in understanding everyday activities like storytelling, it is not feasible to focus on specific parts of the brain (like episodic memory) in isolation; rather, it is necessary to consider the storytelling activity as a kind of system that is organized around a number of cortical resources, from specialized parts of the brain, to associative areas in the brain, as well as cultural tools and artifacts, to other persons' resources.

An implication of this in a social psychological perspective is that brain injuries must be seen as affecting these functional systems, rather than affecting an isolated part of the brain, and thus persons' abilities to do things together.

INJURIES TO THE BRAIN AND DEMENTIA

The brain can be injured in many different ways and for different reasons— by trauma, tumors, stroke, or intoxication—all different types of *acquired brain injuries*. Injuries to the brain can also be caused by neurodegenerative processes, as is the case with Alzheimer's disease (although the term *acquired brain injury* is not used in those cases; instead, the term *dementia* is used). As mentioned in Chapter 1, the term *dementia* does not refer to a specific disease, but rather to a syndrome, that is, to a cluster or pattern of symptoms. These symptoms develop as a result of a disorder. One way to divide the "dementing disorders" is by making a distinction between neurodegenerative disorders and vascular disorders.[11]

In neurodegenerative disorders (like Alzheimer's disease and frontotemporal lobe dementia), the pathological process is characterized by a degeneration of neural brain cells and the connections between these neurons. In most cases, knowledge of why the degenerative process starts is lacking or is fragmentary; not even the actual degenerative process is fully described and known today. The neurodegenerative process may start in different areas in the brain and may also involve different pathological processes, thus resulting in injuries of different parts of the brain, which in turn result in different clinical symptoms. Alzheimer's disease, the most common among the neurodegenerative disorders, often starts in the medial parts of the temporal lobe, primarily affecting the hippocampus. It is generally argued that the hippocampus is central in differentiating between old and new experiences, and thus is important for forming long-term memories, especially so-called episodic memories. Over time, the pathological process spreads to the parts of the lateral temporal lobe, thus affecting linguistic abilities. When the neurodegenerative process spreads further, it affects primarily those areas in the brain where information from several areas are used and integrated. Only in very late phases of the disease process are areas having to do with processes like primary visual analysis affected.[12]

In frontotemporal lobe dementia, the neural degeneration starts in ventral frontal lobes of the posterior temporal lobe. Compared to Alzheimer's disease, the pathological process has to do with the regulation of social behavior (frontal lobe). In some cases, the degenerative process starts somewhere on the temporal lobe, resulting in a version of the disorder that sometimes is called *semantic dementia* or *progressive aphasia*.

Vascular dementia is caused by some kind of cerebrovascular disease; it can be the result of a subcortical infarct in the medial thalamus, or one or more ischemic strokes. The result is often a cognitive impairment, such as decline in memory function.[13]

Alzheimer's disease, frontotemporal lobe dementia, and vascular dementia are by tradition not considered to belong to the group of the acquired brain injuries, as they are progressive neurodegenerative diseases. Neuropsychologist Maria Medved points out that the differences are often overstated:

> Although it might seem easy to come up with a list of differences and similarities in relation to dementia and brain injury, it quickly becomes complicated. Even something that initially seems as clear-cut as different etiologies dissolves on closer examination. Take, for example, vascular dementia. Although it is considered a form of dementia, it is the result of repeated minor strokes, so in a sense it is also a brain injury.[14]

In dementia, as the disease progresses, the injuries to the brain become greater. As certain areas in the brain are associated with specific functions, this implies that these specialized functions no longer contribute to the functional systems that are part of the realization of specific activities— something that will have serious consequences for the individual. Which areas and systems in the brain are affected, as well as the type of injury, will decide whether the injuries will be permanent or not, and what consequences they will have for the brain to function as an organ for coordinating actions and interactions.

Historically, dementias were thought to affect the brain in a general and unfocused way, making it almost impossible to assess the effects. More recent research has modified this view somewhat, and it has become clear that the neurodegenerative disorders like Alzheimer's disease at first affect those areas of the brain that integrate information from more specialized areas. One example is those areas that integrate information from sub-areas involved in the analysis of sounds with visual information and bodily sensations, together with the categorization schemes that are based on bodily experiences. Only in the very late stages of dementia are primary areas affected—if at all.

Although the various types of neurodegenerative disorders and vascular dementia often are presented as "clean" cases, it is important to note that persons encountered in clinical practice may exhibit complex patterns of symptoms that may indicate more than one underlying disease. Thus vascular dementia and Alzheimer's disease, or any other neurodegenerative dementia, are not mutually exclusive. Furthermore, persons with Alzheimer's disease may also be depressed, thus exacerbating some of the typical "symptoms" of the disorder.

An implication of this is that in dementia (as well as in acquired brain injuries) there is rarely a loss of an entire function, but rather a change in and of functional systems as the neurodegenerative disease affects specific areas; that is, the functionality of the brain in relation to specific activities becomes compromised. Thus the individual will have access to a decreasing number of resources as the disease progresses, and these resources will lose some of their functionality. Studies of how especially Alzheimer's disease progresses in the brain indicate that brain areas that integrate the more specialized areas will be affected first by the neurodegenerative processes.[15] Thus the person with Alzheimer's disease may perceive and understand aspects, but will have difficulties with those meaning-making processes that involve the integration of aspects, for instance, recognizing the sounds of someone speaking but not the meaning.

THE BRAIN'S PART IN STORYTELLING

Storytelling is part of a joint activity that engages at least two persons. It is a very complex activity based on coordination of spoken words, gestures, facial expressions, eye movements, emotional attachment, and evaluation—but also a movement between the events in the storytelling situation and the events taking place in the story. It is easy to see that it is an activity that puts a heavy load on the brain as an organ of coordination and regulation. Thus a brain disorder will have severe effects on the individual's ability to participate in the activity.

As indicated in Chapter 2, there are at least two different theoretical views on how stories are produced. One idea is that story production is a linear process based on an abstract mental model of the story events, and these cognitive elements are then "put into" words and spoken. The base structure of a story is thought to consist of a *microstructure* (a hierarchically organized list of micro-propositions about factors like action and setting), a *macrostructure* (core content expressed as a list of more general macro-propositions), and a *superstructure* corresponding to the genre rules for organizing the text. According to this model, a story is constructed by transforming micro-propositions into macro-propositions, which are then transformed into a more complex surface text by using superstructure rules.[16] In other words, stories are generated through the application of abstract rules to micro-propositions. The processing results in a *mental model* that represents the events, characters, settings, and so on, found in the story. This mental model or representation is then mapped onto linguistic structures, ranging from simple words (lexis) to sentences (syntax) and into larger discursive units (macrostructures, genres). In other words, stories are seen as a result of a combination of abstract amodal knowledge stored in the semantic memory, and linguistic knowledge also stored in semantic memory.

The cognitive processing involved in storytelling is dependent on a well-functioning semantic memory and executive functions, that is, on the ability to plan and sequence cognitive and linguistic elements into a coherent whole. As both semantic memory and working memory (part of the executive functions) are affected by Alzheimer's disease, this will have severe effects on the abilities of persons with this type of dementia to comprehend or tell stories.

This theoretical conception of stories and persons with dementia may seem plausible, given the experimental design of the research; the focus is on the decontextualized individual with dementia and on that person's discursive performance, evaluated in terms of coherence and cohesion. The stimuli often consist of pictures and the task is to tell or retell a story or answer questions about the content of this story. The methodological design follows from—and at the same time results in—a conception of both storytelling and story comprehensions as basically an internal process, taking place *inside the head* of the individual storyteller. As a consequence, problems in the discursive performance, whether cognitive or linguistic, can be interpreted as the consequence of dissociations between internal faculties/units.

One of the central problems with this theoretical model of story production and comprehension is that it is conceived on a quite narrow idea of storytelling; stories start with a memory that can be formed into a mental model and then can be put into words. Much of the everyday storytelling, especially autobiographical storytelling, is rather opportunistic and constructive and involves other people. It is an opportunistic process in that much storytelling starts with previous tellings of a story. Although it happens that stories are told for the first time, most stories are retold stories; that is, they have been told previously.[17] Using a previous version of a story of course makes storytelling an easier, quicker, and less energy-consuming process. It is possible to use both whole stories or parts of stories. In both cases, these already told stories can easily be revised in such a way that they fit into the new situation. The basic opportunistic principle guiding conversational storytelling is to use whatever story or story element that can fit into the ongoing conversation—as long as the other participants have heard the story before, because they then must be advised about having heard the story before.

The interesting thing about telling previously told stories is that there is no need for an original memory that has to be identified and turned into a propositional model and then put into words. Instead, a host of different "memories" of the previous telling can be used as sources for the story, from the storyline, to the linguistic constructions used, to phonological aspects, to various bodily "memories" of the telling, as well as to the responses from others. In other words, it is "memories" of the innumerable aspects connected to previous telling of the story that is "remembered," rather than the "original" memory of an event. These "memories" are *multimodal*, that is, it is "memories" of the voice used, bodily responses and reactions that were part of the telling, the visual perception of others listening to the story, and so on. All these different "memory" sources can be used by the teller as *resources* in order to *construct* a story that fits into the ongoing conversation.[18] Using these semiotic resources is less about delivering a predefined text and more about using these resources in order to construct, express, and negotiate meaning in an emerging story that must fit into the expectations and understandings of the participants.

This constructive and opportunistic view of storytelling has implications for how the brain as an organ of coordination is involved in storytelling. Considering storytelling to be opportunistic in using all available types of resources for constructing a story of course also involves using other parts of the brain besides the areas traditionally connected to linguistic production. Above all, areas of the brain connected with bodily movement as well as visual perception are involved, and as a consequence the functional brain systems established in storytelling span a wide network in the human brain.

If storytelling is an opportunistic and constructive process that uses multimodal resources, it could be expected that the neurodegenerative processes involved in Alzheimer's disease might affect different areas in the brain, while sparing others. As a result, there would be no loss of storytelling because "memories" were "lost," for the simple reason that many different kinds of "memories" related to different areas of the brain are involved in storytelling, and not all these parts of the brain are affected. It would thus be expected that persons with dementia, rather than losing storytelling abilities, have to engage in storytelling using fewer available cognitive and semiotic resources; that is, persons with dementia are challenged in their storytelling activity, rather than being the victims of loss.

This is also something that fits fairly well with the fact that several researchers have argued that persons with dementia actually "have memories" of the past, although they have problems using specialized linguistic means for communicating these memories. Pia Kontos has shown, for instance, that persons with quite advanced Alzheimer's disease are able to enact memories; using their bodies, they can show "memories" of themselves rather than telling stories.[19] Autobiographical memories of autobiographical events or event fragments seem to exist as *embodied memories*, something that has rarely been investigated. Numerous similar examples can also be found in the literature around validation (i.e., various techniques for accepting and validating people with dementia, often in quite advanced stages).[20] This theme will be discussed further in Chapter 6.

"THINKING FOR SPEAKING"

A specific problem that persons with dementia face when telling stories is to transform and translate embodied resources into language, that is, talk. As psycholinguist Dan Slobin pointed out, "language requires us to categorize events as ongoing or completed, objects as at rest or as at the end point of a trajectory, and so forth."[21] Many of the "memory" resources used for storytelling exist as embodied "memories." It means that they often have the character of being whole and syncretic, like an image; everything is there at the same time. Language, on the other hand, is analytic and sequential; wholes must be analyzed into smaller parts and ordered on some kind of time scale, because that is how talk is produced (or texts written). As a consequence, many of the resources used to tell a story cannot just be mapped onto a linguistic structure, but have to be *transformed* and *translated* in order to fit the categorical and syntactic structure of language. This what Slobin, drawing on Russian psychologist Lev Vygotsky's ideas, has called "thinking for speaking"[22]: "[t]he world does not present "events" and "situations" to be encoded in language. Rather, experiences are filtered through language into verbalized events. A "verbalized event" is constructed online, in the process of speaking."[23]

Using Slobin's idea, it can be argued that narrative is a sociocultural form that puts certain demands on the teller. Words, with their forms and combinations, have to be selected in a certain way in order to produce a story, that is, something that can be recognized by the listener as a story. The organization of events into a story is a process that joins together multimodal recourses, and produces a story that is not only organized as a *text*. Storytelling is multimodal in the sense that the story *gives* the teller the opportunity to use a number of different communicative *channels* or semiotic resources. These can be not only words, but also gestures, facial expressions, and changes in the voice, voice quality, and rhythm.[24] Hence in the telling the story is organized as a multimodal event and cannot be reduced to just one *channel* or semiotic resource, often the verbal *text*. This is something that has important consequences in those cases where a person loses some of his or her communicative resources, like verbal abilities, which then can be substituted for by gestures, for instance, as will be further discussed in Chapter 6.

Here it will be suggested that Slobin's basic idea about "thinking for speaking" could serve as an interesting analytical framework for understanding autobiographical storytelling and for understanding those challenges that persons with dementia face in telling autobiographical stories. In autobiographical storytelling, tasks at hand in the ongoing conversation originate in the activity of remembering something that potentially could fit into the conversation, through the transformation of this multimodal, global, and synthetic memory into a linear structure that can be fitted into linguistic constructions. These linguistic structures are then used in the production of the speech itself. If memories are thought of as being multimodal, this also makes it natural that various bodily, communicative resources are used in a synchronized way with the verbal utterances in the telling of the autobiographical story, from gestures and gaze to physiological processes.

One example of this comes from a joint interview with a woman, Ann, and her husband, Carl. Both are around 70 years old and have been married for over 40 years. Ann received an Alzheimer's disease diagnosis seven years previous to the interview. She has profound problems identifying events and sometimes also constructing utterances. In this example one of the interviewers has asked Ann to describe an ordinary day at the day care center (Example 3.1). She at first suggests that she cleans, but when her husband protests, she says that she doesn't clean (Line 1).

Example 3.1.

1	Ann:	no we don't clean but
2		we want it to be good (moves left hand back and forth horizontally)
3		we can move things if they are in another place (continues left hand horizontal movement)
4		if we think
5		no (also moves right hand horizontally) let's take that instead (puts both hands on her knee)
6		yes
7		that's what we basically do

It is obvious that Ann has severe problems with both finding specific words (lines 2–3, 5) and expressions (lines 3, 5). She obviously has some idea of what she wants to say, but when she cannot find words to construct an utterance, she uses gestures and illustrates her cleaning activity. The gestures basically enact one aspect of cleaning by mimicking cleaning movements. This gesture is also used to express tidying up.

Thus, in order to be able to tell conversational stories, a person needs to have access to a number of both linguistic and other semiotic resources, as well as cognitive resources including the translation between "thought" and speech. If these resources are not available, the person needs to compensate by using alternative semiotic resources; it could be expected that persons with Alzheimer's disease in particular would encounter certain types of challenges.

The first type of challenge would have to do with the change of cognitive resources, especially the ability to create and remember new memories, as well as problems with identifying, for instance, events or persons (to remember). These changes will result in difficulties in telling "new" stories or even in just telling stories, although the person may be in command of linguistic resources.

The second kind of challenge would have to do with changing linguistic resources; the person may have difficulties in finding words and expressions, and in constructing utterances, although he or she might have an image of the event.

A third type of challenge has to do with changes in both linguistic and cognitive resources, making it difficult to organize narrative discourse[25] (see Chapters 3, 6, and 7 for examples).

LIVING WITH A CHANGING BRAIN

As the brain changes due to the neurodegenerative processes involved in Alzheimer's disease, this means that the brain as an organ for the coordination and regulation of joint activities also changes. Previously available options for action for the person with dementia become difficult or almost impossible. As a consequence, the relationship between the person with dementia and the world—the physical as well as the social—becomes challenged. Furthermore, as the neurodegenerative processes are progressive, the changes in the brain are not just as sudden and abrupt as when a person suffers from a stroke, but slowly continue. Most people with dementia learn to live with this changing brain—although this is often a complicated and emotionally difficult process.

A recurrent idea in much of the research and writing on dementia and acquired brain injuries is that there is a specific, almost causal, relationship between the pathologies in the brain caused by the disease and the consequences of this injury. A common notion is that acquired brain injuries as well as dementia will result in loss of functions. The loss can be sudden, as in a stroke, or gradual, as in dementia. Second, these supposed losses are expressed as specific symptoms. These symptoms in turn can be conceptualized as psychological dysfunctions. Identified pathologies in, for instance, the hippocampus will translate into pathologies in certain memory functions. As a consequence of this perspective, symptoms and psychological dysfunctions can be seen as the direct result of pathologies in the brain. A further consequence of this is that symptoms may indicate what part of the brain is injured.

This is a very old idea in medicine in general and especially in neurology. It is based in clinical practice where observations of the patient are compared to the results of an autopsy of the patient. In this way, the clinician and researcher can combine clinical observations and signs with the report about pathologies found in the brain. It was by using this method in the 1860s that French neurologist Paul Broca could identify a certain part of the brain's motor center as being important for speech production. Alois Alzheimer some fifty years later could argue that Auguste Deter's behavior could be explained by the neurofibrillary tangles and neuritic plaques he found in the analysis of her brain.[26]

This idea and method has been very successful in terms of identifying and understanding the structure and functions of various parts of the brain, as well as diagnosing persons with brain lesions. At the same time, it is a practice that has been criticized for missing important aspects not only of the patient's behavior, but also of how the brain actually functions.

One of the central problems with the idea that brain lesions result in specific symptoms is that these symptoms are regarded as meaningless as such, being merely signs of an underlying dysfunction in the brain. This idea was criticized in the early twentieth century by a number of neurologists and psychologists. Two of the most prominent voices belonged to German neurologist Kurt Goldstein and Russian neuropsychologist Aleksander Luria. Both of them criticized the classical conception of a correspondence between brain dysfunction and symptoms by invoking not only clinical cases that contradicted these ideas, but also by developing examination methods that could show other aspects of the patient's behavior.

The case descriptions presented by Goldstein in the 1920s and 1930s in particular appealed to phenomenological philosophers, as these cases could be used in refuting the classical division between body and mind. One of the philosophers who draw heavily on Goldstein's writings was phenomenologist Maurice Merleau-Ponty. In a discussion of the relationship between brain injuries and behavior, he pointed out that brain injuries do not directly "concern the content of the behavior but rather its structure and consequently that is not something that is observed but rather something which is understood."[27]

What Merleau-Ponty is saying is that brain injuries are not primarily visible as losses—that is, as the absence of a behavior that used to be there, which is the traditional medical view of symptoms. Rather, he argues, it is how behavior is organized that matters, and this organization can only be grasped by "understanding" what the injured patient is doing. A consequence of this is that symptoms instead ought to be seen as attempts of a person with a brain injury to adapt to a situation when his or her brain has changed, or even is still continuing to change, as is the case with Alzheimer's disease and other dementias. Furthermore, Merleau-Ponty points out that understanding rather than observing the patient and his or her behavior would imply an attempt to identify the *function* of the actual behavior (the "symptoms") in a specific situation, rather than just seeing them as bodily or verbal behavior without meaning and connection to the specific situation.

The idea that "symptoms" could be seen as meaningful and as part of functional behavior was one of the fundamental ideas in neurologist Kurt Goldstein's book *The Organism*. He wrote,

Symptoms are answers, given by the modified organism, to definite demands; they are attempted solutions to problems derived on the one hand from the demands of the natural environment and on the other from the special tasks imposed on the organism in the examination.[28]

Taking the clinical examination as his typical situation, Goldstein points out that patients with brain injuries often try to do what they are asked to do. As their brain injuries may create challenges for them, they try to find new ways to accomplish what they were previously able to do with ease. In taking what Kurt Goldstein calls "detours," that is, other ways than the usual, they may do what is requested but also may produce behaviors that are new to them. What Goldstein wanted to point out was that behavior that generally is dismissed as symptoms actually could be seen as a person's meaningful and functional attempt to adapt to a situation when his or her brain had changed, or is continuing to change.

Referring back to Luria's ideas in the previous sections, it can be argued that the symptoms found in acquired brain injuries as well as in dementia are the result of a *reorganization* of functional systems, that is, the system that includes the brain and its systems as well as "external tools," in order to cope with situational demands. This means that persons with acquired brain injuries or dementia rarely just lose a previous function. Instead, persons with acquired brain injuries and dementia engage in social situations and attempt to fulfill situational demands, for instance in a conversation, but certain of the resources previously available are no longer there. This of course will result both in anxiety and attempts to compensate for the resources no longer available (both of these themes are further discussed later).

For persons with dementia engaged in storytelling, the progressing brain injuries will result in an increased number of *resources becoming unavailable*; certain choices and possibilities are no longer available, and hence the task of engaging in storytelling will become an increasing challenge. In Alzheimer's disease it is associated in particular areas with being able to remember and recognize new events and information (hippocampal area), as well as using language (temporal areas) and planning (prefrontal area).[29] When these brain resources no longer are available, this challenges the person's storytelling. But, as we will see, it does not imply that the person with dementia has lost the ability to engage in conversational storytelling. It just means that the person with dementia will face some new and often quite challenging demands in the activity. One response to these challenges can be withdrawal from the activity, but it can also imply a reorganization of the ways the person engages in the storytelling activity. One possibility is to engage new external aids, for instance the resources of other participants, thus reorganizing not only the participatory framework but also the functional systems.

Stories, Confabulations, and Creativity

An interesting example of the creative use of stories using the remaining resources has to do with what in medical terms is called *confabulation*. This is often thought of as a typical symptom of dementia. In the broad sense, confabulations are usually defined as false narratives or statements about world and/or self, due to some pathological mechanisms (i.e., loss of the ability of temporal framing), but with no intention of lying. Against this medical interpretation, it could be argued that rather than being viewed as a neuropsychiatric symptom, confabulation could be seen more productively as the result of an active and creative *meaning-making* or *sense-making process*, using constrained discursive and interactive resources.

For most persons living with dementia, their resources for understanding, communicating, and negotiating their current situations are constrained. However, as has been argued in this chapter, dementia does not obliterate the discursive and cognitive resources, but merely changes them. Therefore, using a contextualized description of confabulation could allow an understanding of it as a social and discursive phenomenon with productive features and certain functions, rather than merely as a neuropsychiatric phenomenon.

During an ethnographic fieldwork at a residential care home for persons diagnosed with dementia, two elderly women—Martha and Catherine—both in their mid eighties, were observed in many different situations over the period of almost a year.[30] Both women were diagnosed with Alzheimer's disease and got to know each other at the residential home. In Example 3.2, Martha and Catherine are sitting in a corridor at a residential living for persons with dementia. At the same time, the staff are preparing to serve afternoon coffee. Sitting in the corridor, Martha and Catherine overhear the assistant nurses talk about the afternoon coffee, but do not realize that the coffee is already being prepared by the assistant nurses in the kitchen next to them. Instead, Martha and Catherine become uncertain about the coffee and they start discuss *who* should take care of the coffee arrangements. Martha suggests that the two of them should arrange for the coffee. They look around, trying to locate some "dining-hall," and search through the notices on the walls in the corridor for information. Finally, Martha suggests that they should order some coffee to be brought in.

Clearly there is a gap in Martha's and Catherine's understanding in this situation: a kind of borderland emerges, and the women cannot find the right "map"—or story—to orientate themselves by. Within only a few minutes, the assistant nurses accompany Martha, Catherine, and the other residents into the day room, where the coffee is to be served, and serve them coffee and cookies. However, the idea of being responsible for the coffee arrangement may have been planted in Martha.

Having served the coffee, the assistant nurses withdraw to the kitchen. In the dayroom, a scene follows that might be found in any ordinary coffee party—sociability and chitchatting about the weather, childhood memories, what is on TV, and similar topics. The situation is to get considerably more complicated, though, as it seems that Martha has an understanding of the situation that differs from that of the others, one that also turns out to be problematic. Somewhere along the way, Martha assumes the status of the gracious hostess—a part that obviously has been her role innumerable times throughout her life. Equally innumerable are her stories found in the fieldwork data about how she, like her mother before her, has taken pride in welcoming everyone to her home and in sharing her food and hospitality with other people, especially those in need.

Given this, it can be assumed that Martha construes her current situation by using a storyline that describes the situation as an afternoon coffee party and casts her as a hostess. This storyline is challenged several times during the afternoon coffee party as other participants do things that do not fit well into Martha's adopted storyline. A first instance that indicates that there may be something problematic about Martha's understanding of the situation takes place as one of the residents, Gertrude, starts behaving in a way that appears to bother Martha somehow. Having finished her coffee, Gertrude leaves the table early. She does not leave the scene once and for all, though, but keeps reappearing in the dayroom, wandering about the space and keeping busy rearranging some chairs in the corner of the dayroom. In doing so, she makes some noise that is quite difficult for Martha to ignore. Martha repeatedly turns to her friend Catherine, sitting next to her, to ask her whether or not "she" (pointing at Gertrude) has had any coffee. Catherine confirms that she has, but as Gertrude continues moving about, Martha does not seem content. She thinks out loud, "I should have asked her if she's had any coffee." Finally, she approaches Gertrude and offers her a cup of coffee, which is accepted, and the two ladies accompany each other back to the lounge suite. Martha asks Gertrude to sit down.

The way Martha takes on responsibility in the situation indicates that she may have assumed the role of the hostess of the coffee gathering, thereby assigning the situation to a series of situations that are familiar and are recounted in a certain way. In doing so, she also introduces a set of guidelines for her own conduct and for the conduct of others. As the gracious hostess of a coffee party, she is supposed to behave in a certain way, to make sure that everybody is treated to coffee and that everybody is made to feel welcome. The guests, on the other hand, are supposed to sit down properly and have some coffee, be polite and sociable, and, at some point, show some hospitality in return, or at least some gratitude. This would explain why Gertrude's conduct bothers Martha. Gertrude does not act in accordance with the part that Martha is trying to attribute to her. She simply does not follow the "script." Not only does she leave the coffee table unsuitably early, without taking part in the customary small talk and without thanking Martha or even saying goodbye, but in moving about the space and rearranging the furniture, she clearly does not respect Martha's alleged private property. As Martha offers Gertrude a cup of coffee and asks her to sit down, Gertrude's part in the situation at hand is, however, subject to negotiation. Martha tries to pour coffee from a thermos standing on the table but cannot open the thermos. Instead, Martha makes an effort to go to the kitchen to search for another pot, but returns to the coffee table only seconds later, empty-handed. Leaning over the table, she asks her friend Catherine, "But they already had coffee, didn't they?" Catherine nods and confirms that at least she herself has already had some, while Gertrude responds in the negative (see Example 3.2).

Example 3.2.

1	Martha:	haven't you had coffee?
2	Gertrude:	no
3	Martha:	who on earth has been here then?
4		you were =
5		[(points to the empty seat next to Catherine, right in front of her)
6	Gertrude:	[= I don't know. =
7	Martha:	= but you were seated here
8		[I was seated over there
9		[(points to the empty seat next to Catherine)
10	Catherine:	yes you were
11	Gertrude:	(taps Martha's back)
12	Martha:	and you were seated =
13		[(points to Catherine's place)
14	Catherine:	[= and I was seated *here*
15		I was seated *there*
16		(moves her coffee cup an inch as if to show the exact location, as she produces the last word in her line)
17	Martha:	we all had coffee in these cups
18		(simultaneously pointing towards the cups)
19	Gertrude:	yes. yes. I believe you

Apparently, Martha is not quite sure what has happened. Gertrude and the others have already had coffee, but Martha is obviously not aware of this. Thus, from Martha's point of view, she must check weather Gertrude has had coffee: and if not, Martha must deal with the fact that she might have missed some of her duties as a hostess and must serve Gertrude some coffee. At the same time, having missed serving Gertrude coffee is a potential threat to Martha's face.

Although Martha is uncertain of what has happened, she is prepared to argue that Gertrude has already had coffee, and thus save her face. In order to support this position, she even points to the used cups on the table, trying to recall the way they were all seated (lines 3–5). This seems to be an effective way of convincing the other women (guests) to support her position; and Gertrude finally agrees (line 19).

Martha's argumentation is made partly in collaboration with Catherine (although Catherine never actually confirms that Gertrude has had coffee). Catherine agrees with Martha (line 10) and then contributes with a collaborated completion (lines 14–16). Thereby she demonstrates involvement in the ongoing interaction and in the task of determining who has been drinking from the used cups. Martha's using the coffee cups as clues to what had happened is repeated later on, as Martha counts and points at the cups in order to establish the fact that they have all had coffee.

This example is about problem-solving and thinking by using a story. Martha is making use of a storyline about herself as a hostess, and this helps her to structure and understand what is going on, and further, to act in the situation. Although the storyline Martha uses seems to be clear to her, the others are less obvious participants in the story. The example shows how Martha can make use of the storyline also to build an argument in order to convince the other women present about what is going on, and in particular, about how she as a hostess has acted correctly.

This example thus has some implications concerning the concept of confabulation. First, it suggests that confabulation might serve as a way of *making sense* of the current situation by organizing one's experiences according to a plot within the scope of a storyline that is familiar, using one's usual stories as easily accessible resources. "Confabulation" is in this case the solution to a problem involving a lack of orientation in time and space: "What kind of situation is this?" and "Where (and when) am I and what is happening?"

Second, it can also be argued that the storyline is used in order to *preserve a sense of self*. The storyline involves a presentation of a self that is consistent with Martha's life history and thus has some stability. Martha's confabulation thus allows her to recognize herself as a certain kind of person, and thus to establish and maintain a preferred identity in interaction with others. In the analyzed episode, it is not just *any* storyline that is applied, but specifically one that allows Martha to describe and act as herself—the generous sharing person that she, according to her many stories, was brought up to be.

Third, neither "sense-making" nor "self-making" are enterprises of a single individual. Rather, they are dependent on interaction with other participants. The way Martha understands the current situation, as well as her personal identity, depends on others confirming and acting upon it. Confabulation thus not only serves to describe the world, but is also *world-making* in its organization of joint action and its legitimization of the conduct undertaken. What is perceived as right or wrong, or true or false, has thus very little to do with what can be experimentally tested. It is rather a matter of "what one can live with among those with whom one interacts in the setting where one must operate."[31]

The example is also an illustration of how persons with dementia can make use of their remaining linguistic and cognitive resources. It is obvious that Martha is severely challenged in using her episodic memory, that is, in remembering events. She solves this challenge by using an old storyline, together with the physical arrangement of coffee cups and pots, and the way her companions are seated around the table. This results in a new problem: Martha makes sense for herself but not necessarily for the participants, and thus she has to negotiate with them.

CATASTROPHIC REACTIONS

A change in the brain as a result of an acquired brain injury or dementia will result in a *disruption* in the relations between the person, the environment, other persons, and the current tasks. Much of everyday life is built on actions that have become *habits* and *routines* and that operate outside awareness. These habits and routines include simple behaviors like walking through a familiar room and avoiding collisions with furniture, as well as more complex behaviors like preparing a meal. Most of these habits and routines function together with various *things* in the environment; the furniture is in its ordinary places in the living room, and spoons, knives, onions, and so on, are found in their ordinary places in the kitchen. Together they make up habitual action systems. Furthermore, quite a few habits and routines are *coordinated* with other persons' habits and routines. Typical examples of coordinated habits are getting dressed in the morning, brushing teeth, and preparing breakfast. Other habits and routines are not individual but can only work if they are performed together with other persons. An example of such a joint routine and habit is turn-taking in conversations.

As a consequence of the changing or changed brain, some of these habits and routines do not work anymore; the cognitive and semiotic resources connected to certain networks in the brain used previously *are no longer available*. In cases of dementia, disruptions initially often occur when a person has problems recognizing everyday things and the way these function, as well as recognizing persons and environments, or finding words and names.

Goldstein pointed out that this disruption of the previous relationships and the availability of resources almost always resulted in what he called a *catastrophic reaction*, in contrast to what he calls a normal or "ordered" reaction—that is, a "reaction" based on habits and routines.

> The catastrophic reactions [. . .] are not only "inadequate" but also disordered, inconstant, inconsistent, and embedded in physical and mental shock. In these situations, the individual feels himself unfree, buffeted, and vacillating. He experiences a shock affecting not only his own person, but the surrounding world as well. He is in that condition we usually call anxiety. After an ordered reaction, he can ordinarily proceed to another, without difficulty or fatigue. Whereas, after a catastrophic reaction, his reactivity is likely to be impeded for a longer or shorter interval. He becomes more or less unresponsive and fails even in those tasks he could easily meet under other circumstances. The disturbing aftereffect of catastrophic reactions is longlasting.[32]

What Goldstein points out is that persons with acquired brain injuries may respond with strong anxiety when they cannot face demands in a situation by invoking their ordinary resources. Add to this that persons with brain injuries often have difficulties in predicting what will happen in situations or consequences of action, and are therefore often caught in situations without a warning, exacerbating the anxiety reaction. The person's catastrophic anxiety has to do with an experience of *disorganization* or a *disruption* of everyday life *routines* and *habits*. Central to this disruption are problems with or loss of abilities to recognize the situation and its tasks, as well as artifacts and their functions, words, and names. The habitual action systems lose their meaning and hence their affordance to actions, something that leads to anxiety and an *avoidance* of the situation that provoked the strong emotional response.

In an extract (Example 3.3) from the third joint interview with Kate and her husband Keith, Kate tells about what happens as a consequence of her illness. She has been living with a dementia diagnosis for many years, but the last year both she and her husband have begun to notice severe changes. Just before the start of the extract, Keith has told about what he thinks has happened to Kate during the year since the last interview. Kate tells about her everyday life.

Example 3.3.

1	Kate:	it has gone so fast (0.4)
2		I'm fully aware of what to say and everything
3		but when I open my mouth it is just jibberish or what it is
4		and what (0.6) <u>not</u> (0.4) keep this (1.2) part any more
5		I used to at least to grasp and understand
6		but now this part (0.7)
7		I can't get it together what he says (1.1)
8		and I've become afraid of walking alone (1.1)
9		'cause I won't find my way home
10	Interviewer:	no:
11		(0.7)
12	Kate:	and then I become stressed (.) that I can't (0.6)
13		take my eh (0.4) walks on my own
14	Interviewer:	have you ever lost your way
15	Kate:	(1.1) eh: (0.6) I can't remember

In the example, Kate's telling illustrates her experiences of catastrophic reactions: the changes in her life caused by her illness are unpredictable. She finds it hard to talk and understand her husband, and her personal freedom has become restricted as a consequence of her memory challenges. It is also obvious that Kate faces severe difficulties in telling her story, as she cannot find words and construct utterances.

It is easy to associate the term "catastrophic reaction" with a massive emotional and bodily reaction. For some persons that can be true, but observing people with dementia in conversation, these massive reactions are rarely noticed. Rather, the main sign of a catastrophic reaction is the *averted gaze*. In conversations, the participants regularly make eye contact, for instance, when they want to change turn and let someone else say something, or when the topic is especially sensitive or emotionally loaded.[33] In conversations with a person with dementia who encounters severe challenges that he or she cannot solve, the person often averts his or her gaze and looks away or down—often with an unfocused gaze.

An example (Example 3.4) of this was when Laura in an interview could not remember how she got in contact with a medical doctor about her cognitive problems—something that resulted in her diagnosis with Alzheimer's disease at the age of 48 (see Chapter 6 for discussion about Laura). Laura answers that her sister established the contact with the medical doctor (lines 1–6).

Example 3.4.

1	Laura:	SHE
2		Monica
3		my sister
4		eh
5		she had some
6		something in on
	Gesture:	(raises right hand and makes circular movement with right index finger; stops and moves finger to lips)
	Gaze:	(unfocused gaze turned downward)
7		(pause 3s)
8		Damn, I don't know

But then Laura is unable to tell what happened. She gestures, then gives up by turning her gaze downward. She keeps her gaze unfocused and directed downward and after a pause (three seconds), says: "Damn, I don't know."

As already indicated, Goldstein mainly wrote about catastrophic reactions as a clinician in a clinical situation, but he rarely included himself in the analysis of the patients' behavior. Persons with brain injuries not only do things on their own, as is the case in clinical test situations. As pointed out, for many persons most of their everyday life is spent doing things together with other persons, like taking walks, preparing food and eating together, talking with others, and telling stories. In this kind of situation, the demands can be very complex; for instance, just following an ongoing conversation about something, identifying a possible contribution, and at the same time keeping track of the possibilities to deliver this contribution in such a way that the relations between the participants are kept are extremely difficult. It is a kind of situation that easily may result in a catastrophic reaction and a *withdrawal* from the situation. In this kind of situation, the other participants may experience the affected person's behavior as strange or even deeply disturbing and thus also withdraw from the situation, thereby severing the relation.

This generally also has consequences for future interactions; there is a heightened risk that the participants will avoid doing things together in the future. Psychoanalyst Paula Freed and psychologist Christian Salas have both argued that catastrophic reactions in situations that involve other persons may result in what they call a "disencounter" of people, that is, a loss of relations with others. Ultimately this may result in a generalized loss of human relationships, thus leaving the person with a brain injury socially isolated.[34]

Compensatory Adaptation

Persons with acquired brain injuries quickly develop ways to avoid catastrophic reactions by either avoiding the situation that gives rise to the anxiety, or by inventing and instigating new and more effective ways to perform old tasks.

Most persons in situations where the everyday habits and routines do not work, and even more so when they result in strong emotional responses, find that actions come to a halt and the person reconsiders the situation afresh. He or she will start a new analysis of the situation, by back-tracking what went wrong, then imagine new possible solutions to the situation and finally test these solutions in order to find out how to continue. A problem for persons with acquired brain injuries and dementia is, of course, that their abilities for analyzing the situation and finding new responses are more limited than before due to the brain injury; they must use their limited resources to find new ways to deal with everyday situations, both individual actions as well as actions coordinated with others and performed jointly with others.

Goldstein called these new ways or responses "detours"; other researchers have used the terms "adaptation," "coping," or "coping strategies," while others talk about "compensation" or "compensatory strategies" or "self-regulatory strategies." As British linguist Michael Perkins has pointed out, there has been a lot of discussion around this terminology, especially of whether these terms imply conscious decisions or not, and whether the "compensation" is intentional or not.[35] As a way out of this discussion, Perkins suggests the use of the term "compensatory adaptation" because "the term is deliberately neutral with regard to issues such as whether or not the adjustment is effective, whether it is under conscious control and/ or voluntary, how it is brought about and whether it may be learned or taught."[36]

Compensatory adaptations can be classified in many different ways. Psychologists Roger Dixon, Douglas Garrett, and Lars Bäckman have suggested a number of what they call "compensatory mechanisms":[37]

- investing more *time* and *training* in order to be able to continue a practice;
- *substituting* a latent skill for one that is declining—that is, using a skill that was not used much before the brain injury.
- developing *new skills* to take over the lost ones;
- adjusting or *accommodating* one's goal to the new situation;
- modifying or *adjusting* the environment and other's expectations.

Although these categories may not be exhaustive, they still capture many of the basic strategies that are available for individuals with acquired brain injuries. There are at least three important limitations to the traditional way of depicting compensatory adaptations that need to be reconceptualized.

Reconceptualizing Compensation

The first limitation is that compensatory adaptation is often considered to be a linear process of finding new goals and paths. In particular, research around the rehabilitation process has shown that it is not a straight process that can be fashioned in terms of goals, motivation, and so on. Rather, the development of compensatory adaptation is better thought of as an explorative and experimental process in which various solutions are tested to see what works and what is feasible. New tests could then be seen in terms of iterative and testing action in order to find new solutions.

One way to conceptualize the compensatory process would be to see it as similar to the *repair* process in conversations.[38] In conversations, one of the participants may notice some kind of trouble in the ongoing conversation; one participant may not have heard what was said, or the speaker may mispronounce a word. One of the participants then indicates that some trouble has been noticed; this can be done saying something like "uh?," or "sorry, I didn't hear." In the next step, the speaker attempts to *repair* his or her utterance by, for instance, repeating a word or a part of an utterance. In a final step, the other participant then acknowledges acceptance of the repair—or requests further repair, and finally accepting—and then the conversation can continue. In the literature around conversational repair, it is also argued that there is a preference for self-correction. That means that when a speaker indicates trouble, having for instance mispronounced a word, the speaker prefers to self-correct the word. If the listener indicates a problem having to do with the speaker, then the speaker prefers to self-repair the problem. The reason for this preference is that being the source of a trouble is face-threatening, and self-correction is thus a way to save face.

This repair sequence is similar to the process of a person with dementia encountering a problem in doing something. A first step for the person with dementia is to indicate that a problem is found. Next, the person tries another action, and if it works, the activity continues; otherwise a third action is tested, and so on. If no alternative action is found that works, there is a high risk of withdrawal from the situation.

Second, there is often an exclusive focus on the individual without considering the use of "tools" or artifacts. The reason for this is that it is often only "internal" tools that are considered, that is, cognitive tools. But quite often, the person with dementia makes use of "external" tools, like pen and paper, a notice board, or a photo. The following example (Example 3.5) indicates how "external" tools can be used as part of compensatory adaptation.

Example 3.5.

> In an interview a woman diagnosed with dementia told about how she found it difficult to bake due to her "memory problems." When measuring and adding flour, eggs, and butter to make a cake, she often lost track of the quantities. Had she measured one cup of flour or three, and what about the sugar? She solved her problem by using spoons as external measuring signs. For every cup of flour she added she put a spoon beside the bowl, and then she could check the number of spoons and know what quantities she already had added. She thus adapted quite creatively to the situation by using an external mnemonic tool; the spoons were used not as spoons but as signs and as such they turned into a new answer to an established situation.

In line with Luria's argument, she had revised part of a previously working functional system used for keeping track of her sequential activities by adding an external tool (or sign) and thus expanded her "working memory" to include things "outside her skull." Cognitive scientist David Kirsh has pointed out that most people tend to organize their surroundings, especially their kitchens and other workplaces, in such a way that the organization may function as an external memory tool. By arranging all the jars in a cupboard in a certain way, it becomes much easier to find a specific jar.[39]

This example clearly shows that compensatory adaptations may involve avoiding certain situations, but also may involve the use of external tools. Finding new ways to use external tools as a part of a compensatory adaptation may increase the person's ability to deal with situational demands.

The third limitation has to do with compensatory adaptations in relation to other persons. For persons with dementia, many everyday situations involve other persons, whether they are living together with a spouse or family, or in supported facilities. This in turn implies coordinating actions with other persons, as well as doing things together, for instance talking. Although the dementia affects one specific individual, the disease has consequences for all other persons because both coordination and joint activities become more complicated. Compensatory adaptations that are executed in these contexts only by the person with dementia have a limited efficacy compared to instances when all participants take part in the compensatory adaptation. If other participants are also involved, it becomes possible to jointly avoid certain situations, or to organize the conversational interaction in such a way that the person with dementia is supported, for instance. Furthermore, in doing things together, participants are generally very eager to complete the joint activity and thus tend to support each other.

Thus, in everyday situations involving other people, one way for the participants to avoid catastrophic reactions is to engage in what could be called *collaborative compensatory adaptation*; that is, participants support each other, and they particularly support the person with dementia. The person with dementia uses the other participants' resources as a way of supporting his or her remaining resources. The collaborative compensatory adaptation could thus be defined as a *reconfiguration* or *reorganization* and *redistribution* of resources, particularly the semiotic and cognitive resources that are used by the participants together in order to accomplish the joint activity. This could, for instance, imply that persons who are challenged in remembering events could get support from someone else just through the right questions, by asking specific, "closed" questions instead of using "open" questions without indication of what kind of answer to give.

Collaborative Compensatory Adaptation

Collaborative compensatory adaptation is a field that needs to be further explored. Often support is described in very general and global terms, as what the healthy persons need to do in order for the person with dementia to take part in an activity. Treating support as a global term means that there is a risk that support results in what has been called "micromanagement" of the situation,[40] in which the healthy person "takes over" and provides the word, name, sentence, or action that the person with dementia has difficulty producing. Or, the healthy person tries to support and "help" the person with dementia by asking questions that aim at testing and supporting memory. For instance, he might ask questions about what day it is, or if the person with dementia may recall the name of the grandchildren.[41] This kind of micromanagement—although often well intended—may result in positioning the person with dementia as being either unable or at least as being a less capable participant in the interaction. This positioning comes very close to the kind of situation that results in withdrawal; that is, the person with dementia experiences failure in engaging with other persons.

There is thus a need to look closer into how collaborative compensatory adaptation can be organized in order to actually support and enhance personhood and agency. Later in this book (Chapter 5), the organization of this kind of collaboration will be discussed in terms of *scaffolding*, detailing how the healthy participant and the person with dementia together can solve problems that emerge in the interaction.

An important conclusion from this is that persons with dementia have not *lost* their cognitive or linguistic abilities to take part in storytelling. Rather, the persons with dementia are tellers who are *bounded* in terms of the possible contributions they can make on their own to the storytelling. In other words, persons with dementia are bounded by the restricted internal cognitive and semiotic resources available to them. The concept of collaborative compensatory adaptation indicates that it could be expected that persons with dementia could use the resources of others.

Cultural Aspects of Compensatory Adaptation

The approach to dementia and acquired brain injuries presented in the preceding implies that traumas and diseases do not have given or automatic consequences. The fit between the changed or changing brain and the way a person responds to these changes is not linear, but rather is fairly loose. This highlights the fact that the consequences of acquired brain injuries and dementias are very complex and depend on a wide variety of factors. A number of quite different factors are important in understanding how persons with dementia respond to and adapt to a life with a changing brain. In this context, at least three aspects are worth mentioning.

First, research has shown that factors like education, work complexity, social networks, and leisure activities may contribute to maintaining a "reserve" cognitive function in old age, as well as in cases of brain injuries.[42] This implies that the incidence of dementia diagnosis can be expected to vary between cultures (and countries) depending on the educational system and the ways in which work is organized. In countries with a comprehensive educational system, engaging children early in education, and with a complexity in later work experience, it can be expected that the symptoms associated with dementia will be presented later in the life course as compared to countries with a less well functioning educational system.

Second, the meaning of dementia, in particular the symptoms associated with dementia like memory challenges, vary quite substantially between cultures.[43] Studies of people living with what would be diagnosed as Alzheimer's disease in, for instance, Japan and India indicate that the interpretation and understanding of the symptoms are quite different. In Japan, as people grow older, concern is about a general decline known as *boke*:

> For the most part, *boke* is expressed through symptomatic features that tend to be associated with patterns of diminished cognitive status in nondemented older adults. Although these may be precursors to or very early stages of pathological conditions among those same individuals, *boke* itself is not usually presented as symptomatically representing pathology in the way that AD or other forms of dementia do.[44]

In contrast to persons living with a dementia diagnosis in the Western world, *boke* allows the person agency, and thus the ability to sustain central cultural values and commitments. In northern India, Lawrence Cohen reports that, for instance, neighbors often use the term "weak brain" to describe and understand the physical consequences of aging. Further, "most forms of old age weakness in Banaras make sense [. . .] in terms of the relationship between an old person and his or her children."[45] This means that when an aging person has a "weak brain," his or her family may be considered to be a "bad family."

Thus the categories used both in Japan and India for understanding similar types of behavior and experiences associated with Alzheimer's disease in the West shift between cultures. Different aspects of the "symptoms" are stressed, allowing for different notions of agency and participation in family and communal life.

Third, the social consequences of dementia can be expected to vary. In countries with a low level of technology and less social interactions with strangers, there is probably a more forgiving attitude toward people with early dementia, as compared to cultures based on complex technology and a high dependence on social interactions with unknown persons. Cultural notions and expectations concerning both aging and dementia will affect the individuals' experience of their changing brains, as well as those practices that are connected with the cultural responses to aging and dementia.

Given this, we might expect that people encounter and deal with the pathological brain processes connected with dementia in quite different ways due to cultural, social, and psychological factors—and interactions among these factors. In other words, the consequences and meaning of the brain changes associated with dementia are not universal, but rather something that is constructed in interactions between people, given certain social and cultural concepts and practices. In that sense, the pathological brain processes involved in dementia can be fairly universal, but the consequences are highly variable.

THE INJURED BRAIN AND HUMAN LIFE

All brains change as a consequence of learning and of experiencing new things, relationships, and persons, as well as a consequence of persons who stop doing things they used to do. These changes in and of the brain are most often concurrent with changes of identity and self. Thus there will be little discrepancy between changes in the brain and changes in the person; the brain and its functionality are not experienced as at variance with what the person is engaging in. It is only when the changes of the brain have no direct relation to what the person is doing or striving to do (and thus is thwarted from accomplishing) that the person will experience problems. This happens when parts of the connections in the brain start to degenerate and rob the brain of some of its abilities. This is what Thomas DiBaggio experienced when he was diagnosed with dementia; "Meaning is lost in a hurried moment, a word lost in confusion is never recovered."

A starting point for this chapter was the conception of the brain as an organ that has a central part in realizing and regulating interaction with both persons and artifacts. The brain is thus part of activities and becomes organized into functional systems that facilitate cooperation with "other brains," as well as with artifacts. These functional systems consist of relationships between various specialized parts of the brain, and are mediated by semiotic systems. The brain's functional systems constitute *resources* for action, made up of basic skills like word finding, sentence construction, attention, and working memory. As pointed out at the beginning of the chapter, these resources have evolved to work together with the language sound system, gestures, and other bodily movements, as well as artifacts like pictures and texts. As the dementia progresses, the cognitive and linguistic resources become less functional and less available in forming and performing actions in activities. This means that fewer and fewer choices are available for action, thus leaving few if any choices for action.[46] The changes in the brain's functionality imply, for instance, that words may be recognized but not their meanings; ideas and images can be conjured up but cannot be told, as words cannot be found. Abilities are not lost, but rather function differently. Most everyday routines are challenged and need to be reorganized and accomplished in new ways, using available resources in novel ways.

As a result of the progressive change of the brain, persons with dementia face a double risk. They risk failure in solving problems on their own, or being micromanaged by someone else taking over the tasks. Both these possibilities are likely to result in the person with dementia withdrawing from the situation and thus exiting social interaction, as well as abandoning relations with other persons. One way to avoid withdrawal is for the participants to collaborate in such a way that the person with dementia can actually find ways to contribute to the ongoing activity without losing face. It has been suggested that collaborative compensatory adaptation is central, that is, attempts to *compensate* for loss in functionality by performing actions in new ways. The person with dementia must perform the task at hand by using other resources, particularly those provided by other participants. Not finding a word might imply using a related word or substituting the word for a gesture. In other words, alternative resources can be used.

It has also been argued that storytelling is less a linear, automatic process where remembered ideas are fitted into words, than it is a constructive and opportunistic process. Stories are constructed in order to fit into a specific social context, with a specific audience, and thus every word matters. Telling a story might mean telling the same story—or parts of a story— again, rather than remembering an "original" event. How stories are constructed and told collaboratively is the theme of the next chapter.

NOTES

1. Thomas DeBaggio, *Losing my Mind* (2003), pp. 14–15.
2. Sabat, 2001.
3. The evolution of the brain as part of the development of more complex relations and in human society of institutions is a recurrent theme in modern evolutionary theory. See, for instance, Bowles & Gintis, 2011; Richerson & Boyd, 2005.
4. Recent brain research has in many ways revolutionized our understanding of both the way the brain functions and how it has evolved. See, for instance, Arbib, 2011; Jeannerod, 2006; Panksepp, 2005; and Rizzalotti & Sinigaglia, 2008.
5. Barrett, 2011; A. Clark, 2006, 2008; Thelen, 2000.
6. Suddendorf & Corballis, 2007; Sugiyama, 2001.
7. Luria, 1973, p. 31.
8. Gillispie & Zittoun, 2010, p. 50.

9. Herman, 2003. Also see Wertsch, 1985, for a discussion about "tools."
10. Luria, 1980, p. 21.
11. See Lezak, Howieson, Bigler, & Tranel, 2012.
12. For a detailed description of the neurodegenerative process in Alzheimer's disease, see Braak & Braak, 1991, 1995.
13. Lezak et al., 2012, p. 237.
14. Maria Medved, 2014, p. 92. Also see, Clare, 2008.
15. Braak & Braak, 1991.
16. Cf. Kintsch & van Dijk, 1978.
17. See Neal Norrick, 1998, 2000, about retold stories in conversations.
18. The section about resources draws on Michael Perkin's inspiring work *Pragmatic Impairment* (2004), in particular Chapter 4.
19. Kontos, 2004.
20. See <IBT>Naomi Feil & Vicki de Klerk-Rubin, *The Validation Breakthrough* (2012).</IBT>
21. Ibid., p. 91.
22. Slobin, 1996. Also see Quaeghebeur & Reynaert, 2010.
23. Slobin, 1996, p. 75.
24. Cf. McNeil, 1992.
25. For further discussions of these kinds of problems, see Aleksander Luria's books on aphasia (1970, 1976).
26. See Stephen Jacyna's *Lost Words* (2000) for a historical account.
27. Merleau-Ponty, 1963, p. 64.
28. Goldstein, 1997, p. 35. This book was first published in 1934.
29. For a general review of which parts of the brain are engaged in various narrative activities, see Mar, 2004.
30. For more information about the study, see Örulv & Hydén, 2006, and Örulv, 2010.
31. Bruner, 2001, p. 36.
32. Goldstein, 1997, p. 49.
33. See Kendon, 1990. Also see Cheston & Bender, 1999.
34. Freed, 2002; Salas, 2012.
35. Perkins, 2007, pp. 147–148.
36. Perkins, 2007, p. 148.
37. Dixon, Garrett, & Bäckman, 2008; cf. Bäckman & Dixon, 1992.
38. Cf. Schegloff, Jefferson, & Sacks, 1977, and Clark, 1996.
39. Kirsh, 1995.
40. This observation and term have been suggested by my colleague Professor Nicole Müller.
41. This resembles a practice that is typical of teaching in classrooms. My colleagues Professor Anna Ekström and Professor Ali Majlesi have very cleverly argued that the same kind of interactional practice can be found in conversations involving couples with dementia.
42. For a general overview of the concepts of brain reserve or cognitive reserve, see Stern, 2002. For dementia, see Fratiglioni & Wang, 2007; and Valenzuela & Sachdev, 2006, for a review of studies concerning dementia.
43. For an example, see Cohen, 1998.
44. Traphagan, 1998, p. 82.
45. Cohen, 1995, p. 318.
46. Cf. Perkins, 2007.

CHAPTER 4

Stories

Making Worlds and Selves

(1) Starting the main point of the story

V: when you look back over your past Tina, what is it that stands out most?

T: ah [. . .] well I guess the thing that stands out the most is
    ah my memories of my illness
    and ah the fact that I couldn't even really walk
    [. . .] and ah I

(2) Support for the main point by focusing on an event

    Daddy used to have to carry me and ah [. . .] you know
    it was a bad situation
    but it brought us all close together
    [. . .]

(3) More detail about the event

    and ah you see
    they cut this wound on my back without anesthetic
    [. . .] and I was just a teenager
    and ah it was ah
    my mother didn't know they were going to operate on me

(4) Restating the main point

    and ah
    and on
    and I guess they felt they had to do something

(5) Restating stanza 3: her mother's anger

> and I guess my mother was furious when she found
> out that they had cut this hole in my back
> and ah

V: what about other memories Tina?

*(6) Conclusion on the narrative despite interruption. Restating points
articulated in stanza 2*

T: it was a painful situation
> well I have ah
> my my daddy used to carry me
> and ah everywhere
> and brought us really close together because ah
> it was that kind of situation

This story was told by a woman called Tina to interviewer Vai Ramanathan. At the time of the interviews, Tina was 65 years old and was diagnosed with mild to moderate Alzheimer's disease. She had been a teacher of math and English, but decided to quit her job when she was diagnosed with dementia. Vai Ramanathan, a sociolinguist, interviewed Tina repeatedly and in various settings (at home and at a day care center).[1]

Ramanathan parses the story into six parts. The first part starts with the interview question that Tina responds to by introducing the main theme of the story, which is her illness as a child and her inability to walk. This theme is then elaborated on in the next part, while part 3 introduces a new theme, the operation, which is again reiterated in part 4 and further developed in part 5 by her mother's anger. Then the interviewer tries to introduce something new by asking Tina for other memories, but Tina sticks to her story by going back to part 2 and repeats it almost verbatim. Part 6 also functions as an evaluation and conclusion of the story. In the transcriptions presented by Ramanathan, it is not possible to see her own contributions to the interaction with the exception of her interview questions. Interestingly, the last interview question ("What about other memories, Tina?") could potentially function as a discontinuer by impeding on Tina's ongoing talk, but Tina ignores the question and thus is able to conclude her story. Tina incrementally adds new lines and parts to her story and thus is able to develop both the structure and the topic of her story. Her voice throughout the story is clear, and in overriding the interviewer's attempt to introduce a new topic, Tina forcefully expresses her own voice in the conclusion.

This interview was conducted in Tina's home, in her living room. Early on in the extract, both the listener and the readers are carried away to a different setting, Tina's childhood somewhere in the United States, and to a time not further specified. The movement is from the "here-and-now" not only of the interview, but also away from the actual situation of reading the story, and to a world placed "there-and-then." What transpires in the story is not happening in the here-and-now of the interview, but in the world of there-and-then. Both of Tina's parents are present, they talk, think, and have emotions. At some points in the storytelling, Tina steps out from the story world and comments on the events in her childhood—that it was a bad situation, but it brought the family together—and evaluates what her parents did for her. Although the interviewer attempts to move on by asking Tina to move to a new story world, Tina prefers to remain in her childhood, thus declining the invitation.

By "traveling" to the world of her childhood, Tina constructs not only a story world, but also a *self*, the self of the child with an illness, cared for by two concerned parents. This childhood self is constructed by a teller, again struck by illness, although this time by Alzheimer's disease. Tina's present self, existing in the here-and-now of the storytelling situation, is thus juxtaposed with the childhood self, making a comparison possible. What is the same, what is different, and what does the comparison tell about Tina?

Autobiographical stories, like all stories, obviously have the ability to engage their audience in "traveling" to constructed worlds and to take part in a "re-enactment" of events. Storytelling thus entails construction as well as collaboration and the sharing of both thoughts and emotions. It is these constructive and collaborative elements that will be presented and discussed in this chapter, together with considerations about how persons with dementia use stories in the construction of self. From a theoretical point of view, it is stressed that many notions about stories and storytelling use written stories as their typical example of a story. As a consequence of the theoretical norms derived from written stories, the stories told by persons with dementia appear to be fragmentary, incomplete, or even confabulatory. This in turn has been used as an argument in favor of the notion that a person with dementia does not have an identity.

This chapter challenges these theoretical notions in favor of taking the conversational story as the best example of what a narrative is in the field of dementia studies. Much of the research on dementia and narrative—as well as in the field of narrative gerontology—has been based on the often implicit assumption that written stories can serve are the best examples of what a narrative is. A consequence of taking the written narrative as the norm is that it becomes more likely to regard the stories that people with dementia tell as expressions of a life story that can be revised and amended and thus become true. In contrast, stressing the importance of theories around conversational storytelling might help to focus on stories and storytelling as a collaborative activity, negotiating joint meaning and thus shared story worlds—and shared imagination. In this perspective, neither people living with dementia nor other persons have one life story. Instead, they might tell many different stories about their lives in different contexts and in collaboration with different persons. Thus, stories as expressions of identity are then not merely the business of a single individual, but a joint accomplishment of several participants.

For these reasons, this chapter is primarily about issues around narrative theory; although dementia is discussed in the chapter, it is obviously in the background.

NARRATIVE NORMS

A problem in the narrative field is that many social scientific researchers have tended to conceive and analyze stories told in interviews or identified in observational data as if they dealt with a written story. Hence, the focus is often on the *discursive organization* of the narrative in terms of coherence, plot, and so on. Generally, it also implies that the *meaning* of the narrative can be found *in* the narrative text as such. And finally, it implies that the narrative primarily is a *representation* of events in the past. This approach implies that narratives told in interviews or in some other kind of interaction are analyzed in relation to norms for written text production as if they are instances of *written* autobiographical texts.

A problem with these literary norms is that social scientific researchers, especially those working with stories told by persons with dementia or other communicative disabilities, often expect and hope to elicit, find, and collect stories that conform to the literary norms. Most storytellers with communicative disabilities have problems telling stories that conform to these norms and expectations, either in interviews, or in clinical or everyday settings; they quite often tend to upset the often implicit and taken-for-granted *narrative norms* of the researcher. In fact, researchers often judge people with communicative disorders to be too difficult to interview, and therefore many of these individuals have been excluded from research, even though the ambition is to be inclusive.[2] One way for researchers to deal with this situation has been to compile narratives themselves from the interviews in order to create a coherent narrative with a beginning, middle, and end—that is, a story that adheres to the norms of written text narratives. Another way has been to use stories told by others (relatives, caregivers, professionals) *about* the person with dementia. As a consequence, it is not the person with dementia (or other communicative disabilities) who tells the story; the story is rather an analytical construction by the researcher or the relative or caregiver, who join and order fragments from an interview, and give them the kind of temporal order and coherence prescribed by their narrative norms and expectations.

This procedure has, in fact, profound consequences both for the theoretical conception of what a narrative is and for the ways narratives are analyzed—something that is rarely discussed. Due to the fact that interviewees with communicative disabilities often have severe problems telling stories, the question emerges of *whose story* it is that is being told and then presented in research, and *whose voice* is heard in the storytelling.[3] Is the story told by the researcher actually the story that the person with the disability tried to tell, or is it the story that the researcher believes that the interviewee wanted to tell? Another important consequence is that persons with communicative disabilities tend to appear as less competent storytellers than they actually are. Telling stories that don't comply with the established narrative norms often results in the idea that the teller is incompetent and hence a person whose personhood is questionable.

DEFINING STORIES

Defining what a story is in general is difficult, almost impossible. Psychologist and narrative researcher Jens Brockmeier argues that today no single encompassing definition exists either of what a narrative is, or what narrative research is and can be. This is due to the fact that materials and media "considered to be relevant for narrative practices have metastasized." Thus, he concludes, a unifying notion of narrative and narrative research "cannot exist any longer."[4]

One way to avoid using an overgeneralized notion of narrative is to limit the field of interest. *Narrative* in this book most generally refers to stories told in conversations and thus does not refer to written stories, or to stories appearing in other media. It is also a very specific kind of story that is discussed, namely autobiographical stories (sometimes called life stories), and hence not fictional stories, or stories about events in the world in general. Thus, in this context the definition presented by literary theorist Barbara Herrnstein Smith can be quite fruitful. She suggests that we "might conceive of narrative discourse most minimally and most generally as verbal acts consisting of someone telling someone else that something happened."[5]

This definition is simple and in many ways overlaps the everyday notion of a story. The definition refers to stories told in everyday conversations between people, and may not necessarily be valid and productive in discussing other kinds of stories (for instance, written stories). It is also a definition that fits well with autobiographical storytelling, as this kind of story often refers to the personal experiences of events. It is important to note that her definition stresses the fact that storytelling is an interactive and collaborative activity; one tells stories in order to tell someone else "that something happened." Thus, the teller must tell the story in such a way that the other can understand what happened and must assist the listener or be assisted if problems emerge during the telling. The aim is obviously that both teller and listener share the same story about what happened, something that implies *joint meaning-making*. Thus this conception of narrative connects to Brockmeier's suggestion that narrative is a "mode of meaning-making."[6]

One further aspect can be added to this concept of conversational storytelling as an act of meaning-making. As early as 1977, literary theorist Mary Louise Pratt pointed out that in telling a story, the teller is "inviting his adressees [sic] to join him in contemplating it, evaluating it, and responding to it."[7] Mary Louise Pratt emphasizes that storytelling is about *inviting* others to take part and share experiences. That is, storytelling is a kind of exchange between the participants, where everyone is supposed to make contributions of various kinds (telling stories, being attentive listeners, etc.). This means that storytelling is an activity that is about *mutual emotional engagement*, where the participants have to attune to each others' emotions and the emotional content of the stories.

STORY WORLD MODEL

The meaning-making activity in storytelling draws on the fact that one of the wonderful and emotionally exhilarating aspects of telling stories is the possibility of creating new realities—the there-and-then of the *story world*—that exist in the *here-and-now* of the speech event. Tellers and listeners can travel thousands of miles, visit other times and places, and even familiarize themselves with events that may never have taken place at all, at least not in historical reality. The story world is made up of events that took place somewhere else at some other point of time. It is a "world" that is jointly imagined and in a sense exists in the space between the participants in the storytelling situation. Characters who are not present in the world of storytelling populate the story world; the events take place in locations other than the present, and are not equal to the ones in the speech situation. Fictional storytelling suspends expectations about truth, thus letting imagination run freely, while nonfictional storytelling is committed to some kind of truth, or at least proximity to truth.

The story world is the result of what literary theorist David Herman calls "narrative worldmaking."[8] In some situations, a person's action is under-specified, questionable, or deviant—or it is possible to see the person in this way. It is typically in these situations that a teller can evoke a story in order to cast light on the teller by creating a context, reasons for actions and events, and so on. Storying of the world is thus a way of meaning-making; what at first appears to be hard to understand is placed in a story world. By creating a story world, it becomes possible for participants to explore the story world by "worlding" the story world;[9] that is, by using everyday experience and knowledge, the participants can understand and make sense of events in the story world.

The story world is inserted into the *realm of the conversation*, that is, the ongoing joint activity involving the participants. Thus the story world constitutes an enclave in the conversation. Between the story world and the realm of the conversation a further realm exists, namely the *realm of the telling*. This realm is constituted when the teller indicates a shift from the ongoing conversational discourse to a narrative discourse. This is often done by some kind of linguistic cues, like "I remember once . . . . " This sig-nals to the participants that a different kind of discourse is going to follow, and that it is specifically a story. Inside this realm the teller also can add information about the story as well as evaluate it (see Figure 4.1).[10]

As a result, a very complex situation unfolds and emerges; in a way, sev-eral "worlds" exist side by side simultaneously in the conversation, differ-entiated only by the complexities of linguistic constructions. As has been suggested by many researchers, the activity of storytelling is *layered* or *laminated*.[11] Erving Goffman was one of the first to point out that ongoing activities can be transformed and that it would be convenient to think of each transformation as adding a layer or lamination to the activity. One can address two features of the activity. One is the innermost layering, wherein dramatic activity can be at play to engross the participant. The other is the outermost lamination, the rim of the frame, as it were, which tells us just what sort of status in the real world the activity has, whatever the complex-ity of the inner laminations.[12]

The here-and-now of the conversational activity is a first layer, the sto-rytelling as a specific kind of discourse is a second layer, while the there-and-then story world is added as a third layer, inserted into the others.

Each realm and "world" is what phenomenological philosopher Alfred Schütz called a "finite province of meaning." Instead of using the concept of layering, he argued that we as humans live in "multiple realities" at the

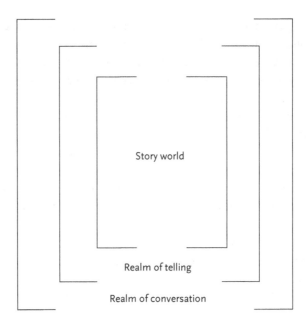

Figure 4.1. Realms of storytelling.
Adapted from Young (1987).

same time, going from one "reality" to another. An instance could be going from a state of sleep and dreaming, to being fully awake, to giving a lecture. Schütz argued that each of these "realities" "show a specific cognitive style" that, for instance, guides the person's

- view of reality (dreams do not have the same ontological status as the everyday realm of coffee-making in the morning);
- type of activity (play is different from work); or
- experience of the self (for instance in terms of agency—dreaming versus solving a problem).

Moving between the realms of storytelling similarly involves, for instance, a change in belief (events are imagined while events in the conversations are perceived), the self (as a projected character), and actions (events in the story world).[13] Following Schütz, it is also possible to argue that movements between these realms must be signaled and marked in some way in order for the participants to be able to coordinate the way they approach the various realms.[14]

Shifting between worlds occurs when someone begins to tell a story, moving from the realm of the conversation, to the realm of telling, and finally to the story world (see Example 4.1). Example 4.1 is taken from a joint interview with Kathy and Martin, with a focus on their life together and how dementia has affected it. They have been married for more than 50 years; at the time of interview they were around 80 years old. Kathy has severe memory problems, although she is fairly fluent linguistically. This extract is from the very beginning of the interview, just some 30 seconds from the start.

Example 4.1.

1	I₁:	we are a bit curious
2		could you tell us (0.5) when you met the first time
3		(2.6)
4	Kathy:	°heh°
5	Martin:	(turns towards Kathy)
6		maybe you could try to tell about it
7	Kathy:	heh no
8	Martin:	(turns towards I₁ and puts his hand on Kathy's)
9		we would like her to talk as much as possible
10		(removes his hand from Kathy's)
11		and remember
12	Kathy:	yes but I don't remember as well as
13		(puts her hand on Martin's)
14	Martin:	(takes Kathy's hand)
15		well I'm sure you do
16		the first times
17	Kathy:	eh
18	Martin:	and where (.) heh (0.3).hh think
19	Kathy:	well it was probably the first time I met Martin
20		I think it was at my parents' home (0.3)
21		(0.4).hh (0.4) then he just popped up (pats Martin's hand)
22		out of nowhere (1.2)
23		and I fell
24		(looks at Martin and takes his hand) (1.2)
25		for his charm
26		he was so kind and cute
27		and we've been a couple since then

The first interviewer (in line 1) says that "we are bit curious . . . ." This refers to something that belongs to the realm of conversation—it is about the research interview situation. The couple has just before this question been informed again about the project and they have signed an informed consent form. Martin supports the question (line 6) and Kathy expresses some concerns about this. Continuing inside the realm of storytelling, Martin connects bodily with Kathy and at the same time addresses the first interviewer that "we" would like Kathy to talk as much as possible (lines 8–11). Kathy again expresses her doubt about whether she can remember.

After some more support from Martin, Kathy on line 19 leaves the realm of conversation and enters the realm of the telling: "well it was probably the first time I met Martin." It is a comment that does not primarily refer to something going on in the conversation, as it refers to something that belongs to the story world: the first time she and Martin met each other. After this Kathy moves into the story world and starts by introducing the place ("at my parents'") home. Mentioning her parents also implies a different *time*, as her parents were still alive. Then, Martin suddenly popped up from nowhere and she fell for his charm and he was kind and cute (lines 25– 26). Kathy is moving around in the past: she fell for his charm *then* at her *parents' home*. In her final comment (line 27) Kathy moves out of the story world and into the realm of telling and the here-and-now of the interview.

As this example illustrates, the moving back and forth between the different realms or "worlds" makes storytelling a complex activity and highlights the fact that storytelling is not just a delivery of an already composed story text, but is actually a collaborative, constructive, and interpretive activity in which participants must coordinate their understanding of the progressing story. The complexity at the same time gives the participants the possibility of jumping between the layers, creating new relations between the layers and thus giving the story new interpretive possibilities—something that often is used in autobiographical storytelling.

COLLABORATIVE STORYTELLING

In order for people to tell about "something that happened" and move from the world of here-and-now to the story world, they must construct the story in such a way that it is possible for them to understand each other. The participants in storytelling events are thus never passive recipients of a story text delivered by the teller, but rather active participants who closely follow and anticipate the evolving story. Although some researchers sometimes seem to argue that stories are delivered straight on by the teller, linguist Wallace Chafe has pointed out that the teller—or the tellers— construct the story by building on small parts that he calls *idea units*. An idea unit consists of one piece of new information added to the emerging story in the conversation.[15] The idea unit in the telling is marked in different ways, often prosodically, thus making it possible for the listener to discern the unit.

This point has been taken up by James Gee, who argues that oral stories are divided into what he calls main *parts*, then *strophes* that are organized around happenings or events, and finally *lines*, which are the basic elements expressing ideas. The teller prosodically marks various elements in a narrative, helping the listener to follow and understand the story as he or she hears it; this makes it possible to identify what the teller thinks is important, funny, noteworthy, or connected. Gee's understanding of stories also stresses that stories are told incrementally; that is, new elements ("lines") are added one at a time as the story is told.[16] (As a consequence, transcripts of stories could be organized with the line as a basic unit—something that has been done in this book.)

In practical terms, this means that a storyteller never tells a story in one long sequence, but rather structures the telling of the story into smaller parts, each part corresponding to an idea unit. This could be conceptualized in interactional terms as the teller making *contributions* to the ongoing storytelling activity, with each contribution corresponding to an idea unit. Example 4.2 is an extract from a joint interview with a woman and her husband about their life with dementia. The wife has had a dementia diagnosis for a couple of years and has quite severe memory problems. They are both around 70 years old at the time of the interview and have been married to each other since their early twenties. The interviewer asks them if they can tell about the first time they met; the husband, Carl, starts the story.

Example 4.2.

1	Carl:	yes
2		well it was nineteen seventy
3		(2.0)
4		it was
5		(.)
6		in January

Listening closely to the recorded interview and taking special care to notice even very small pauses, the start of the story is parsed into a number of smaller units, marked by pauses of various lengths. On line 1, the "yes" is a response to the interviewer's request for a story, followed by a brief pause (under 0.5 seconds). On line 2, Carl gives the year they met, followed by a longer pause (2 seconds). He then starts saying something, but pauses for half a second, and then in line 6 adds information about which month they met. His pause might be an indication of him being unsure about the month, but we will never know. This beginning of the story thus consists of three contributions, each a meaning unit: the response to the request, the year, and the month. Each contribution is marked by pauses, helping the listener to identify the central idea element that Carl contributes to the story.

So parsing the story into units facilitates the understanding of central elements of the story, but constructing the story this way also has important interactional consequences. Psychologist Herbert Clark suggests that the listener at each end of a contribution has the possibility to indicate whether he or she *acknowledges* his or her *acceptance* of the teller's contribution. The acceptance has many potential functions:

- signaling that the listener actually *heard* the contribution, something that is not obvious if the teller has problems with speaking or the listener with hearing;
- signaling *understanding* of the contribution; the listener might be unfamiliar with something, the contribution can be unclear, etc.;
- signaling *agreement* with what was said; the teller may have gotten something wrong or is telling about something that is contested.

The acceptance can have many different forms, from the implicit acceptance of the listener's continued attention, to continuers (like "mmm") or assessments (like "really?"), or demonstration or display of understanding by repeating a small part of the previous utterance or by nonverbal means, like nodding. The implicit acceptance is the strongest, as it demands less time and effort as compared with verbal demonstration of understanding and acceptance. If a contribution to the storytelling is accepted, the storyteller continues the story.[17] An example of the contribution-acceptance sequence is found in Example 4.3.

Example 4.3.

1	Carl:	yes
2		well it was nineteen seventy
3		(2.0)
4		it was
5		(.)
6		in January
7	Ann:	yes that's true
8	Carl:	yes at Heaven in the city center
9		a dance hall
10		that's where we met the first time
11	Ann:	that's where we met

In lines 1–6, Carl has given his wife plenty of opportunities to request a repetition or to challenge his contribution, but she has continued to listen and, moreover, to signal her attention to his story by looking at Carl. On line 7 she explicitly acknowledges her acceptance of his contributions by saying, "yes that's true." Carl then continues with a new contribution, adding more information about where they met (lines 8–10). Then again, in line 11, Ann explicitly accepts Carl's contributions so far by repeating parts of his previous utterance ("that's where we met").

In storytelling, as well as in conversations, the listener may have problems hearing or understanding what the teller is saying. The reasons for this may range from external disturbances making it difficult to perceive what is said, to the fact that the speaker may have problems producing an intelligible utterance. In those cases, no acceptance is possible; the contribution needs to be repeated, rephrased, or elaborated and explained. In other words, a *repair* is necessary. This can be accomplished through a number of repair strategies, from a paraphrase of the utterance filling in missing information, a request for clarification, to explicit questions about the meaning of the utterance, or a request for a total repetition of the utterance.[18]

Much research shows that the person with dementia will face increased challenges in telling a story due to problems with finding words and constructing utterances, as well as understanding others' contributions. This will result in an increase in the number of trouble episodes, and conversations and storytelling with persons with dementia are often fraught with troubles and repairs.

In conclusion, storytelling can be seen as a collaborative activity that is built around *contributions* and their *negotiation* and *acceptance*, as has been suggested by psychologist Herb Clark and his colleagues.[19] Although Clark has written primarily about conversations, his ideas also work well for storytelling in conversations:

> Contributing to conversation [. . .] requires the collaborative effort of both speaker and addressees. [. . .] In the collaborative view, the speaker and the addressees try to do something more at the same time: establish the mutual belief that addressees have understood what the speaker meant. [. . .] The speaker and addressees try to ground what is uttered, to establish what the speaker meant as common ground.[20]

CONVERSATIONAL STORYTELLING

In many studies of stories told about personal experiences, a story is often thought of as a clearly identifiable discursive unit, with a beginning and an end; it is linguistically, temporally, and causally coherent, often with a clear point and moral evaluation. In many respects, these ideas reflect narrative norms often associated with written stories and the type of personal experience story that sociolinguist William Labov made familiar through his and Joshua Waletzky's article published in 1967 about oral storytelling: "Narrative Analysis: Oral Versions of Personal Experience."[21]

Sociolinguist Elinor Ochs and psychologist Lisa Capps argued against this canonical idea. They stated that personal experience stories often vary, and hence deviate from the prototypical case of the Labovian interview stories. They suggest that personal experience stories told in conversations vary in five dimensions:[22]

- *Tellership*: who the teller of a story is can vary from one active teller to multiple active tellers;
- *Tellability*: to what degree a story can be said to have tellability (that is, whether it has a point or reports a canonical breach, thus making it worth telling), which can vary from a high degree to a low degree to the point of having no tellability at all;
- *Embeddedness*: a story can be presented as detached from the surrounding conversation or can be embedded in the ongoing talk;
- *Linearity*: a story can be built on a closed temporal and/or causal order on one extreme or have a very loose and open temporal and/or causal order on the other;
- *Moral stance*: stories can convey a certain and constant moral stance or be uncertain and fluid.

As a consequence of these variations in stories and storytelling activities, it could be expected to find stories in conversational storytelling activities that lack the classical marks of being clearly discernible discursive units in talk. Those stories can involve several tellers, and may be highly integrated into ongoing conversations, and hence may be less easy to spot and delineate from an analytical perspective; they also may show considerable fluidity concerning both the order of events referred to in the story and the moral evaluations of those events.

In storytelling involving persons with dementia, the deviations from the established narrative norm are even greater and more frequent. This can be expected especially concerning tellership; persons with dementia can be expected to have many troubles telling stories on their own, but will be more successful telling stories with support. Thus, many of the features of stories and storytelling that are considered to be typical for persons with dementia (weak coherence, multiple tellers, a weak point, etc.) in many ways are typical for conversational storytelling and are not an obvious sign of an inability to tell stories.

AUTOBIOGRAPHICAL STORIES

One type of story is the genre of autobiographical stories. These are thought to have a real-life importance because they help to construct both a sense of self and an identity; that is, they are stories that have vital functions in peoples' lives. As already mentioned, the interest in the relationship between stories and identity in persons with dementia is connected to a re-evaluation of the person with dementia and a stress on the potential for maintaining self-identity.

Sociolinguist Charlotte Linde has argued that what sometimes is called a life story actually consists of all the stories told by an individual during the course of his or her lifetime; they are stories that are about the individual, and are told and retold over the course of a long period. "A life story consists of all the stories and associated discourse units, such as explanations and chronicles, and the connections between them, told by an individual during the life course of his/her lifetime."[23]

According to this definition, persons don't have *one* life story, but rather a set of stories that are told at various points in time and to various persons. These stories have what Charlotte Linde calls "extended reportability," that is, they can be told repeatedly in many different settings. She also points out that life stories have the teller as their primary evaluative point; that is, life stories do not have a point about how the world is in general, but rather aim to highlight something about the teller.

One critical note on Linde's definition could be worth adding. To her, life stories are told by individuals and belong to individuals. This focus on the individual is often the result of a research design favoring interviews with individuals. If this design is changed to include, for instance, couples, it becomes evident that the spouses share quite a few life stories. Thus, Linde's definition needs to be amended in order to also include the notion of *shared life stories* told by *multiple tellers* (this theme will be further discussed in Chapter 5).

Life stories or autobiographical life stories can be used by persons in several ways in order to tell or show something about who the teller is, and what kind of person he or she has been, presently is, and intends to be in the future. Sociolinguist Deborah Schiffrin writes about most stories that they convey a "self portrait" of the teller:

> Telling a story provides a self-portrait: a linguistic lens through which to discover people's own (somewhat idealized) views of themselves as situated in a

social structure. The verbalization and textual structure of a story (analogous to the creation of form and composition in a portrait) combines with its content, and with its local and global contexts of production, to provide a view of self that can be either challenged or validated by an audience.[24]

One obvious possibility inherent in narratives is to connect the past with the present by telling stories about how events in the past have led to the situation at the time of telling the story. The life story can stress the sameness of the person by stressing continuity in life over time, as well as point to a fundamental disruption and change in life, through events that have been halting or changing the course of the life process, and thus tell a story that includes turning points.[25]

This concept of an autobiographical story draws on certain genre norms that help to define what an autobiographical story is, as well as its limits. Social historian Philippe Lejeune writes that an autobiographical story consists of

> retrospective prose narrative written by a real person concerning his own existence, where the focus is his individual life, in particular the story of his personality [...] . In order for there to be autobiography [...] , the author, the narrator, and the protagonist must be identical.[26]

Put in other words, what Lejeune is saying is that the teller of an autobiographical story must personally have witnessed the events that make up the story, also implying that these events must have in fact taken place. If the teller of the story is recounting events that have taken place, but were not witnessed or experienced by the teller, then it's not an autobiographical story—but it perhaps may be a historical story. So autobiographical stories presuppose that the teller *owns* the experience and *remembers* and communicates it correctly.

As literary scholar Paul Eakin points out, breaking the rules and conventions of autobiographical storytelling has a "disciplinary potential confronting those who fail to display an appropriately normal model of narrative identity."[27] In this perspective, it is obvious that persons with dementia will face problems easily if their stories are not well defined and coherent, true, based on accurate individual memories, and dressed in an adequate linguistic outfit. If their stories don't live up to these norms, there is always the risk that they will be considered to be "failed" stories. These narrative norms thus risk excluding the stories of persons with dementia, which makes these norms quite problematic.

Storytelling is an activity that is about the events and characters in the story world, but also about the meaning of the story for the relationship between the participants in the storytelling situation—the interactional and relational function of the story. It could even be claimed that both the relations and the identities of the participants in the storytelling situation are interdependent; what one of them does, not only has consequences for the other, but also is implicitly designed on a conception of the other.

In telling autobiographical stories, other times, places, persons, circumstances, and events are introduced, compared to those present in the situation of telling. These other times, places, persons, circumstances, and events are set right into the middle of the ongoing speech event, in order to define and redefine the teller or tellers. In telling autobiographical stories, the teller introduces a "double," the speaker as a character or figure in a story. This character is often the protagonist of the story or a witness to the transpiring events, and the listeners generally witness what takes place in the story world through this character's perspective. It is important to remember that the character in the story is not simply the teller, but rather a *version* of the teller. The character is often a previous version of the teller, for instance the teller as a young person, sometimes as a small child, at other times as a teenager or as a young adult—or the person before a disease. In some autobiographical stories, the character may even exist in several versions. For instance, the character may appear in a story as a teenager commenting on himself as a child. There is not only a temporal difference between the teller and the character in the story. The story probably takes place somewhere else, in other geographical and social places, and in different kinds of situations. As a consequence, the character in the story may have different properties from those of the physical teller in the storytelling event. The character may share certain things with the teller, but probably has different experiences, knowledge, outlook, moral values, and so on. This fact gives the teller the possibility to introduce and display other possible identities or to revise existing identities. The projected version (or versions) of the teller's self and identity thus exists side by side with the self of the teller in the here-and-now conversational situation.

Narrative researcher Michael Bamberg argues that this layering (or lamination) of selves allows the teller to *position* him- or herself, and to be positioned, at three different levels:[28]

- First, the teller can position him- or herself through the self that is constructed alongside other characters and their relations in the story world. Focus is on the events in the story world and the ways the characters act, with a particular emphasis on the teller as character. Pertinent are questions related to agency: being in command, acting in a responsible way, being unable to control actions and circumstances, and so on.

- Second, the teller in the speech situation might position him- or herself in relation to this projected self, often through the evaluation of the self and the events that involve the self in the story world. In the terms introduced earlier, this would imply that the teller takes a step back from the story world and into the realm of the telling and positions him- or herself in regard to the characters in the story world. Thus the teller might claim identity with the character, may stress differences, or abject self as character.

- Third, the teller can use these two different positionings in order to position him- or herself in relation to the listeners and thus define their relationship in the present. In the terms introduced earlier, the teller positions the events in the story world, as well as the evaluation of these events in the realm of the conversation.

Of course these three positionings can be seen as steps in one process; the teller first positions him- or herself in the story world, then evaluates this character and her action, and finally positions him- or herself vis-à-vis the other participants in the storytelling situation. Even a more pragmatic point of view could be suggested. Bamberg's levels of positioning could be seen as different possibilities for the storyteller to position him- or herself in the most effective way given the available resources and possibilities in the situation. This is especially interesting in relation to persons with dementia, given that these persons often have limited access to their cognitive and linguistic resources. They thus often have to simplify their storytelling by using a simplified positioning strategy, for example by contrasting now and then.

In the interview with Tina that started this chapter, it is obvious that she juxtaposes her identities as a sick child cared for by her parents and her present situation as a person ill with dementia. This is obviously a way to connect the past with the present by finding a common denominator and to compare the situation, and thus to potentially evaluate a life with illness. This kind of comparison between the past and the present is often found in interviews with persons with dementia. In Example 4.4, Ann, who was diagnosed with Alzheimer's disease five years earlier, reflects together with her husband on her current situation.

Example 4.4.

1	Ann:	[well:] yes there's a lot happening around my alzheimer's (0.4).hh
2		'cause it goes like this
3		(hand movements going up and down)
4		but now it has like become quite flat
5		(hand movements in horizontal plane)
6		(0.5)
7		and this is something that affects me (0.3) us
8		'cause I have a temperament now so this-.ehh (0.4)
9		and I can (0.5) become sorry for something (0.7)
10		and I cannot understand why I become like [this] eh
11	I$_2$:	[m:]
12	Ann:	although I know how it is (0.6)
13		but (0.9)
14		it's not much you can (1.0)
15		but still it is (1.3)
16		it's not I who do things like this
17		become angry and things like that.hh (0.8)
18		so so I think that (.)
19		things happen
20	Carl:	(looks at his spouse) a: you are quite sorry for the disease =

This is the second interview with Ann and Carl, one year after the first. One of the first questions in the interview is about what happened during the year since the last interview. As a character in the story world, Ann has lost some of her agency, as she has become a "victim" of her Alzheimer's disease. Ann starts by saying that her "alzheimers" has become much more volatile. With her hands she illustrates the roller-coaster development she has been experiencing, although the development of the illness for the moment seems to be slower. After a brief pause she starts to tell about how she has been altered by the illness, in particular becoming more aggressive and moody. Her utterance "things happen" in many way sums up her experiences. Going through her story, she makes an evaluation of the new situation. This is accomplished through comparing the present to previous situations. The disease has gone from a roller-coaster phase to a steady phase (lines 4–5) and it affects her temper in a way she cannot understand (line 10). The person who cannot understand is not the character in the story world, but rather Ann, the teller of the story. She continues this evaluation on line 12, saying that she, Ann in the realm of telling, knows about the disease and acknowledges her inability to do anything to change the course of events.

When Ann's husband turns to her and says, "you are quite sorry for the disease," the events in the story world, as well as Ann's comments in the realm of telling, are brought to bear on the present relationship between Ann and Carl.

Ann thus moves between the different story realms and positions versions of herself in these realms in order to be able to both evaluate these versions, and to bring them to bear on her life in the present, especially her relationship with Carl.

CO-CONSTRUCTED STORIES

The point that Elinor Ochs and Lisa Capps make about the variation in tellership indicates that storytelling in conversation is not a monologist activity with one teller delivering a story. The term *joint storytelling* may refer to the fact that all participants in the situation are engaged in the telling in different ways. A listener may contribute to the story through simple tokens of listening ("hm" and head nods) or by comments ("wow," "yes/ no"). These tokens of listening give the teller feedback and also indicate potential disagreements between the teller and the listener, thus giving the teller a possibility to adapt the evolving story for the specific listener. Sometimes the participants can refer to the fact that two (or more) persons might be telling a story together.

The typical example would be when two persons are telling about their *shared experience* of something, typical in family storytelling when family members often share the experience they are telling about. Quite often, although not always, the tellers also have told this story previously. This means that the tellers have the same *epistemic* relationship, both to events in the story and to previous tellings and versions of the story. It is also possible that the joint tellers do not share the experience of the events in the story, but just of previous tellings of the story, thus making it possible for them tell it jointly. This is of course particularly interesting when one of the tellers for some reason—for instance, memory problems connected with dementia—has problems with remembering either the story or parts of the story. The other teller can then support and supplement the first teller.

Autobiographical stories are mostly told together with others, especially in families or other close relationships. Storytelling about past individual and family events is a way for many families to share experiences, as well as to express and communicate belonging and identity. Shared memories and stories are cherished and important for most couples and families, as they manifest and express their common history and values. Sociologist Jenny Mandelbaum has even argued that a couple's joint storytelling about their shared experiences is an important means of expressing and displaying their "couplehood."[29] Thus autobiographical stories are often part of joint identity projects. As such they are co-constructed, that is, there are two or more tellers who collaboratively construct the story, thus challenging one of the norms that Ochs and Capps discussed critically, namely the idea of one author and one voice.

Co-construction of stories also becomes important in another way. When both cognitive and linguistic resources become challenged though the dementia, most spouses and family members try to remediate the communicative problems by taking over some of the functions lost by the person. Spouses and family members can support the person with dementia by helping to identify memories, suggest words and expressions, as well as asking questions at the right point or in the right way. The taking over of interactional and narrative functions by other participants also implies taking over some of the responsibility for initiating and engaging in the storytelling. This redistribution of activities and responsibilities in the storytelling resembles what developmental psychologist Jerome Bruner once called *scaffolding*. By taking over responsibility and linguistic and cognitive functions, the listener prospectively scaffolds the storytelling activity in order for the storyteller to be able to participate in the conversation. Narrative scaffolding indicates that it is important to include the activities and interpretations of other persons (the listeners) involved in the storytelling situation. A focus on just the person with the communicative disability will only capture what that person is able to generate without support from other participants. Including other participants in the analysis and understanding of the person with communicative disability will make it clear that storytelling abilities are best described as *socially distributed* abilities across a network of participants, implying that different persons may actually be involved in carrying out various cognitive and linguistic functions lost by the affected participant. This will be further discussed in Chapter 5.

VOICES AND VICARIOUS VOICES

If autobiographical stories are co-constructed as a consequence of scaffolding, what happens to the perspective of the person with dementia—that is, having events related from a special individual perspective? One way to talk about this is to use the concept of *voice*, which is associated with Michail Bakhtin, Russian philosopher and specialist in comparative literature.[30] Bakhtin developed his ideas primarily in relation to the novel and other fictional texts. His ideas were adopted by Erving Goffman in the 1980s in his deconstruction of the concepts of "speaker" and "listener."[31] In his analysis Goffman discerned three different relationships between the words that are uttered and the physical speaker.

First, voice can refer to the sounding voice or the *animator* (i.e., the physical voice that others can hear). Every sounding voice is personal, because its acoustic image is unique; it is always possible to "hear" who is talking because the voice can be recognized. The second is the *authorial voice*. Telling about something is to express "authorship" of the special experiences and special perspective of the world and of life that are connected to an individual, but also to that person's biography. It is the authorial voice because here it is not the acoustic image that is in focus, but rather the process by which the thought is clad in words, to use a metaphor of the Russian psychologist Lev Vygotsky,[32] and thereby can be heard. The third aspect of voice is what Goffman called the *principal* voice, which expresses the relation of responsibility between what is said and a potential speaker.

The animator voice can for various reasons become silent or very quiet. This might happen when a person has severe problems with finding words and producing an utterance. They might start, but not finish, constructing the utterance. This is what happens in Example 4.5. The extract is from a joint interview with Oswald and Linda, who have been married for the better part of their lives. Oswald has severe linguistic problems. In the extract the interviewer asks Oswald if he studied at the university in X city.

Example 4.5.

1	I_1:	did you study at the university in X city?
2	Oswald:	yes
3		eh yes
4		it was
5		in ffffff
6		e
7		it was
8		not
9	Linda:	yes at that time the program you studied was in X city

Oswald answers this question in the affirmative, but then apparently would like to add some more comments or information. He makes several attempts to construct an utterance, but fails several times. The fact that he says in lines 7–8 that "it was not" gives an indication that he was trying to either oppose or complement the information about his studies at the university in X city. He might have wanted to say that since he had studied, that program had moved to another university and another city, although that is a guess. His wife Linda confirms in line 9 that Oswald studied in X city and also indirectly verifies that his university program had moved from there since then.

Although Oswald actively makes contributions to the conversation, his animator voice is fairly unarticulated, but it is obvious that Oswald claims his *authorial* voice, that is, wanting to add something personal to the ongoing story. The authorial voice brings out, links together, and communicates that which is the individual's special experience and perspective of the world. The authorial voice starts out as an intention and a gesture, and must be clad in words in order to be communicated. Memories, thoughts, and associations can all exist in compressed form, but in order for them to be communicated they must be converted into (for example) the form of language, as was discussed in Chapter 3. Otherwise, thoughts and experiences remain inaccessible both to the individual and to others. In this sense, the authorial voice is not given, but rather constitutes a process by which it is formulated through the words and their organization. But, as was discussed in Chapter 3, one of the challenges persons with dementia face is difficulties with translating a syncretic whole to the analytical and sequential organization that language demands. This is probably what happens to Oswald in Example 4.5; there are some indications that he might have an idea about what he wants to say, but cannot transform this idea into a full utterance. As a result, both his animator voice and his authorial voice become challenged and tend to fall apart.

The third voice in Goffman's argumentation is the principal, that is, who is held responsible for the utterance. The typical example of this is when a politician reads a speech that someone on his or her staff wrote. The politician is animator, but not the author, of the utterances that he or she produces. Although not the author, it is the politician who is held responsible for the utterances. In Example 4.5, although Oswald has severe problems with both animating and authoring a new contribution, his wife Linda obviously holds him responsible for the utterance he might have produced.

Most persons with dementia will face increasing challenges in articulating their animator, authorial, and principal voices as time passes. Having these problems in being able to verbalize in social situations implies a risk of not being invited to take part in conversations or not being expected to make any contributions because other participants find it difficult to deal with the challenges the person with dementia faces. If this becomes an interactive pattern, there is always a risk that no one expects the person with dementia to say anything, nor do they leave space for his or her attempts to make a contribution. The person with dementia might also withdraw from the situation, and eventually this will result in the person with dementia being considered "socially dead."[33] In the example, Oswald is far from being "socially dead." Here he is the addressee of the interviewer's questions, and gets all the time he needs to formulate a contribution, while Linda supports his utterance and views him as responsible for the facts about where he studied.

In her utterance in Example 4.5, it is also possible to see something more than Linda affirming Oswald's contribution. Linda implicitly adds some new information—the university program he belonged to has actually moved to another city. As indicated earlier, it might even have been this that Oswald wanted to say in his turn, but failed to find the words. In a sense, Linda is then acting as a *vicarious voice* for Oswald; she animates and authors what Oswald himself cannot do.

When a person with dementia is challenged in terms of animation and forming an authorial voice, it is not only the sounds that are missing, but perhaps more important, the words that "clothe" the authorial voice— words that are organized, for instance, into a narrative. The thought, the perception, and the memories lack not only the sounding aspect, but also the words that transform the thought or the memory into something communicable. This means that a vicarious voice not only has to loan out the sounding voice, but also acts as an organizing voice. The vicarious voice thus attains a double function, both as "sounding box" and as "author."[34]

An example of the complex interaction between many different voices in storytelling is when a couple tells about their shared life. In Example 4.6, Martin and Kathy (also described in Example 4.1) tell about where they received their basic training and education. They have just started to tell about their early history together and their educational background.

Example 4.6.

1	I_1:	and where (0.3)
2		did you work (.) eh (.)
3		did you study in Y city?
4	Kathy:	yes:
5		(1.3)
6	I_1:	and where did you work as a clerk later on?
7		(1.3)
8	Kathy:	(aaa).hh =

9	Martin:	= can you tell
10		(leans towards Kathy and puts his hand on hers)
11		.hh a bit about your education.hh (0.5)
12		it wasn't (.) a straight journey
13	Kathy:	no no I cannot
14		no I don't remember heh =
15	Martin:	can you tell
16	Kathy:	= it is lost (0.7)
17	Martin:	no she studied in Y city
18		(removes his hand from Kathy's hand)
19		and she had problems with her bronchitis.hh
20		so after eh h some years she moved (.) to the north
21	Kathy:	yes I did yes

The extract begins with the interviewer asking Kathy about where she studied and works. He does this by posing two questions, first an open question about where she worked, but changes this to a specific question of whether she had worked in Y city (lines 1–3). Kathy affirms that she did study in Y city, but does not expand her response, resulting in a brief pause (line 5). So far, Kathy is the animator, as well as author and principal. The interviewer then asks a specific new question about where Kathy had worked (line 6). Kathy apparently has problems answering this question (lines 7–8)—her voice becomes quite weak. At this point it is obvious to the interviewer and probably also to Martin that Kathy has severe problems remembering where she did study and work. At that point, Martin apparently decides to support Kathy actively, probably in order to avoid having her integrity become even more threatened, or even worse, that she will lose face.

Martin establishes a close bodily relationship with Kathy by leaning in toward her and putting his hand on her hand (line 9–10). This bodily closeness is obviously meant to support his effort to get Kathy to tell about her education. In doing this, he not only explicitly supports Kathy to tell about her education, but also adds some more information: "it wasn't a straight journey." This might be a comment that is directed toward Kathy, but it can also be seen as a comment directed at the interviewers, saying something about the difficulties Kathy has encountered. If that is true, Martin's comment might also function as an account directed at the interviewers for the problems Kathy has with telling about her education.

When Kathy says she cannot remember (lines 13–14), Martin once more tries to get her to tell (line 15) and Kathy reiterates that "it is lost." At that point, Martin obviously shifts strategy and takes over as the teller of the story. As if to mark this shift between Kathy as the teller and the author of the story, he, as teller and author, removes his hand from hers, as if to point out a distance and a shift in voice (lines 17–18). Martin goes on and says that Kathy had been sick, resulting in her moving from Y city to the north, implying that the northern air was better for her bronchitis. At the end (line 21), Kathy confirms Martin's rendering of her education and educational experience. Her affirmation also indicates that she acknowledges herself as being the principal of the small story Martin has told (lines 17–20), although she could neither animate nor author it. Martin also constructed his story in such a way that he just described the events, but didn't analyze or comment on what happened. That is, his own voice became quite silent and his animator voice instead took over a story that could have been authored and voiced by Kathy.

Thus what happens in a storytelling situation like this, where the person with dementia is challenged in voicing a specific position and experience, is that an asymmetrical relationship is established between the voices of the participants. Both the sounding and the authorial voices of the person with dementia are weak and have difficulty asserting themselves on their own. The vicarious voice, however, not only is intact, but also tries to reconstruct the authorial voice of the other person with dementia. There is, however, always the possibility that the vicarious voice will incorporate the voice of the other person with dementia into his or her own voice. Over time, as the disease progresses, the sounding and authorial voices of the person with dementia will become even more weak, and eventually it is only the vicarious voice that will be heard.

IN CONCLUSION: STORYTELLING AND ENTANGLED STORIES

In conclusion, there are three concepts that have been important in this chapter. First, the stories told by persons with dementia rarely fit with everyday as well as theoretical *narrative norms*. Conversational storytelling is a cultural practice based on the premise that stories are told in such a way that others can take part in this event and understand what is going on both in the situation and in the story. Like all social and cultural practices, conversational storytelling is often guided by implicit and embodied norms that help the participants by showing them how to produce a story that will be recognized as a certain kind of story. It will also guide them in how to organize the performance, as well as enhancing listening and understanding the story, and evaluating both the storytelling event and the story. Thus all participants have certain expectations about the organization of the story, how the story should be told, and so on. These norms are learned by the participants from an early age, and as a result most people not only become very versatile storytellers, but also are able to appreciate a wide variety of stories, told by different people, in different contexts. These narrative norms often exclude the stories told by persons with dementia, as their stories are experienced as being fragmented and broken.

Second, in autobiographical stories the teller is presented as a character, and thus it becomes possible for the teller to *position* him- or herself in relation to this character, for instance, by making comparisons between the actual teller and the character. Both the present teller and the character in the story world can be evaluated in such a way that a moral point can be derived, and thus contribute to a moral negotiation of the identity of the teller.

Third, autobiographical storytelling is rarely an individual pursuit, but is accomplished through *collaboration* with other persons in conversations. This means that the participants are oriented toward each other and try to cooperate in telling and understanding the stories. This also implies that they collaborate in order to compensate for those narrative resources that are not available to the person with dementia, as discussed in the previous chapter. Thus the autobiographical stories are co-constructed, often implying that the voice of the person with dementia will also be affected.

In Chapters 1 and 2 it was argued that autobiographical stories told by persons living with dementia could be characterized as *entangled stories*. Given the discussion in this chapter, the notion of entangled stories can be identified at several levels.

The concept of entangled stories first refers to the fact that stories told by persons living with dementia often violate everyday narratives norms. One reason for this was pointed out in Chapter 3: the person with dementia is linguistically and cognitively challenged and thus cannot adhere to the implicit everyday narrative norms. Violating these norms implies that the linguistic and discursive organization of the story becomes problematic because words are missing or words choices are made that might confuse the listener; discursively the story might start in the middle of a chain of events and lack an ending. Thus the story told by the person with dementia becomes entangled in itself.

The concept of entanglement also refers to the interpersonal or relational level as the audience can become confused not only by the discursive organization of the story, but also by the fact that the person living with dementia is challenged in remembering her relations to and the identities of the other participants in the storytelling event. This threatens to turn all relations into a jumble, and it is often a difficult and time-consuming process to try to disentangle the relations.

Finally, the entanglement of relations also affects the collaborative relations, especially the repair work, something that will be further discussed in Chapter 5. The linguistic and cognitive challenges make collaborative repair work difficult and time-consuming, and imply a shift in the interactional labor in storytelling: the healthy person must take on much of the responsibility for the organization of the storytelling.

NOTES

1. Ramanathan, 1997, p. 33.
2. Carlsson et al., 2007.
3. This question was raised by American anthropologist Sue Estroff in her work with former mental hospital patients; Estroff, 1995.
4. Brockmeier, 2013, pp. 262–263.
5. Smith, 1981, p. 228.
6. Brockmeier, 2013, p. 266.
7. Pratt, 1977, p. 135.
8. Herman, 2013, p. 179.
9. The terms *storying experience* and *worlding the story world* are David Herman's.
10. This model was developed by Katherine Young and is found in her book *Taleworlds and Storyrealms: The Phenomenology of Narrative* (1987).
11. Clark, 1996; Goffman, 1974; Young, 1987.
12. Goffman, 1974, p. 82.
13. About suspense of belief in art, see *Mimesis as Make-Believe* (1990) by Kendall Walton.
14. Schutz, 1962, p. 230.
15. Chafe, 1994.
16. Gee, 1986.
17. Clark & Schaefer, 1989.
18. Clark & Schaefer, 1987, 1989.
19. Clark & Schaeffer, 1987, 1989; Clark & Wilkes-Gibbs, 1986.
20. Clark & Schaefer, 1987, p. 19.
21. Labov and Waletzsky, 1967. Also see later versions of the article in Labov, 1972.
22. See Ochs & Capps, 2001, Chapter 1.
23. Linde 1993, p. 21.
24. Schiffrin, 1996, p. 199.
25. McAdams, 2006; McAdams, Josselson, & Lieblich, 2001.
26. Lejeune, 1989, pp. 4–5.
27. Eakin, 2001, p. 120.
28. Bamberg, 1997.
29. Mandelbaum, 1987.
30. Bakhtin, 1984.
31. Goffman, 1981, Chapter 3, "Footing."
32. Lev Vygotsky, 1987.
33. Sweeting & Gilhooly, 1997.
34. Ibid.

CHAPTER 5
Collaborative Compensation

Scaffolding

Oswald:	I remember when we were at at
	the point
	we were going to ttt
	turn
Linda:	o yes
Oswald:	and that
	it was good
Linda:	mmm
Oswald:	we had a
	one that
	we went like
	so (*makes gestures with his hands outlining the turns of the boat*)
	and then down
	right so (*makes gestures with his hands outlining the turns*)
	and then that one out
	so (*makes gestures with his hands outlining the turns*)
	it went okay
Linda:	yes
	thanks to
	the kids who knew more than we did
Oswald:	Linda she knows
	she knows a lot

Linda:	well no
	I'm not good at marine things
Oswald:	yes you are
	at least you know some things
Linda:	I didn't know anything about the boat
	wasn't interested
Oswald:	but I
Linda:	you were very clever with the boat
Oswald:	yes I was aaaa
	I aaa
	it was yes

The story is from an interview with a couple who had been married for almost 50 years—Linda and Oswald. Oswald has mid-stage Alzheimer's disease and has severe problems with both finding words and constructing complete utterances. (They have figured in a previous chapter.) The story the spouses tell about and remember together has probably been told many times before. It is probably part of what William Randall calls their "narrative environment," that is, stories about the family's past events, and is a way for this family, as well as other families, to express and communicate their belonging and identity as a family and as individual family members. Telling stories about shared personal experiences implies that the tellers must *collaborate* in the actual telling, as well as in the rendering of the shared events, experiences, and evaluations of those events. Often in such situations, other persons may be present as audience, not sharing the experiences depicted in the stories. This is frequently quite common in family storytelling.

When one family member or spouse gradually loses the ability both to tell stories and to remember shared events and stories due to dementia, this is often experienced as very distressing by other family members—especially in families that honor storytelling.[1] In those cases, not being able to tell stories and cherish the common history is a potential threat both to the experience of belonging together and to the participants' individual and shared identities, and their stories about their past, as discussed in the previous chapter. Most spouses and family members try to remediate the communicative problems caused by the progressing dementia by taking over some of the functions lost by the person with dementia—what in Chapter 3 was called *collaborative compensatory adaptation*. Supporting the person with dementia by helping to retrieve memories or asking questions at the right point can do this. Other participants who take over interactional and narrative functions also assume some of the responsibility for the storytelling. In this sense, *collaborative storytelling* becomes an important way for couples to retain their relationship.

Not much research has been conducted on this kind of collaborative storytelling involving persons with dementia, as research has often been focused on the changes in the ability of the person with dementia to tell a coherent and informative story. There is a need to know more about how persons tell stories together and in what ways the presence of dementia alters how persons collaborate. This is important because knowledge about how collaboration is reorganized can contribute to what advice should be given to persons who receive a dementia diagnosis.

In the following, three issues are discussed. First, the concept of joint activity is discussed, as it gives some background to the analysis of Oswald and Linda's stories. Second, special attention is paid to those features that are closely connected with collaborative storytelling involving a person with dementia (repairs), and with keeping the person with dementia actively involved. Third, as the person with dementia progressively loses some of the cognitive and linguistic abilities that are important in collaborative storytelling, the person without dementia will have to take on a greater responsibility for the storytelling activity. It is suggested that this can be discussed in terms of the creation of "scaffolds" that both parties can use in order to negotiate shared meaning and hence be able to continue their joint storytelling—something that will be called *narrative scaffolding*.

OSWALD'S SAILBOAT STORY

The interview with Oswald and Linda was part of a longitudinal research project involving joint interviews with couples in which one spouse had been diagnosed with Alzheimer's disease. The interviews involved several *narrative tasks*, that is, they were given questions that would solicit joint storytelling. Although Oswald had severe problems finding words and constructing utterances, he and Linda succeeded in covering a great deal of their joint life history in the interview. They accomplished this mainly by Linda's active support and help for Oswald, for instance by asking clarifying questions in a format that he could follow, and presenting possible interpretations of his utterances. In that way it became possible for Oswald to continue as an active partner in the storytelling.

At several points in the interview, Oswald had severe difficulties finding words for communicating events he appeared to remember. One such occasion was when Oswald initiated a small story (presented at the beginning of this chapter) about how the family took part in a sailing race although none of the family members was a good or experienced sailor. The description of this specific event was part of the couple's telling about their various summer activities, especially when their children were small. They had been talking about the sailboat they had for a couple of years and how the family used to sail together for a couple of weeks every summer. After a few years they became a bit more confident as sailors and decided to enter a race.

In the example, Oswald tells about one specific episode—one of several the couple talks about—that involved making a quick turn with the sailboat in order to avoid hitting land. As in all storytelling, the listeners are transported from the here-and-now of the storytelling situation to the then-and-there of the story world, among some islands in an archipelago along the coast many years ago. The family is in the sailboat and they are about to turn the boat around a point; they first make one turn and then two more rapid turns before they successfully round it. Then Oswald leaves the story world and moves back to the realm of conversation by commenting "it went okay" (Example 5.1, line 1).

Example 5.1.

1	Oswald:	it went okay
2	Linda:	yes
3		thanks to
4		the kids who knew more than we did
5	Oswald:	Linda she knows
6		she knows a lot
7	Linda:	well no
8		I'm not good at marine things
9	Oswald:	yes you are
10		at least you know some things
11	Linda:	I didn't know anything about the boat
12		wasn't interested
13	Oswald:	but I
14	Linda:	you were very clever with the boat
15	Oswald:	yes I was aaaa
16		I aaa
17		it was yes

So far it is a story about a dramatic sailing event that the family successfully coped with together. This episode and its evaluation is followed by another, joint evaluation, not only of this episode but rather of the couple themselves (lines 5–17). Linda praises the children for their know-how about sailing, while Oswald extols Linda, who in turn praises Oswald, who seems to accept this acclaim. At this point the meaning of the story shifts somewhat. It is not the dramatic events that are the focus, but instead they are used by the spouses in order to mutually evaluate and praise each other. It has become a story about two persons who appreciate each other and who want to convey this appreciation to the two interviewers listening to (and recording) their story—and also to each other.

In listening to the story told by Oswald, it is also obvious that he has severe problems finding words and constructing utterances. All his contributions come to a stop and are never completed, as he cannot find the linguistic constructions he is searching for. It is as if he has a "syncretic" memory of the events; he seems to be able to remember an *image* of the events. His problem seems to start when this image must be analyzed into sequences that fit in certain kinds of linguistic constructions ("first this, then that, then . . . and at the same time we . . ."). As a result of these problems, Oswald had to restructure the relationship between spoken language and other bodily, communicative resources, as discussed in Chapters 3 and 4. Instead of primarily relying on words, he used gestures in order to get Linda (and the two interviewers) to understand what he was referring to, while the few spoken words assume a more general indicative function. His gestures trace the turns of the boat and are used instead of describing the events with words. In telling his story and using both words and gestures, he refers to events that not only he had knowledge about. Both he and his wife were on the boat and hence share experience of the events he is telling about. Early on in the telling, Linda also confirms that she knows what events he is referring to, and later she silently listens to Oswald without either adding information or questioning his rendition of the episode. A problem with substituting words for gestures is that the gestures in this case are connected to a concrete knowledge of the coastline. Using verbal language means invoking more abstract descriptive words, which also makes it possible for the two other participants in this situation—the interviewers—to track and understand the events. So in a sense gestures take away some of the abstract quality of words.

Oswald and Linda are jointly engaged in the storytelling activity. Although it is Oswald who is the main interlocutor in this episode, Linda is eager to show both him and the two interviewers that she is a co-author and co-principal of the story by affirming Oswald. The episode is about a shared experience in relation to which they have the same epistemic status. Oswald and Linda's current relationship is also mirrored in the story, as Oswald refers to "we" in the episode. This "we" depicts both the family and probably also the couple, but that also is a kind of agent deciding to turn the boat. Oswald only refers to himself as "I" when he introduces the story: "I remember." The closeness of the spouses is further pronounced when they both evaluate their contributions to the family's sailing experiences.

Although Oswald had severe problems telling his story using spoken language and instead had to use gestures in order to show what happened, he is successful as a storyteller; he and Linda jointly construct meaning. Furthermore, both Oswald and Linda use the storytelling and the story as a way to confirm their relationship and their shared identities as a couple, in the here-and-now situation as well as in the there-and-then situation. As a consequence, it is apparent that both the storytelling and the story have a wider function; they are used as means to present, instantiate, and negotiate Linda and Oswald's relationship and identities. It is also obviously performed and organized as a joint activity in which both Oswald and Linda collaborate in order to tell the story and cope with Oswald's communicative challenges.

JOINT ACTIVITIES

The concept of joint activity was introduced in Chapter 1, but might still need more discussion. Many researchers have used the concept of activity. The linguist Stephan Levinson's definition captures many of the central theoretical features when he suggests that activities are "goal-defined, socially constituted, bounded, events with constraints on participants, setting, and so on, but above all on the kinds of allowable contributions."[2]

What Stephen Levinson argues is that activities can be seen as a number of events with boundaries that put constraints on participants and actions. What is less clear in Stephen Levinson's definition is the distinction between activities with one participant, and activities with two or more participants. When participants do things together, this could be considered to be a joint activity.

Joint activities can be of many different kinds. Having a conversation and telling stories are good examples of a joint activity, as having a conversation would be impossible without collaboration with another person(s). Some joint activities have more or less clear goals set out beforehand, as in many work-related activities, or are more or less an end in themselves, as when people sit around the dinner table going through what happened during the day. Furthermore, some joint activities are unique and may not be repeated, while other activities are part of ongoing, long-term relations, are hence repeated with the same participants many times, and are part of the participants' joint life project or "couplehood," as will be discussed in Chapter 7.[3] Joint activities that are part of life projects of course become especially vulnerable when one of the participants loses his or her ability to actually take part in and accomplish these activities.

In joint activities, participants must *coordinate* their actions in a special way. Following Margaret Gilbert, it could be argued that the participants share a commitment to the joint activity, in the sense that they constitute what she calls a *"plural subject."*[4] That is, the participants together constitute a "we" unit that is doing something together. The use of the collective pronoun "we" is often central to the phrases most people would use if queried about what they are doing, either in the middle of the activity or in retrospect, when they account for their actions. This means that the participants in joint activities constitute themselves as something more than just a collection of individuals who happen to have similar intentions; instead they *share* intentions.[5] In some cases, the shared intentions come close to more or less clearly stated goals—especially in joint activities that are part of formal organizations. In other cases, the shared intentions are more or less equal to the activity as such, as in just spending time together, talking about whatever comes to mind.

Sharing intentions in activities also implies sharing a *commitment to cooperation*; that is, the participants are committed to act in such a way that the intentions or goals of the activity can be achieved. This *procedural commitment* is expressed in the way that joint activities progress and implies that the participants must be *mutually supportive*, that is, that they must help each other when they encounter problems in the interaction.[6] Working toward shared ends means that the participants must be cooperative not only in making contributions, but also in fulfilling these contributions, which implies that they must help each other to create a shared meaning or understanding of their contributions. This may, for instance, entail talking in a loud voice if the other person has problems hearing, repeating contributions to a conversation that were not heard or understood, or repairing, expanding, or explaining other contributions.

There are several potential risks and problems connected with mutual support.[7] Some of those are of particular relevance in understanding interactions involving persons with dementia. First, there is a risk that giving support may jeopardize the supporter's ability to make his or her own contributions by taking over the contribution; this is a form of what was called micromanagement in Chapter 3. A second risk may be that the person giving support may think that the support costs too much in terms of effort, hence making the joint activity not worth the time or energy. This is what often happens in interactions involving persons with dementia who tend to repeat stories over and over again; other participants may find it tedious and hopeless to correct the story or listen to the story over and over again. A third problem is that the supportive activity may develop into an almost new activity of its own and hence risk replacing or taking over the original activity—something that might be a problem in certain circumstances and will be discussed later. The same kind of problems and risks can be identified for the person needing support. The occasional, repeated, or constant need of support may make participation in a joint activity such an effort that it is not worth it, thus adding to the risk of not being able to pursue the joint commitment. This is what often leads the person with dementia to withdraw from interaction and choose to become a passive onlooker.

In Chapter 4 a model of collaborative storytelling was presented. A basic idea was that joint activities like storytelling advance through individual *contributions* to the activity. Each contribution has to be noted and understood by the other participant; otherwise, some kind of repair becomes necessary until both participants can accept the (negotiated) meaning of the contribution. One way to facilitate this process is to design contributions in such a way that they fit into the previous contributions while adding something new; that is, contributions generally have to be responsive to what already has occurred, but add something new in order not to be a repetition. At the same time, contributions also have to be forward-oriented both in relation to the joint activity and in opening up possibilities for other new contributions by other participants. In this way, the process of making a contribution and negotiating its meaning forms a small *joint action* project with a starting point (the individual action), the negotiation phase—including repair if necessary—and finally the acceptance.

Herbert Clark argues that in order for people to do something together, they need to cooperate and coordinate their actions at several levels. First they need to share their *attention*; that is, they need to focus on the same thing, in this case an action (utterance). This joint attention allows the participants to focus on hearing and perceiving *what is said* (or done in other ways). Joint attention and hearing in their turn allow for an *understanding* of the action and eventually the *uptake* of the action, for instance answering a question. All these concepts will return in the analysis of Oswald's and Linda's storytelling.

COLLABORATIVE COMPENSATORY ADAPTATION

In Chapter 3 it was suggested that participants in joint activities together make compensatory shifts in the conversation in order to facilitate participation in the conversation for the person with dementia.[8] It is important to note that collaborative compensatory adaptation may entail that the person with dementia is only able to participate using a very diminished and restricted set of communicative resources. This may imply that in collaborations, persons with dementia may make use of fragmented cognitive and linguistic resources or, especially at later stages of the disease, mainly use basic bodily actions like gaze or touch. Nevertheless, they are still displaying what is often called a "cooperative attitude";[9] that is, the person with dementia, although having extremely restricted cognitive and semiotic resources available, actively attempts to be part of the interaction and to sustain agency.[10]

Living with a person with dementia or being a caregiver in most cases implies that over time a set of specific problems that emerge in collaboration become well known and identified by both participants because they are frequent and reoccur incessantly. Over time, these problems most likely even increase in frequency and severity as a result of the progressing disease. This means that some of these problems tend to occur irrespective of what the participants do, while other problems only occur under certain conditions and in that sense are *potential* problems. As a consequence of the increased number of problems, the need for support in joint activity increases. The participants will then organize and reorganize their collaboration in order to still be able to do things jointly. This reorganization then functions as a collaborative compensatory adaptation, although the participants may not be aware of what they are doing. The reason for this is the tendency to "normalize" everyday interaction and to experience changes as part of the "new normal."[11]

The emergence of these kinds of collaborative problems, and the way the participants deal with them, are central to all studies of joint activities involving persons with dementia. This means that it is important to try to describe and understand these problems and collaborative compensatory adaptations in terms of how the joint activities become organized.

If dementia and its consequences are seen from the perspective of joint activities, then there must be a focus on how the participants deal with the challenges and troubles that result from the impairments caused by dementia; that is, the idea would be that the disease as such does not automatically result in certain consequences or problems. Rather, the interesting point is what kind of problems people themselves identify in collaboration involving people diagnosed with dementia, and what strategies they use to deal with these problems. This would also change the description of the impairments from an individual property, to a property of the interacting participants, and from an impairment with given consequences to a practical problem in the form of interactional troubles identified by the participants. As indicated in Chapter 4, research on problems in conversations involving persons with dementia indicates a number of problems that are frequently identified. These range from problems with *participating* in the interaction and *managing* discourse topics to problems with *understanding* and making *responses*.

SCAFFOLDING

The fact that interactional problems occur frequently and increase in joint activities involving persons with dementia makes it necessary to include this aspect in a theoretical framework. In more general terms, it would probably be possible to suggest that one basic way to deal with actual and potential interactional problems is a *change in the division of interactional labor* between the participants. The person without dementia will have to make contributions that facilitate for the person with dementia to both understand and respond to contributions, as well as to make further contributions; the person without dementia must also engage in fairly advanced, extensive, and comprehensive interactional work together with the person with dementia in order to establish joint meaning.

This redistribution of activities and responsibilities in interaction in many ways resembles what the developmental psychologist Jerome Bruner called *scaffolding*. Bruner and his colleagues argued that when an adult helps a small child with how to solve a problem (how to tie shoelaces or how to solve an arithmetic problem), the adult acts as an "expert" knowing how to accomplish the task, while the child does not. The "expert" constructs a scaffold by arranging tasks, support, and feedback in such a way that the child with this help will be able to solve the problem on his or her own:

> Scaffolding is a process that enables the child or novice to solve a problem, carry out a task or achieve a goal which would be beyond his unassisted efforts. This scaffolding consists essentially of the adult "controlling" those elements of the task that are initially beyond the learner's capacity, thus permitting him to concentrate upon and complete only those elements that are within his range of competence.[12]

There are at least three problems with the original model suggested by Bruner and his colleagues in relation to activities involving persons with dementia. First, the model focused exclusively on situations with a limited number of possible solutions (the toys used in the experimental situation had to be built in certain ways). In interactional situations when people are, for instance, making conversation, telling stories, or cooking together, the possible options are often numerous.

Second, their formulation was also based on a situation constructed in such a way that the roles were fixed (tutor and tutee) by the fact that the tutor was the "holder" of the solution. This could be interpreted as the learner having the more or less "passive" role of being the "receptor" of instructions.[13] A similar everyday situation could be when one person tries to get another person to remember a specific event, helping him or her by suggesting cues. In that situation, one person might be conceived of as "knowing" the solution, although the participants have to find a solution between them in order to be able to proceed with what they are doing. This means that we will have a situation where both participants have to be very active in trying to find and negotiate the meaning of the contribution. In other words, in most everyday situations "roles" are more open and flexible as compared to the experiment devised by Bruner and his colleagues.

A third critical point has to do with the fact that in the experiments designed by Bruner and his colleagues, scaffolding referred to a learning situation; the child had to learn how to solve a specific problem—that is, the activity and the aim or goal of the activity was to learn some new abilities. In conversations involving persons with dementia, the problems the participants have to solve are more varied, and above all, the problems and their solving are sub-parts in an ongoing activity with a different aim or goal than the problem-solving. The problem-solving is not the goal of the joint activity, but is rather a sub-activity organized around the necessary mutual support.

These critical points suggest that all participants have to be regarded as being active in scaffolding, attempting to construct a joint meaning in order to pursue their ongoing activity. It also suggests that interactional support that has mostly been discussed in terms of one person supporting another (as discussed in the preceding) is instead better conceived of as *mutual support*, as participants working together in order to achieve a shared understanding of contributions.

Given these reservations and remarks, it is still possible to use the metaphor and idea of scaffolding suggested by Bruner and his colleagues. A basic similarity is that meaning-making in conversations, like the problems presented in the experimental situation, could be thought of in terms of problem-solving. That is, the participants must work out a shared understanding of each contribution made by the participants in order to proceed with their activity, for instance the conversation. Scaffolding is based on a renegotiation of the division of interactional work, implying that although both participants are active, the person without dementia has the responsibility for setting up tasks (and the situation) and using semiotic resources in such a way that it becomes possible for the other person to take part in problem-solving (i.e., the meaning-making).

OSWALD AND LINDA

In the interview conducted with Linda and Oswald, themes were introduced as starting points for the interviewees to identify one of several story topics, that is, a certain set of events, persons, and experiences that were treated by the tellers as belonging together. The suggestion of a topic almost always came after a short pause, indicating a borderline from previous talk and topics. The topic was then elaborated by the telling of stories. These were organized around a presentation of events, persons involved in these, and thoughts and feelings connected with the events. The theme generally resulted in four to six topics before the interviewees indicated that the theme was exhausted, with the exception of a large number of topics generated around the theme of "everyday life."

The stories were told in rounds, exhausting a topic and then moving on to the next topic, or to a new theme suggested by the interviewer. Most stories were embedded in the surrounding talk, but a few times Linda told stories that were more detached and were marked as specific units. The end of a story topic was always marked by a pause, as was the start of a topic round. This indicates that the interviewees themselves organized the storytelling around separable topics, and mutually indicated when a topic was exhausted.

Chapter 4 introduced Ochs and Capps's critique of the idea that conversational stories could be seen as having a more or less linear organization. They instead argued that stories told in conversation can vary in terms of tellership, tellability, embeddedness, linearity, and moral stance. Applying at least some of their suggested dimensions to the stories told by Oswald and Linda, it turns out that much of the storytelling in the interview is characterized by *co-tellership*, where Linda was the main contributor to the storytelling and Oswald the one who accepted (or rejected) her contributions (with some exceptions).[14] The stories were *embedded* in the interview conversation with a limited number of freestanding stories. It was also characterized by a fairly *low tellability*, stressing the shared experiences rather than any strong points, moral or otherwise. The storytelling could at best be said to be *meandering*, rather than following a straight line. Finally, what stands out as the most characteristic feature of the interview is the amount of *troubles* and *repairs*, which leads to a multitude of side sequences and contributes to the meandering character of the interview. The amount of repair work contributes strongly to the meandering character of the storytelling, following a line that suddenly digresses and then later returns to the storyline. Given this, throughout most of the interview it is quite clear when Oswald is the principal of the stories, even though his animating and authorial voice might become weak. Linda is very intent on respecting Oswald's voice throughout the interview, while often contributing a vicarious voice, especially when animating Oswald's voice.

The interactional pattern in the interview can basically be characterized by contributions made in turns. Example 5.2 is from the first part of the interview and is in many ways typical of the interactional and collaborative structure of the storytelling. Linda is the one who basically elaborates on the topic "Where did we meet?" and Oswald acknowledges her accounts.

Example 5.2.

1	Linda:	but it wasn't you and me who met then
2		it was mostly Leonore and Harvey who met then
3	Oswald:	it was yes
4	Linda:	but you had to travel with him
5	Oswald:	I don't have such a big
6	Linda:	no (laughter)
7	Oswald:	no
8	Linda:	but you know
9		eh Harvey had the car so you had to wait for him
10		and stay overnight
11	Oswald:	mm yeah
12	Linda:	and I was Leonore's friend
13		but then the next day all of us went to X town
14		do you remember that?
15	Oswald:	yeah that's probably true

In this example, as well as throughout the interview, Linda presents her utterances in small segments marked by micropauses. These installments constitute an intonational unit, represented in the transcription by a line.[15] As a consequence, her speech becomes structured into easily discernible smaller parts. Every intonation unit represents one new idea in relation to previous talk. Linda often presents two or three lines and then Oswald acknowledges these contributions, generally by a "yes" or "yeah." The exception to this is when Linda engages in an extended turn when she tells about a particular event. In those cases, Oswald's acceptances are placed at non-disruptive places in the story, mostly near the end.

In lines 1 and 2, Linda makes her contribution in two installments presenting two ideas (who actually met, and then she introduces Harvey and Leonore). In line 3, Oswald acknowledges his understanding of Linda's contribution, both the understanding of what she has said and the reference to their common history. In line 5, he acknowledges his understanding of Linda's contribution in line 4, although he is not sure about the historical circumstances. In line 5, Oswald uses words that are a bit strange ("such a big") something that indicates that he has problems finding the correct phrase, probably "I don't have *any* recollection" or "I don't remember anything at all." In line 14, Linda directs a question to Oswald ("do you remember that?"), something she does quite often. This is probably a way to make sure that Oswald understands, that they agree on the memory, and that Oswald participates in the conversation.

This structure reflects the basic structure of the storytelling activity in the interview; Linda structures her contributions into intonational units, each presenting a new idea (or information), marked by micropauses. Hence she gives Oswald a chance to acknowledge his understanding, something he does almost every time by saying "yeah" or "it's true," or by some similar phrase. The exception from this is when Linda makes her contribution in an extended turn, telling what Ochs and Capps would call a freestanding story. In those cases, Linda speaks faster; although as she parses her story in idea units, it is obvious that she is not seeking confirmation but wants to continue by using devices like shorter pauses.

At some points at the end of the interview, Oswald tries to both introduce and elaborate on a topic on his own. This happens when they are talking about hunting and sailing. Just before the beginning of Example 5.3, the interviewees have been talking about the fact that they have several summer houses, but that getting older means that they just visit one of them.

Example 5.3.

1	Oswald:	hm
2		I went to the K mountain
3		just like
4	Linda:	yes
5	Oswald:	back and forth
6		sometimes
7	Linda:	no not back and forth but
8	Oswald:	yes I did

9		(pause 6 sec)
10	Linda:	so you discover that you want everything closer to yourself
11	I₂:	yeah that's true
12	Oswald:	did you come along at that time
13	Linda:	what when
14	Oswald:	eh with
15		when we went and
16		yes
17		of course you did
18	Linda:	what when
19	Oswald:	sorry
20	Linda:	what what are you thinking about
21	Oswald:	what did I think about
22		yes
23		I forgot it now but
24	I₂:	had it anything to do with the K mountain
25	Oswald:	yes that's true too
26	Linda:	yeah
27	Oswald:	it
28		it was it
29	Linda:	how come you thought about that
30		because we talked about it the other night
31	Oswald:	yes
32	Linda:	yes (laughter)
33	Oswald:	hm that's right

Without any introduction, Oswald introduces in line 2 a potentially new topic, his travels to the big K mountain in the very north of the country. Linda acknowledges this (line 4), and then Oswald expands this topic and adds that he went back and forth (lines 4, 5). Linda indicates that she has heard his elaboration but she doesn't agree (line 7), but Oswald insists (line 8). This results in a standstill—a very long pause (6 seconds). After that, Linda resumes the topic she had been elaborating on just before Oswald suggested his new topic, before the start of this example. This is something that is acknowledged, not by Oswald, but by one of the interviewers (line 11). Oswald pursues his self-selected topic and tries to reintroduce it again on line 12, something that seems to confuse Linda (line 13). She is puzzled, both by what events Oswald is referring to, and when these took place ("what when"). Hence Oswald tries to explain what he means (lines 14–17). Linda still seems confused and she asks Oswald about what he is trying to say, something he cannot answer. Then the interviewer suggests an interpretation of Oswald's attempts that is accepted by both Oswald and Linda (lines 25, 26). Finally Linda tries to understand why Oswald persists in talking about the K mountain and comes up with a suggestion ("because we talked about it the other night"), accepted by Oswald (line 31). The laughter and further acknowledgment in lines 32 and 33 close this topic, and the conversation moves on to a new topic.

This example shows the problems that Oswald encounters when he tries to introduce a new topic. He finds it very difficult to elaborate on his topic by telling about events and persons. The sequence of presentation of a new contribution and its acceptance, which is typical of the main part of the interview, is broken here, because Linda identifies different kinds of troubles. As a result, all the participants in the interview—including the interviewers—become involved in repair work, trying to find out what Oswald is trying to tell. This results in several side sequences, mainly having to do with establishing what events Oswald is referring to and when they took place.

TROUBLE AND REPAIR

Example 5.3 clearly indicates a characteristic of the spouses' storytelling, namely the multitude of necessary *repairs* mainly having to do with Oswald's linguistic and cognitive problems. Due to his hearing problems, he often had difficulties hearing Linda's utterances and needed repetitions. At other times, he had problems identifying the events she was referring to, due to memory problems. When Oswald made contributions, these were almost always incomplete due to his problems with either finding a certain word or name, or with pronouncing certain words. This always resulted in self-repair, asking for help or giving up. Rarely did Linda initiate a repair sequence, although it happened, as in Example 5.2, but she could help Oswald when he requested help by using indirect repair. The multitude of repair work in the interview resulted in a *meandering storyline*, digressing into side sequences specifying an event, repeating an utterance, or searching for a word, and then coming back to the main story topic.

Repair in conversations involving a person with dementia is connected to at least three different problems. First, unsuccessful *self-repair* by the person with dementia may result in this person being unable to continue participation in the conversation, generally ending up in silence (a hint of this can be seen in Example 5.2, line 9). Second, repair initiated by the other participant can be potentially *face-threatening*, as the person with dementia may be positioned as an incompetent participant.[16] This is especially true if the repair is *direct*, that is, involves a correction. One way to deal with this issue is to use *indirect repair*, that is, by repeating a small part of the previous utterance and adding some information.[17] A third and more general problem is that the troubles that the person with dementia indicates are often quite *complex* and generally need quite complex repairs. This is something that is also indicated by Milroy and Perkins in connection with aphasic discourse.[18] Generally this means that the person without dementia will have to take on a greater responsibility for the conversation and the repair work. The person without dementia may do this by organizing the repair work collaboratively, and in such a way that the person with dementia may be able to figure out the meanings and events. As a result, the person with dementia will be able to continue, not only as a participant, but also as an active and fully competent participant. Taking over this kind of interactional responsibility could be thought of in terms of *scaffolding the interaction*.

In the interview, three different kinds of troubles and repair strategies are frequent and recurrent, and are connected to the different problems just discussed. One kind of trouble that occurs frequently during the interview—in 40 out of 302 repair instances—is related to Oswald *requesting* Linda to repeat what she said. Oswald's hearing problem is probably one of the main reasons for these requests; it is also possible that his cognitive disabilities affect his understanding of Linda's utterances (Example 5.4).

Example 5.4.

1	Linda:	I guess it was due to your job we moved
2	Oswald:	what did you say
3	Linda:	it was due to your job that we moved
4	Oswald:	well it probably was

As in Example 5.4, these repair sequences often had a four-turn structure: (1) Linda makes an utterance, (2) Oswald asks her to repeat it, (3) she obliges, and (4) Oswald acknowledges hearing and understanding her utterance. The main variations of this sequence have to do with what phrases Oswald uses for requesting a repetition and whether it takes one or two repetitions for him to acknowledge his understanding. The repair sequence in this example is quite straightforward and not face-threatening, and it does not involve an extended sequence of turns or Linda doing much more than repeating her first utterance.

Almost a third of Oswald's turns are *incomplete*, in most cases lacking a word or half a sentence, often making it difficult to understand what he actually wants to say. He has a particular problem with finding nouns and names of places and persons. In those cases when Oswald chooses an incorrect word but it is possible to understand what word he intended and hence what he means, Linda generally acknowledges his utterance without any comment. At other times it becomes more difficult for Linda to understand what he wants to say, resulting in more complex repair sequences. In Example 5.5, Oswald and Linda have been telling about how they moved to their current address after their retirement (lines 1 and 2).

Example 5.5.

1	Linda:	and later on
2		we moved here into the city
3	Oswald:	but then
4		but then we got a
5		like I said
6		a
7		a
8		mmmmmmmove to a
9		a
10		(heavy exhalation)
11	Linda:	when we moved here
12		is that what you are thinking about
13	Oswald:	yes
14		no
15		yes too that
16	Linda:	yes here yes
	Oswald:	yes
17	Linda:	yes
18	Oswald:	not not fr
19		not from there and to
20		and to
21		well
22		(sigh)
23		(pause)
24	Linda:	well you are thinking about
25		the big house we used to live in
26		we don't live there at all now

Oswald indirectly acknowledges that he has heard and understood Linda's utterance, but he apparently wants to elaborate further on this topic. He starts with a phrase indicating this, but cannot find either the words he needs or some event (lines 3–9); this is a sequence involving self-repair. In this self-repair process, he also has problems pronouncing some word (line 8) and finally he acknowledges his difficulties by a deep exhalation. This apparently makes Linda suggest an interpretation of what he intends to say (lines 11, 12), which Oswald then acknowledges. Oswald then makes one more attempt to elaborate on the topic (lines 18–21) but once more gives up (line 22), and Linda once more tries to interpret what he attempts to say.

In this example, Oswald is not very successful in his attempted self-repair, something that may threaten not only his trying to contribute to the story, but also his status as an active participant in the conversation. Linda steps in and suggests a possible meaning for Oswald's utterance. She does this by basically *paraphrasing* her own previous utterance (in lines 1–2). By making this suggestion, she avoids pointing out Oswald's problems, but rather suggests that Oswald actually is intending something ("is that what you are thinking about," line 12; "you are thinking about," line 24). In this way she helps to pursue Oswald's own intentions, avoids his losing face, and as a consequence at the end of the example Oswald is still part of the conversation. In other words, Linda is taking on a role as storytelling "expert" by holding on to the storyline and helping Oswald to align his potential contribution to this storyline. She does this by paraphrasing and hence interpreting his contribution. By taking on the role of expert, she scaffolds the interaction, helping Oswald to find a way forward.

At other times, Oswald has severe problems understanding what Linda means, demonstrating the third kind of repair. Example 5.6 is from the very beginning of the interview. In this example, Oswald has problems with at least two things besides finding words. First he has trouble with the meaning of the question "where did we meet?" It takes at least seven turns and a pause before both Linda and Oswald have agreed about the meaning of the question. Then the next problem has to do not only with the historical reference—that is, when and where they met—but also about what actually took place, specifically that Linda and Oswald met.

Just before the example starts, the main interviewer has suggested a theme ("Where did you meet?") and Linda responds to this by posing a question to Oswald (line 1) that he then repeats.

Example 5.6.

1	Linda:	where did we meet?
2	Oswald:	where we met
3	Linda:	Yes
4	Oswald:	met on what

5	Linda:	first time
6	Oswald:	first time
7	Linda:	yes
8	Oswald:	yes (hesitant)
9		(pause 3 seconds)
10		Yes
11		first time
12		yes yes it must have been whewhewhen iiiit we was when we were newnewnew
13	Both:	(laughter)
14	Oswald:	new new neewl newl
15		what's it called
16	Linda:	but the first time that we met
17		we were at a party
18	Oswald:	mebbe so (maybe so) yes that was the way it was
19	Linda:	Yes
20	Oswald:	but then it was
21		then it was like that yes
22		that SOMEONE
23		YOU
24	Linda:	Yes
25	Oswald:	who met someone
26	Linda:	yes I met YOU then yes
26	Oswald:	Yes

Oswald's repetition in line 2 is a signal that he hasn't grasped the question, that is, he doesn't signal acceptance, so Linda affirms that he got the question right (line 3). Then it becomes evident that Oswald has problems understanding the question, and he asks a question in order to get a clarification ("met on what"). When Linda answers "the first time," Oswald repeats this and then he takes a long pause (line 9). The pause seems to give him time for thought because he returns again, and this time he introduces a suggestion about when they met (line 12). Due to his problems with finding words, it is unclear what he really wants to say, although he is trying to identify a specific word, and he finally says that he can't find the word. In lines 16 and 17, Linda repeats a phrase about the first time they met, but adds some new information, "we were at a party." Oswald seems to use this information in order to establish not the reference to the historical event but the reference to the involved persons, "YOU met someone." When Linda confirms this and fills in that she met Oswald, both confirm this understanding.

In this example, several of the troubles and repair strategies noted in some of the other examples are present, including Oswald's troubles with finding words and pronouncing words, the requests for repetition and clarification, and so on. This example also involves the risk of Oswald becoming an incompetent participant in the conversation by not being able to understand and contribute to the start of the story.

To meet this, Linda is again quite clearly *scaffolding*; she repeats her initial question and narrows it down to the "first time." By repeating the phrase several times, she erects a sort of scaffold that makes it possible for Oswald to try different "pieces," as in a jigsaw puzzle. By being there through the repetitions, this scaffold helps Oswald to figure out and test various possible answers to the meaning of Linda's initial question and to the historical reference to their first meeting. Hence this scaffolding helps Oswald to finally understand what the story is going to be about, as well as the structure of the historical event, and to remain an active participant.

TYPES OF SCAFFOLDING

By keeping to both Bruner and his colleagues' original model and to the concept of joint activity, at least three types of scaffolding in collaboration involving persons with dementia can be suggested. These types of scaffolding range from support for joint activity to support in constructing joint meaning, and imply an increase of responsibility for the healthy person to select:

(1) *Activity frames* (environment and general preconditions for the activity and format, perspective, wording, topic) that will increase chances for contributions from the person with dementia;
(2) *Actions* (contributions) that will increase the likelihood for constructing joint meaning;
(3) *Repair activity* that will help to produce an acceptance by either of the participants.

At an activity level, one of the most important kinds of scaffolding has to do with when the conversational partner helps to *frame, reframe*, and *remind* about the joint activity. One way to deal with some of the collaborative problems is that the person without dementia is *proactive* by organizing the interaction beforehand in such a way that the risk for certain problems to emerge is minimized. This means thinking ahead: (i) to be at least one step ahead of the next turns in the interaction, (ii) to imagine and predict what will come if nothing is done, (iii) to predict the possible problems that may emerge, and (iv) to find alternatives like changing aspects of the situation, as well as projecting alternative possible turns.

Being proactive in this way may imply things like changing certain aspects of the physical and social situation. This could, for instance, be done by reducing distraction from other stimuli in the environment or persons, in order to enlist the attention of the person with dementia and help him or her to keep it focused on the joint activity. It could also mean adapting the general pace of the talk and turn-taking, allowing more time for the turn-taking, as well as other measures that increase the probability for successful participation.[19] In a similar vein, *emotional support* is important in supporting persons with dementia to continue their participation in joint activities. Emotional support may function as a guide, indicating that the participants are on the right track.

At a second level, scaffolding is also possible in constructing and performing joint *actions*, that is, negotiating the meaning of new contributions to the joint activity. This could, for instance, imply projecting subsequent turns that are possible for the person with dementia to use and hence to continue to participate in the activity. Many persons with dementia, especially in the later stages, will provide only minimal responses or turns, as has been pointed out by Heidi Hamilton.[20] One way to deal with this situation could of course be for the person without dementia to talk more and in that way minimize the need for contributions by the person with dementia. Another, more proactive way, would be to project a possible format of the next turn. For instance, asking an open question would give the next speaker a possibility to answer by telling a story, something that could be difficult for some persons with dementia. The opposite would be to use a closed question that just allows for a simple yes or no or some other specific information, often easier to provide for a person with more advanced dementia.[21]

Mentis and her colleagues, like most other researchers, found that persons with dementia "produced significantly more problematic topic introductions, including tangential shifts and noncoherent topic changes" than persons without dementia.[22] They also found that persons with dementia in general had difficulty in "maintaining topic sequences," often repeating themselves. In other words, persons with dementia often have problems with keeping to the ongoing joint activity, for example by suddenly introducing new conversational topics. One way to scaffold the ongoing joint activity can be for the conversational partner to use questions. Michael Perkins and his colleagues found that listeners tend to use repetitive questions in conversations with people with dementias. Repeating the same question is a way to maintain topical coherence in the conversation and maintain a conversational flow. By using repeated questions around the same topic, it becomes possible both to elicit responses into the conversation and to stick to the same conversational topic.[23]

Finally, scaffolding can also be organized at the level of *repair* of joint actions. The emergence of problems "online" and attempts to repair these are ubiquitous in all conversations and interactions. The common way to describe the identification and treatment of interactional problems is in terms of repair. According to this view, repairs are summoned in response to some kind of identified trouble or problem in a contribution (utterance) produced by one of the tellers. Either the teller (self) or the listener (other) may indicate that something is problematic. This is generally done through the use of some verbal or nonverbal flag (trouble-indicating behavior), either by self or the other. Signaling trouble indicates not only trouble but also what is called the trouble source or source of the problem. This may, for instance, be mentioning an incorrect fact, uttering an unrecognizable sound, producing the wrong word, or something unspecified. Generally the current speaker attempts to repair the trouble (self-repair); in some cases, the other may repair by submitting information or words (other-repair).[24]

Although the concept of repair is valuable for understanding many cases of repair in ordinary conversations, it has been suggested by researchers, including Lesley Milroy and Lisa Perkins, that this concept becomes problematic in relation to speakers with communicative disabilities. There are at least three aspects of the dealings with interactional problems in conversations involving persons with dementia that challenge the traditional notion of repair in interaction.[25]

First, in conversations between persons without communicative disabilities, there is a general preference for persons making problematic utterances to repair those utterances him- or herself. In conversations involving persons with conditions like dementia, it turns out that much of the repair work connected to utterances made by the person with dementia is accomplished by the person without dementia, although the problem or trouble indication may be initiated by both self and other.[26] This indicates that the person without dementia has a fairly important role in the interaction; that is, the functional relation is asymmetric.

Second, repairs may often become more complex when the repair attempts presented by either participant may include a further need for repair[27] (i.e., the repair needs repair, etc.). This implies that the repairs may become very complex, with several sequences added on to the original sequence.

Third, repair that involves persons with communicative disabilities like dementia is often elaborate and involves many turns. In many cases, attempts to self-repair by the person with dementia may imply quite an extensive number of turns and may often result in the need for repair support by the other person.[28] This makes it less meaningful to use the distinction between self-repair and other-repair, as the repair is a consequence of extended and elaborate interaction.

Consequently, it may be more meaningful to reconceptualize the idea of repair in interaction involving persons with conditions like dementia as *extended collaborative repair episodes involving scaffolding*. Extended collaborative repairs are fairly extended sub-activities of the joint activity involving more than three interactional turns. Extended collaborative repairs take up much of the participant's time and effort and also form a fairly delimited part of the activity with a beginning and end, and thus constitute an *episode* of the activity. Extended collaborative repair episodes are less dependent on the distinction between self/other initiator and repairer but are better seen as a joint, *collaborative work* of the participants, striving for mutual understanding of contributions and hence completion of the activity.

Finally, central to the extended, collaborative repair episodes are their character of *joint problem-solving*. Participants are facing a problem concerning meaning, which they have to solve in order to be able to pursue their joint activity. This also implies that the extended collaborative repair work involves the participants' creative abilities; they have to set up the problem (the joint understanding) in such a way that it is solvable for them and so that they can find solutions by using various semiotic resources (words, nonverbal vocalization, gestures, etc).

COUPLES LIVING WITH DEMENTIA

This chapter ends with a return to the beginning and hence to Oswald and Linda—an example of *possibilities*—what a person with dementia actually can do together with other persons, rather than what he or she cannot do. Oswald, like most persons with dementia, lives with another person. Living together implies doing things together: discussing, passing time with small talk, cooking together, remembering both the recent past as well as the distant past. The example at the beginning of this chapter showed Oswald and Linda involved in a joint activity, telling the story of their life together. Framing their storytelling theoretically as a joint activity implies that the cognitive and linguistic losses connected with dementia, as well as coping with these losses, involve everyone in the network—both Oswald and Linda, not just Oswald. Doing things together presupposes that people support and help each other in order to accomplish what they are doing. The example also suggests that the support often has the character of a scaffolded interaction, and that scaffolding can be of many kinds, ranging from support of joint activity to support of joint actions. By scaffolding the collaboration, both participants may successfully be able to jointly tell a story about their shared past.

What the preceding analysis has shown is that storytelling involving persons with dementia can be seen as a *collaborative activity*. Two tellers contribute to the story, although one of the storytellers assumes more responsibility, for elaborating and pursuing the storyline, as well as for organizing the interaction—what has been called *narrative scaffolding*. By scaffolding the collaboration, both participants may successfully be able to jointly tell a story about the shared past. The troubles that are identified by both participants in the interaction represent a constant threat that the person with dementia will gradually fall out of the conversation and ultimately become a non-participant. Not being able to take part in conversational activities, shared storytelling, and remembering in close relationships for many individuals with dementia will imply a threat to identity and personhood. To fall out of conversations and joint storytelling events for most persons means redefining relations with others, becoming a bystander, and being unable to participate anymore. In order to help the person with dementia to remain an active participant, a lot of repair work is needed, in which both participants must be actively involved.

As the analysis has shown, telling stories together with a person with fairly advanced dementia involves extensive repair work. This repair work is best understood as a *mutual interpretive activity*; both parties collaboratively attempt to make themselves understood and try to understand each other. This mutual interpretive activity is probably best thought of as scaffolding—the participant without dementia is able to construct a "scaffold" that can be used by the person with dementia in order to understand and to be understood.

It is important to note that collaborative storytelling and scaffolding activities are linked to *mutual obligations* of at least two different kinds. Given that both participants are committed to the joint activity, each participant is committed to support the other to fulfill his or her part in the joint activity.[29] The reason for this is that not being supportive jeopardizes the joint activity, while mutual support will increase the possibilities for being successful. In that sense, being part of a joint activity entails certain moral obligations that are part of the joint activity as such. It could further be argued that the mutual commitment of the participants is also based on their long-standing relationship and their attempts to sustain this relationship in the face of the progressing disease. Both spouses are attending to each other and making efforts to support and help each other. In this way their collaboration is not only an interactive accomplishment, but also the result of a long and close personal relationship, mutually defined by caring attitudes, mutual attachment, and a wish to sustain their "couplehood."[30]

These two kinds of obligations make the narrative scaffolding a *deeply moral* activity; scaffolding displays the couple's mutual obligations, rooted in a long-standing relationship. This attachment also supports who they are, their identities, and being able to make conversation together; remembering together through storytelling is a way to sustain their couplehood. When one person suffers from progressing dementia, threatening his or her ability to take part in the joint activities, it becomes the other person's responsibility to hold the person in his or her identity through support and scaffolding.[31]

NOTES

1. Small et al., 2003.
2. Levinson, 1992, p. 69.
3. Hellström et al., 2005.
4. Gilbert, 1990.
5. Bratman, 1993.
6. Bratman, 1992; Herb Clark, 1996.
7. Bratman, 1992.
8. Also see Gallagher-Thompson et al., 2001; Ripich et al., 1991.
9. This concept was introduced by philosopher Paul Grice (1975).
10. For an example of a person in a very late stage of dementia who actively cooperates, see my article "Non-verbal Vocalizations, Dementia and Social Interaction" (Hydén, 2011) and Samuelsson & Hydén, 2011.
11. For the concept of normalization, see, for instance, Staske, 1998.
12. Wood, Bruner, & Ross, 1976, p. 90.
13. Cf. the criticism of Rogoff, 1998.
14. Ochs and Capps, 2001.
15. Cf. Chafe, 1994; Gee, 1986.
16. Cf. Hamilton, 1994; Sabat, 1991.
17. Sabat, 1991.
18. Milroy & Perkins, 1992.
19. Müller & Guendouzi, 2005.
20. Hamilton, 1994.
21. Mikesell, 2009.
22. Mentis et al., 1995.
23. Perkins et al., 1998.

24. The classical paper on conversational repair is Schegloff, Jefferson, & Sacks, 1977.
25. Milroy and Perkins, 1992.
26. Watson et al., 1999.
27. Orange et al., 1996.
28. Ibid.
29. Bratman, 1992.
30. Hellström et al., 2007.
31. Lindemann, 2009.

CHAPTER 6
Embodied Memories

[. . .] soon, mechanically, weary after a dull day with the prospect of a depressing morrow, I raised to my lips a spoonful of the tea in which I had soaked a morsel of the cake. No sooner had the warm liquid, and the crumbs with it, touched my palate than a shudder ran through my whole body, and I stopped, intent upon the extraordinary changes that were taking place. An exquisite pleasure had invaded my senses, but individual, detached, with no suggestion of its origin. [. . .] it was a real state in whose presence other states of consciousness melted and vanished. I decide to attempt to make it reappear. I retrace my thoughts to the moment at which I drank the first spoonful of tea. I find again the same state, illumined by no fresh light.[1]

This is the start of Marcel Proust's *Remembrance of Things Past* and is based on what generally is called an "involuntary" memory. Visiting his mother, the author accepts a cup of tea and a small cake. Eating the cake soaked in tea resonated bodily with the protagonist; his state changed, he felt "invaded" by experiences that he could not place at first, but then decided to search for the past. It is the bodily state that starts the novel and the author's search for the times past.

The experience, the change of mood, and the attempt to trace this state form a good example of what could be called an *embodied memory*. In this example, it is the teller and his experiences that are in focus, but as literary theorist Guillemette Bolens has pointed out, in order for the reader to understand this passage, it is necessary to be able to refer to a similar experience.[2] Evoking experiences of being transformed by drinking or eating help the reader to understand further levels of meaning in Proust's text. In this way, both the teller and the listener/reader use their bodies in order to tell and understand stories.

Discussions about both the construction and understanding of a story have often been based on cognitivist assumptions; the "construction" and telling of stories are considered to involve "information processing," based on the rules of some kind of "narrative grammar." The result of this "processing" is then mapped onto linguistic structures and delivered as speech. This idea views storytelling and stories as being disembodied, and excludes the various ways in which everyday, embodied, modal experiences actually are used by both the teller (and listeners, as well as by readers) of stories to construct and interpret stories. Eventually, all the multimodal bodily engagement in storytelling is lost and turned into an amodal cognitive process.

This idea ignores the possibility that everyday experiences are used in telling and understanding stories. It also neglects the fact that experience is modal; that is, experience and hence memories do not exist as abstract, amodal "information" or "representations," but only as part of our bodily sensorimotor activities.[3] This implies that experiences and memories are connected to vision, taste, and so on, as in the Proust example. Creative use of language, from figurative expressions to gestures, also falls outside this understanding of storytelling. Leaving the actual, physical body, as well as creative use of language, out of the analysis and understanding of stories becomes especially problematic in research with persons who have bodies that are afflicted with illness or dysfunction—bodies and brains that intervene more or less in the stories these persons tell or try to tell.

For persons with dementia, engaging in joint activities like storytelling is fraught with challenges related to the fact that fewer linguistic and cognitive resources are available, as compared with before the disease. Of particular importance are challenges concerning finding words and names, constructing utterances and stories, as well as remembering events and stories—and the combined effect of these. Having fewer resources available makes it difficult to tell stories in conversations, to listen to others' storytelling, or to identify and grab a turn in a conversation in order to put in a word, and so on. As was discussed in Chapter 3, not being able to take part in joint activities often implies a risk of others micromanaging and taking over the telling of the story; as a result, the person with dementia may withdraw from the activity. The other alternative is for the person with dementia to attempt to make compensatory adaptations of the situation with fewer resources. This might imply choosing a strategy from the beginning that can be successful, for instance by always relying on gestures when words are hard to find, or to avoid certain topics. Or it can imply trying to initiate repairs when trouble is identified as a result of issues like word-finding problems. Common to the different compensatory adaption is the attempt to use other semiotic means besides language, and to reorganize and restructure the relation between spoken language and gestures.

In this chapter, two issues will be central. The first has to do with how persons with dementia deal with the fact that over time they can use fewer of their linguistic resources. The use of other semiotic resources is of particular importance. Second, persons with dementia will also face challenges concerning their cognitive resources, especially those connected with remembering. This will be discussed in terms of using embodied memories.

EMBODIMENT

The bodily engagement will be discussed in terms of *embodiment*—a concept used by many researchers and with many different meanings. Despite these differences, there are two aspects of embodiment that are of particular interest here. First, individuals who participate in conversational storytelling are physically present with each other. This implies that they can use their bodies as *communicative resources* because bodies are visible objects to which it is possible to ascribe meaning.[4] Conversational storytelling is in that respect embodied. Second, modern cognitive neuroscientists, as well as phenomenological philosophers, have argued that experience and various kinds of knowledge are modally embodied.[5] In telling autobiographical stories, this implies that we make use of embodied experiences like visual perception as well as motor actions and emotions, both when we tell stories and when we listen to stories.[6] Autobiographical memories are thus *modally embodied* and bodily *enacted* through the telling.[7]

Phenomenological philosophers have pointed out that, at least in face-to-face situations, we always encounter other persons as bodies. This implies that although people may be engaged in various activities, in face-to-face situations they are actually body to body. This is also true for most situations involving conversational storytelling. Stories told in conversations are collaborations between teller and audience. Participants are never passive recipients of a story-text delivered by the teller, but rather active participants who closely follow and anticipate the story at several levels. A story told in a conversation is designed for the specific audience, especially in relation to their knowledge about the events depicted in the story or the involved persons, but the teller must also take the participants' commitments, values, experiences, and responses into consideration. This is reflected not only in what a teller takes as given or elaborates and explains in the telling, but also in the teller's choice of words and linguistic expressions. In that sense, stories are co-authored and co-constructed by the audience.

Telling stories in face-to-face situations implies that all participants can see, hear, and maybe also touch each other; in other words, their bodies are in close proximity. As Erving Goffman pointed out, in this kind of situation participants monitor each other for clues and signs having to do both with what goes on in the story world and with the performance of the story.[8] In writing about the body in action, Charles Goodwin notes that in telling stories,

> participants take each other's bodies into account as they build relevant action in concert with each other. Moreover, human bodies, and the actions they are visibly performing, are situated within a consequential setting. The positioning, actions, and orientation of the body in the environment are crucial to how participants understand what is happening and build action together.[9]

What Goodwin points out is that the participants monitor each other's bodies as part of their interpretation of the story. The participants monitor the teller's body in order to see what he or she may mean, by including not only the spoken words, but also gestures, facial expressions, body position, and voice. The participants check each other's bodies in order to search and confirm their mutual understanding of the story—something that is important to both the teller and the listeners, because it indicates whether repetition or elaboration is needed, or if a gaffe has been made and hence needs attention. By the participants' continued attention to both the story and their bodies, the storytelling can continue as the participants incrementally add new parts to their common ground—their shared understanding of the story.

This is part of making the storytelling not just a delivery of a story-text but a collaborative activity. Participants not only respond to each other, but also share a commitment to a common activity in which they are all engaged, displaying their mutual engagement and their present understanding of what they are doing together.

As a consequence, the present bodies of the participants in joint activities are never neutral; bodies always "mean" something. Further, the mutual monitoring makes it possible to use the body as a communicative resource. Stories are told not only by visible bodies, but also through these bodies. Tellers, as well as listeners, use their bodies as a bundle of communicative resources: the gesticulating hands, the angles of the mouth and the brows, as well as the pitch of the voice.

This implies that parts of the body are turned into *semiotic signs*. For example, a pointing finger is no longer a finger stretched out, but rather an index demanding that the viewer follow the direction of the finger in order to find its intended goal. This also applies to a gaze indicating the intended addressee, or hands forming a circle. So the body is at once the biological body producing sounds and other behaviors and, at the same time, a semiotic body. (This double role of the body is something we all become aware of when the biological body becomes ill and cannot function properly, creating problems in the semiotic sphere.)

At the same time, telling stories is not an activity in which the participants make use of itemized, isolated, semiotic units that then are combined into larger units and finally into stories. Telling and listening to a story is not about adding together all these different bodily "channels" or semiotic resources, including verbal talk plus gestures plus eye movements. Rather, telling a story is about "distributing" experiences through many different bodily systems and semiotic resources, as pointed out by psychologist David McNeill.[10] Thought, intention, and gesture are fulfilled in the actual telling. Thus, it is not a question of embodying a thought in verbal and nonverbal signs; instead, it is a process that becomes completed in the embodied performance.

There is basically no limit to what body parts can be turned into semiotic signs and used in telling stories. Some of the most important are the following:[11]

- *The voice*: The human voice has an enormous variability. It can be used to produce a stunning range of vocal sounds—some verbal and some nonverbal—stressing that one basic aspect of language is that it is a physical artifact. As such, it consists of those highly conventionalized sounds that are identified as belonging to the verbal language. But we also produce a number of sounds that are vocal but not verbal. For instance, we mimic other sounds (of a car, of the rain dripping, etc.) and also use a number of fairly culturally conventionalized sounds to express pain, affirmation, protest, well-being, and so on. (Some sounds have become further conventionalized into words, often called onomatopoeic words, that retain some of these mimicking aspects.)

  As a physical artifact, language can vary in prosody, pitch, and rhythm. All these aspects can be used to stress or to clarify a certain aspect of the verbal sound, or to give the spoken words an entirely new meaning, as in irony. The rhythm of the spoken language is also related to breathing (a bodily function important in speaking), contributing to the parsing of speech into smaller units.[12]

- *Hands*: Although it is possible to make gestures with other parts of the body, the hands are most often used. Hand gestures are often divided into three groups: (1) *rhythmic* movements with one or two hands in order to stress or underline something said; (2) forming hands into *iconic* gestures mimicking central features of something described in words ("round," "big"); (3) *conventionalized* hand gestures like the "V" sign or the "OK" sign.[13] Often hand gestures appear simultaneously with spoken words, but they may also substitute for words either partially or totally (as in sign language). Hands can also be used to touch a participant, for instance putting a hand on the other's arm and patting—often interpreted as a sign of closeness.
- *Eyes*: The eyes can of course be used together with the eyebrows to make a kind of gesture of surprise, anger, and so on. Above all, by a steady and intent look at someone or something, the eyes can be used to direct the attention of other participants. Gazing at one person among several may indicate that this person is the addressee.[14] Alternately looking at and looking away is an important tool in the regulation of conversational turn-taking.

All use of bodily organs is perfectly synchronized, down to a hundredth of a second.[15] This indicates that utterances in general, and in particular stories, are not thought up in abstract cognitive models that are later clothed in words and supplemented by other bodily signs. Instead, it seems that stories have their origin in multimodal experiences that are organized simultaneously and as part of a whole, into different bodily "channels."[16]

This view of embodiment and storytelling has certain consequences for understanding storytelling in dementia. When cognitive functions like planning and remembering, as well as linguistic abilities, used in storytelling become impaired, the person with dementia can use other resources in combination with abilities that are still fully functional. Instead of gestures accompanying words in a story, gestures can take the lead role, with words only stressing or supporting bodily gestures, or gestures may even replace words entirely. This implies that the verbal narrating of an event may be partially or totally substituted by the bodily enactment of the event. This adaptive compensation entails a *restructuring* of the relationship between the teller's various cognitive and semiotic resources used in storytelling, as well as between the participants in the storytelling situation. As the person's ability to communicate linguistically declines, the person may resort to other semiotic resources using his or her body to physically enact and perform memories of past events, as well as making use of the conversational partners' semiotic and cognitive resources.

In the following, three aspects of embodiment in storytelling involving persons with dementia will be discussed. First comes a discussion of the use of gestures and the ways gestures are grounded in bodily, multimodal "memories." Second, the use of story fragments and repetitions as examples of embodied storylines will be examined. Finally, the text explores the use of previously told stories as resources in order to understand new situations.

GESTURES

One challenge that persons with dementia face is that linguistic resources become less available as the disease progresses. This often results in word-finding problems, problems with understanding words, and increasing difficulties in constructing utterances. Thus taking part in conversations and especially in storytelling becomes difficult.

As discussed in Chapter 2, in order to be able to communicate and tell about an event or an idea from a psychological perspective, it is necessary to transform the event or idea so it can be expressed in spoken language. Linguistic constructions are based on a *linear* and *sequenced* rendering of an event; it is necessary to identify the subject and the characteristics of the subject, as well as the context, and to add an action, its characterization, and so on. This entails analyzing the event or idea into its constituent parts so these can be transformed into some kind of linguistic construction.

One of the challenges many persons with dementia face is to be able to perform this analytical task, as well as to identify appropriate linguistic constructions, from single words to more complex constructions, for instance subject-verb. Thus, although a person with dementia may in some sense remember an event, it may be difficult, sometimes impossible, to communicate this event by the use of verbal means. One possibility in this situation is to substitute *gestures* for linguistic constructions. Gestures can be defined as "actions that have the features of manifest deliberate expressiveness," to quote Adam Kendon, one of the pioneers in the study of gestures.[17] Gestures can be of different types and can be categorized along what has been called "Kendon's Continuum":[18]

Gesticulation → Language-like gestures → Pantomimes → Emblems → Sign languages.

This taxonomy is based on relationships between spoken language and gesticulation. Starting from the left, gestures are accompanying spoken language, and as the presence of speech declines (moving to the right), gestures will become more language-like; at the very right, idiosyncratic gestures "are replaced by socially regulated signs" as in sign languages.[19]

Gestures have an advantage over linguistic expressions, as the gesture is iconic in nature. It can be perceived as an immediate, synthetic whole and does not need to be analyzed into constituent parts; gestures can be added in a sequence following the actual event sequence. In other words, there is less need for the transformative steps between idea and linguistic expression. It is hence less an individual word that is substituted for a gesture, but rather an idea or "cognitive content." It also makes it possible to use words and, when these fail, to add gestures, implying that the persons with dementia are free to make use of two (or more) different semiotic means as their main "channel" in communicative situations.[20]

Gestures and Words

One example of the use of gestures together with verbal utterances in storytelling may be seen in Example 6.1, where a woman called Laura tells about her son in an interview. Laura is at the time of the interview 52 years old and has early onset dementia, diagnosed when she was 48 years old. She has two children, one daughter in her early twenties, who is married, and a son 16 years old. Laura and her husband separated in connection with her receiving her diagnosis. She also stopped working and she is currently living in an apartment on her own with daily support and help.

The interview was part of a pilot study of couples with dementia. As Laura did not have a partner, she wanted her social support person to be present during the interview. The interview was conducted in Laura's home and was videotaped by two interviewers (I_1 and I_2). In the interview Laura was asked to tell about her diagnosis, her life story, and her present life. (In the transcription, gestures and gaze are rendered on separate lines.)

Example 6.1.

1	Laura:		well my son ehh (1.5s)
		Gestures:	(hands resting in lap—default)
		Gaze:	(gaze directed towards I_1)
2	Laura:		lives with his father (2s)
3			and w-we all lived there (0.7s)
	I_1:		mm

4	Laura:		w-we separated
		Gestures:	(raises both hands in an outward movement)
5	Laura:		and then (0.7s)
		Gestures:	(join hands)
6	Laura:		we had different (2s)
		Gestures:	(outward hand movements—keeps hands separated)
7	Laura:		he came to me (0.8s)
		Gestures:	(right hand in to the body midline)
8	Laura:		and then it was empty (0.5s) (small laugh)
9	I_2:		yes
	Laura:	Gestures:	(left hand in to body midline)
		Gaze:	(shifts gaze to I_2)
10	Laura:		and then (2s)
		Gestures:	(right hand outward and then to midline)
		Gaze:	(shifts gaze to I_1)
11	I_2:		[alternate residence]
12	Laura:		[we did this for a while]
		Gaze:	(shifts gaze to I_2)

The interviewers ask Laura to tell about her son, who had been stay-ing with her for some time after the separation. In the transcription every utterance is represented by one line (cf. Chapter 4). Laura talks slowly, one "idea" at a time, with pauses between; most pauses are quite long, around two seconds. Some of her lines are used to indicate a continuation of the ongoing events in the story rather than to indicate new ideas (lines 5, 10).

When the example begins, Laura's hands are in a default position while she talks; her hands are in her lap and her gaze directed toward the first interviewer, who is presenting the question. She goes on to say that her son lives with his father and that they all used to live there together (lines 1–3). She pauses slightly between the three utterances and speaks slowly. Laura then says that she and her husband separated (line 4). She has some prob-lems producing this utterance, indicated by her stumbling when saying "we" and as if she is sensing a problem with her words. She simultaneously raises her two hands from her lap in an outward movement, as if demon-strating and illustrating the notion of "separation." She then returns her hands to their default position in her lap. This outward movement of her hands also establishes a *gestural space*, a space placed before her body and between the four participants sitting around a low sofa table.

She continues by saying that as a consequence of their separation ("and then" in line 5) the spouses had "different . . ."—but she cannot find the word she is searching for (probably "homes" or "apartments"). Instead, she again uses an outward movement of her hands, but this time she holds them separated when she utters the word "different," as if she wants to underline that their separation was not temporary.

After establishing their permanent separation in this way, Laura continues by shifting her focus to her son—although without indicating this in any other way than by a shift in pronouns from "we" to "he" (line 7). When Laura says that her son came to stay with her, she moves her right hand, still outstretched, in toward her body midline, as if showing her son's movement from his father's home to hers. She uses very few words in describing both the separation and her son's coming to live with her. This is even clearer when she then says, "and then it was empty" (line 8). This expression is probably a proxy for a linguistic expression of the idea that her son then left his mother in order to move back to his father. She then says "and then" (line 10) and at the same time moves her hands from her lap outward and then moves her right hand again in toward her body midline. It is as if the whole concept of her son alternating his living between his parents is impossible for Laura to express in words. She uses words just to indicate the sequence of events and gestures to capture her son's moving back and forth between his parents. This understanding of what is going on is corroborated when the second interviewer fills in the abstract word that can capture the notion she is trying to express, "alternate residence" (line 11), and Laura implicitly accepts this suggestion by continuing her story (line 12).

So one way to understand Laura is that she has problems with finding individual words and making linguistic constructions for more general and abstract ideas ("separation," "alternate living"); instead she uses gestures. Her linguistic constructions have a basic agentive structure ("we separated," "he came to me") but lack all further descriptions by adding, for instance, auxiliary verbs that help to specify the mood of the actions, or adjectives that add information about the setting and characters. Laura also has a clear sense of the sequence of events, although she only uses one "linking" expression ("and then"). Thus, to be more precise, Laura uses gestures to supplement and sometimes to substitute her linguistic constructions at those places where she apparently faces severe challenges with transforming a syncretic image into an abstract linguistic expression. Looking closely at the example will also show at least two other aspects of Laura's gestures, as the gestures seem to have more complex relationships to their referents. Her gestures not only substitute a gesture for a word, but they also add new experiential features to the story, namely a visual aspect. The gestures thus help to shift the listeners' attention between the story world and the realm of telling.

Embodied Gestures

A number of researchers favoring an embodied perspective indicate that an essential part of our cognitive activity is based on everyday bodily experiences. In the field of telling stories, this would imply that we make use of actual experiences (bodily and otherwise) of events (actions, activities, experiences), both when we tell stories and when we listen to stories.[21] This also opens up the possibility to "tell" by enacting part of the story, that is, to perform actions that are central to the story. In narrative terms, this is *mimesis* rather than *diegesis*. Although much conversational storytelling entails enactment—showing rather than telling—this becomes of special importance when people for some reason have lost either the ability to use verbal language or have lost partial command of spoken language. Enactment may assume a greater role, as is the case with persons with acquired brain injuries like dementia.[22]

Traditionally, gestures have been viewed primarily as being visual because hands can be seen. Many phenomenological philosophers, from Maurice Merleau-Ponty to Maxine Sheets-Johnstone, have argued that the lived bodily experience is crucial in forming concepts and an understanding of world, as well as communicating in and about the world.[23] As has been pointed out by several researchers recently, gestures can also involve other senses besides visual perception. One of the researchers proposing this approach is Jürgen Streeck, who writes,

> Although speakers utilize a variety of methods to depict objects, including drawing their shapes or performing schematic acts of making them, the most common method for depicting things by gestures is to perform some schematic act of handling them: lifting them, putting them down, or performing a characteristic motion that identifies the object more specifically.[24]

What Jürgen Streeck points out in this quotation is that it is not only visual drawing of shape that matters in constructing a gesture, but also motor, kinesthetic, tactile, haptic, and other experiences that can be used to inform a gesture. Streeck also notes that

> hand gestures are performed by lived bodies, that is, bodies that have accumulated tactile and haptic experiences and skills in their owners' life-worlds. What the hands contribute to symbolic communication are motor schemata that construe content and/or perform social actions.[25]

Enacted gestures in this sense would involve performing and showing some multimodal actions that are central to the story and that are similar to the actions in the story. Thus the enactment of action is a gesture that has an iconic relation to its referent; that is, the performed action looks and feels the same as the referent action.

Consequently, it must be added that the gestures Laura used in the preceding example actually were iconic, multimodal enactments of embodied meanings. Although Laura had severe difficulties with finding words and other linguistic expressions, she at the same time obviously had embodied conceptual ideas about what she wanted to tell: the separation, the spouses living at different places, the son moving back and forth between his parents, and the emptiness when he was gone. The gestures she forms— separation, coming and going, emptiness—are all synthetic enactments, capturing in a general and thus abstract way the basic relations and coming and going of the persons close to her. It would thus be possible to think of her gestures as a kind of abstract enactment of her embodied experiences. What Laura remembers is less an abstract representation, and more an embodied pattern of relations that she then can use because she does not need to "unzip" these synthetic, gestural signs to fit them into a linguistic, sequenced structure. Laura thus creatively resolves the problems that her declining semiotic resources present to her.

An argument in favor of this interpretation is that Laura sometimes evidently cannot remember either what happened once or stories told about events in the past. In these cases she doesn't use gestures. In the section of the interview just after the one discussed earlier, Laura is requested to tell about circumstances around how she got her diagnosis. Laura starts to tell, but cannot remember anything about meeting the doctor, going through the medical and psychological examinations, and eventually receiving the dementia diagnosis. In contrast to the first example, she does not use gestures when she doesn't remember (Example 6.2).

Example 6.2.

1	I₁:	what happened after that?
2		did you contact
3	Laura:	SHE
4		Monica
5		my sister
6		eh
7		she had some
8		something in on
	Gesture:	(raises right and makes circle movement with right index finger; stops and moves finger to lips)

	Gaze:	(unfocused gaze turned downward)
9		(pause 3s)
10		damn I don't know
11		but I came directly to XXX the right person
12		I did see
13		yes hmmm
14		but I cannot remember who it was
15	I$_1$:	do you remember what happened
16	Laura:	(pause 5 s)
17		noo
18		eh well I was to do certain things
	Gaze:	(gaze turned downward)
19		and I should
	Gesture:	(circle movements with both hands; puts both hands in her lap)
	Gaze:	(gaze down)
20		yes in
21		well
22		(pause 3s)
23		these pills
24		they just fall straight down here
	Gesture:	(right arm and extended hand moves from head and downward; her upper body follows this movement)
25		In order to talk
		(moves body into default position; her arm makes a circle movements and then back to default position in lap)
26		ehh
27		I'm not that old
28		I'm not that old
	Gesture:	(small circle movement with left hand)
	Gaze:	(gaze down)

In this example, it is obvious that Laura has a less clear memory about what happened, and she doesn't remember stories that might have been told about what happened. A guess is that Laura is attempting to tell about how her sister Monica helped Laura to contact a doctor her sister knew (lines 3–8). When Laura is trying to find words and expressions that would work, she raises her right hand and makes a circle movement with her index finger. This gesture is used again twice (lines 19 and 25). It is not obvious from the situation what the circle movement refers to, although it is faintly similar to a somewhat conventionalized gesture indicating that the person is seeking for something in her mind. Laura stops her gestures and is quiet and unmoving for three seconds, then says, "I don't know," thus confirming that she cannot find what she is trying to remember. Slightly before and during the pause, she is not making gestures. Then she clearly moves on to the next event sequence in the story, what happened at the doctor's. She again tries to remember something—whom she met. During her search (lines 11–14) she is not using any gestures, just words. The interviewer asked what happened then (line 15), and Laura is quiet for 5 seconds, doubtless because she cannot remember what happened. She doesn't make any gestures during this sequence, but sits in a default position with hands in her lap. Then (line 18) she suddenly remembers that she was asked to do certain things and when she tries to tell about this she makes gestures, using the circle movement, this time with both her hands. Laura turns her gaze downward, indicating that she gives up and seems to move on to a new event having to do with taking pills (lines 23–25). (From other parts of the interview, it can be conjectured that she is referring to the prescribed dementia medication that is supposed to help her to function better.) In trying to find the linguistic expressions, she again gestures, mimicking something falling down. Then again, she probably gives up (line 26) and says, "I'm not that old," as if commenting on her own situation and her inability to find words and memories.

In the sequences when she is at a loss finding linguistic expressions and probably does not have a clear idea about what she wants to say, Laura doesn't make any gestures. At other places, she only seems to be making a gesture when she talks about the pills. The other gestures (especially the circle movements) seem to refer to her ongoing search for memories and words; that is, they are signs to the listeners about what is going on in the situation. This is something that might indicate that it is important to recognize that gestures have different functions. Some gestures are referring to events in the story world, others to what is going on in the conversational situation. Still other gestures are part of the transformative process from idea to semiotic sign.

Moving from Story World to Conversational Realm

Although Laura has severe problems with remembering and finding linguistic expressions, she keeps her pragmatic abilities related to the "here-and-now" realm of the storytelling activity; that is, she is good at sustaining the relationship with the interviewers in the storytelling situation. This explains her use of the circling hand movements in lines 8, 19 and 28. This gesture is used to shift emphasis from the discursive story world to the social functions of the story. All other gestures that Laura uses, in both Examples 6.1 and 6.2, refer to events in the story world.

The circling hand movements—either with one hand or with both hands—are directed toward the interviewer and primarily have the function of indicating that Laura is searching for something and hence that she wants to keep her turn. In other words, she wants to continue her story. In all three cases she is unsuccessful; she cannot find what she is searching for. She demonstrates this by turning her gaze from the interviewers, thus disengaging the "relation," and turns her gaze downward. Averting her gaze in this way is a sign of withdrawal from the ongoing activity, although she reconnects in the first two instances after a brief pause, and in the last case the interviewer poses a new question (outside the transcription).

USING FRAGMENTS AND REPETITIONS

As was discussed in Chapter 3, autobiographical stories are often considered to be based on some kind of original experiences of the teller. The possible exception may be personal experiences of being born and the like, in which case it is sufficient to use the memories of the mother as a proxy. These "original experiences" are then used to construct new autobiographical stories every time they are told. A problem with this idea is that many autobiographical stories are told repeatedly to both the same and different people, and in a number of conversational situations. This means that many autobiographical stories exist in many versions, with various, often minor, variations.[26] A consequence of this is that when people tell a specific autobiographical story, they may base the new performance of the story on previous tellings, rather than on memories of the experiences of the "original" events that once more are assembled into a story. This makes it necessary to broaden the concept of what kind of experiences are turned into embodied memories to also include the repeated tellings of a story. These embodied, repeated tellings may form a set of possible ways not only to tell, but also to use the tellings.

Persons with dementia quite frequently repeat the same story or story fragment over and over. It is easy to think that these fragments and repetitions are meaningless, often because it is challenging for others to listen, and to think that the repetition is connected to a loss of temporal abilities (remembering that the story has already been told). Although these explanations might carry some truth, it has also been suggested that people with Alzheimer's disease may repeat story segments "that capture, albeit in frozen ways, the teller's attempt at making sense of his or her life,"[27] thereby making meaning-based connections between certain events connected with an overall interpretive schema that remains the same. In line with this argument, it is also possible to regard repetitions as a form of reuse of already existing story elements, from the abstract story structure, to specific "sentences" and verbal expressions, to phonological units. In fact, most speakers employ already used linguistic elements in new situations and linguistic context because it makes speaking quicker and easier, as new forms do not need to be constructed just then.[28] As a consequence, employing already used and established forms and units might be an important help for persons with dementia as they face word-finding and memory difficulties. Thus, repetitions can be regarded as a creative use of already established narrative and linguistic elements in order to solve interactional and communicative challenges. It should also be noted that using repetitions in this way challenges the received way of thinking about autobiographical stories and memories; using old versions of stories and memories implies that the often cherished notion of "original" experiences, memories, and stories is highly questionable. It is instead the repeatedly told stories that are cherished.

One example of repetition and reuse of story fragments was found in the material collected during an extended ethnographic study of an elder care facility. This care unit served eight residents, seven of whom were diagnosed with some form of dementia, mostly Alzheimer's disease. Storytelling between two female persons with Alzheimer's disease without staff present was observed. Martha and Catherine were diagnosed with Alzheimer's disease four to five years ago and seven to eight years ago, respectively. Both have mid-range Alzheimer's disease, although Martha is distinctly more inclined to hold the floor in conversations and generally less impaired in terms of linguistic capabilities. In small talk and in commenting on other persons' stories, Catherine's difficulties are sometimes negligible, but become more evident as she tries to construct a story of her own. In the spontaneous storytelling situations, Martha is almost always the teller of the story, while Catherine is her confidante. Martha's stories, told spontaneously to her friend Catherine, are often autobiographical, emotionally involved, and contain evaluative statements.

It was possible to identify one story that was told several times by Martha on different occasions, in various contexts, and with various audiences. The story is organized around a set of reportable events. The actual story—here called "the driver's license story"—was adapted to these different contexts and audiences and was therefore told in different ways.[29] It is a story about how Martha in her past, perhaps as a young person, decided to learn to drive and to get a driver's license, and then to buy her own car. Her husband questioned her ability, both to learn to drive and to save up for a car by herself, but was proven wrong. In the summer Martha and her family went for a long car ride, visiting relatives in various places. Martha surprised her sister and mother by being able to drive, and later discussed with her sister about being a married woman and learning to drive.

In one sense, this is a story about the different reactions encountered some decades ago by a woman wanting to be able to drive and to have her own car. It is a story that portrays Martha as not only challenging the values of her generation about what women can and ought to do, but also overcoming them, going her own way, and making a statement about herself.

One of several instances of the telling occurred after lunch when the two women walked along the corridor talking, and eventually sat down on a bench. Quite early on in the stroll Martha had started to reminisce, and gradually started to tell a story about her driver's license. Catherine went along and sat close to Martha on the bench. Martha told her story for about 30 minutes. At that time the staff started to move around, and the two women heard snatches of the conversation among the staff. The storytelling came to an end and resulted in a long pause (nearly 2 minutes). After some brief comments about the staff, the two women started to comment on the lights in the corridor. The storytelling episode was over.[30]

Example 6.3 is from near the end of this episode, after some 25 minutes. It's a typical example of the way the storytelling is organized and of the kind of stories Martha told. This is the third time during the episode that Martha tells the story about her decision to buy a car. Just before the example starts, she has been telling about making a down payment on a car. On line 1, Martha makes a general comment about that summer followed by an "and then" (line 2), indicating that new events will be added to the story. On line 4, Martha repeats the "and then" and the new story part, organized around a new theme, starts.

Example 6.3.

1	Martha:	it was it was such a lovely summer
2		[and then --]
3	Catherine:	[yees you] were lucky
4	Martha:	= and then I got and then I [. . .]
5		the instructor he asked me (.)
6		"would you like me to accompany you looking for a (.) car–"

7		'cause he did understand [(xx)]
8	Catherine:	[yes]
9	Martha:	"'cause they won't cheat you then" he said
10		and then he said
11		"I can accompany you and [. . .] look for a car 'cause I could pick the best one"
12	Catherine:	yes that's true
13	Martha:	yes "If you want to" he said
14		"yes I would like that" I said
15		"I've got—my brother has got a driver's license but [. . .]
16		but he eh (.)
17		it's better I get to learn from eh someone who's a real instructor"
18	Catherine:	yes that's true
19	Martha:	= yes "You are really careful, you really are" he said
20		(takes hold of Catherine's arm, leans forwards toward her and looks her in the eye)
21		"so you'll get along okay" he said
22		[(leans back and laughs)]
23	Catherine:	[well that was a nice compliment]
24	Martha:	(laughs) *yees*
25		(laughter in her voice; points to Catherine)
26	Catherine:	she got a nice compliment!
27	Martha:	*yes
28		(makes a pointing gesture toward Catherine again and keeps it during the rest of the utterance)
29		he said that
30		yees* (nods and then exchanges a knowing look with Catherine) ehh
31	Catherine:	yes I believe so (xx xx)
32	Martha:	= yes

In general, the telling of the story in the example is interactionally well organized. Both women position themselves in the turn-taking as tellers and listeners, changing positions so as to leave room for comments. Catherine frequently supports Martha's storytelling with small interjections or comments (Lines 8, 12, 18, 23, 26, 31). There are no gaps in the turn-taking, or long pauses or outright misunderstandings that cannot be solved. In the telling there are some short pauses that mostly have to do with word-finding problems (most notably in lines 15, 16). Thus, there is little indication of problems in the organization of the interaction.

From line 19 to line 31, an evaluative section of the story can be identified. During this stretch of talk it is noticeable that simultaneous talk appears. The simultaneous talk underlines that both participants have recognized and appreciated the evaluation of the events in the story. In this way, closeness between the two women is displayed around some points in the story. The simultaneous talk is further supported by bodily display of closeness and hand gestures; Martha puts her hand on Catherine's arm, leans forwards, gazes at Catherine, points, and so on (line 20 and onward).

Discursively, the telling is organized around a dialogue between two of the story's main protagonists, Martha and the driving instructor. The dialogue is replayed and dramatized. The quotations are generally prefaced or followed by expressions like "he said," "and then he said," "I said," and so on. Martha's narrative voice is found only at the beginning of the story (lines 1, 2, 4, 5) and in the small comments in the evaluative part of the story (lines 21, 24, 25).[31]

There is a problem with unclear word references and sometimes confusing pronouns. On line 4, for instance, Martha says, "and then I got and then I," and in line 6 she quotes her driving instructor. What she probably meant to say is that she got her driver's license and then considered buying a car. In lines 15 and 16, Martha evidently has problems finding words. She resolves this problem by using a phrase that she has used several times previously: "it's better I get to learn from eh someone who's a real instructor." This solution introduces a third problem, namely the fusion of two storylines.

In line 15, Martha introduces a circumstance that probably is important to her, the fact that her brother has a driver's license. Potentially he could help her select and buy a new car. When she has talked about her brother previously, it had to do with her not letting him teach her how to drive. It's this storyline she continues in line 17, that she wants the professional instructor to teach her how to drive. She then continues the storyline by quoting her instructor's approval of her choice. The fusion of two different storylines in this way happens several times during the storytelling episode.

In general, during the whole storytelling episode, when Martha nests the strophes together she doesn't organize her telling around a temporal progression of the events. Normally it would be expected that this type of autobiographical story would be organized around a set of events that are temporally ordered; the order of the events in the telling corresponds to the order in which it is told. This would make it possible for the listener to pose the question, "What happened then?" to the unfolding narrative, and to listen for the next event.[32] What happens when Martha tells her story is that she changes the order of the events and repeats certain events and parts of the story several times, making certain events appear again and again without relating them to the temporal sequence of events.

All this is an indication of Martha constructing her story by using several "ready-made" units. A closer look at all the instances when Martha is telling her story will show that she is actually using both individual words and expressions, as well as storylines and phonological units. This is something that becomes quite clear if some of James Gee's ideas about oral stories are used.[33]

Themes, Stanzas, Lines

As suggested in Chapter 4, James Gee proposed a way of transcribing and analyzing oral narrative by basing it on the prosodic organization of the narrative. He argued that stories are organized around some basic units that are marked by changes in prosody like raising the voice, stressing, pauses, and so on. A narrative is divided into main *parts, strophes*, which are organized around happenings or events, and finally *lines*, which are the basic elements expressing ideas. The teller prosodically marks various elements in a narrative, helping the listener to follow and understand the story as he or she hears it; this makes it possible to identify what the teller thinks important, funny, noteworthy, or connected.

Using this model, it could be argued that the various versions of the story about getting a driver's license are organized around a set of *strophes*, for instance "deciding to learn to drive," "the driving instructor encouraging Martha to learn to drive," "Martha deciding to buy a car," and so on (see Box 6.1). The strophes generally have a clear beginning, some sort of complicating action, and an evaluation resembling William Labov's and Joshua Waletzky's 1967 proposal about the organization of oral stories.[34] The strophes are variations of more general *themes* that could be considered as *parts* of the story; for instance, "getting a driver's license," "buying a car," and "driving on vacation." Taken together, the strophes and the parts constitute a set of temporally progressive events.

The strophes are nested together into stories, and in that way the stories that are told on the different occasions emerge. It's unclear whether the stories that emerge from the nesting process are supposed to be heard as continuous stories, although it's possible to listen to the narrations in that way.

Box 6.1 THE UNITS OF THE DRIVER'S LICENSE STORY

Part I: Martha getting a driver's license
1:1   Martha decides to learn to drive
1:2   The local driving instructor encourages the young Martha to learn how to drive
1:3   Martha's husband questions her ability to learn to drive
1:4   Martha passes her driving test easily

Part II: Buying a car
2:1   Martha decides to buy a car
2:2   Martha's husband questions her ability to save up for a car
2:3   What the car looks like
2:4   Getting help to buy a car
2:5   Martha plans how to pay for the car
2:6   Making a down payment to get the car right away
2:7   Martha buys a car
2:8   Getting the car (right away)

Part III: Driving on vacation and meeting the family
3:1   Practicing before going away
3:2   Making a detour (700 kilometers)
3:3   Surprising her sister (later: mother) and the absent husband/ driver
3:4   Advising her sister about learning to drive: never drive with one's husband
3:5   Competing with her husband for the driver's position
3:6   Stopping along the road, picking berries and flowers
3:7   Driving for several days, visiting other relatives on the way

The strophes could probably be thought of as a set of autobiographically reportable events, in line with Charlotte Linde's (1993) argument. They are also apparently events to which Martha has access. From the fieldwork we know that Martha had problems accessing memories in general and that she tended to use a small number of stories in different types of situations as a way of creating meaning.

The strophes are made up of lines that are often organized around certain phrases. Quite often Martha uses the same line (or phrase), although in two different contexts. This is especially true about lines that express some important emotional or moral content. Some of these phrases can be found in both storytelling episodes.

It turns out that Martha organizes the nesting of the strophes into a larger story in different ways, depending on the storytelling setting. When she is telling the story without staff present, the emerging story lacks a temporal progression of events. As a consequence, strophes can be told several times without comments, or events can be told in reverse order or without any temporal order at all. When Martha tells her story with a staff member present, the assistant nurses support Martha's storytelling, resulting in a temporally well-organized story.

It is evident that Martha's telling about getting a driver's license, buying a car, and getting to drive on her own is a way to remember events that are somehow central to her identity. A constantly recurring theme is Martha's ability to do things on her own and follow her own mind, even if other people were critical or might disapprove of her actions—that is, the stories are about Martha as an independent and capable woman who knows her own mind.

Although combined differently, there is an overall similarity between the versions of the driver's license story as to what units are included. The parts seem to fit together in more than one way, some of which notably diverge from the chronological structure, but still add up to a recognizable story, even with instances of almost identical linguistic phrases. Taken together, this indicates that Martha is using a number of kindred themes, closely related to getting a driver's license and to the consequences of this. In this respect, Martha's way of telling has a close resemblance to traditional oral storytelling, as in Gee's argument. Stories that stand out from standard patterns, he claims, become comprehensible when viewed as *oral* stories, rather than as literary stories.

In line with this, it can also be argued that difficulties in telling autobiographical stories can be handled by (re-)using smaller ready-made units that somehow illustrate a meaning-based connection between events, as suggested by Vai Ramanathan;[35] that is, more or less flexible resources can be reused and combined in a variety of ways, although still in line with the same moral theme, to compose autobiographical stories. In this way, referential aspects of the composed story do not quite add up as comprehensible when scrutinized, but the point or the moral theme remains intact. As a consequence, it becomes possible to use these moral themes in order to sustain the teller's identity.

Furthermore, it also becomes possible to relate actively to loss of memory by using remaining narrative elements in creative ways, and with some support. Martha is capable of combining a set of narrative events, characterized by their tellability and evaluative points, into a storytelling event. Memory loss is thus not a simple loss of memories, but rather a loss of the ability to combine and use memories in stories recognizable by others.

It also turns out that the most important thing is not necessarily the progressing temporal organization, but the tellability of the story and its evaluative points. As long as this works, the teller with dementia can use the telling of stories in order to present and negotiate his or her identity.

Using an Already Told Story as a Recognizable Format

It is rarely noted that a story as a formal structure could be used as a resource or "tool"; that is, the structure of a story can be used as a structure for a new story. Literary theorist Mark Turner argues that stories function as parables that can be projected into new areas as a way of structuring and thus understanding the new area.[36] Stories build on basic "schemas" that, for instance, allow prediction of the consequences of events, evaluation, sets of objects, events, or actors. Similarly, David Herman argues that stories function as cognitive tools helping to make sense of the world and other persons; stories can help to gather experiences into segments, to suggest causal relations between events, and to typify and sequence events and actions.[37] These general story schemas become embodied as a set of possible ways to tell a new story.

With fewer available cognitive resources, it becomes a challenge for persons with dementia to encounter new and unfamiliar situations. Even small deviances from routines may set off a problem-solving activity trying to understand what is taking place, and how to make the situation meaningful in general, but also meaningful in terms of what to do in this situation (if anything). The challenge in this kind of situation has to do with loss of not only categories and typifications, but also the ability to remember similar events and what to do in these situations. The person has a limited accessibility to a small set of interpretive resources, for instance a number of previously told and established stories organized around a common storyline. A storyline is a basic schema, a set of guidelines and constraints for telling a story that conveys it as a story of a certain and recognizable kind.[38] Using a storyline thus makes it possible for the teller to create variations of already recognized and often well-established stories, and thereby helps to create a sense of a situation being familiar and hence meaningful. Using a storyline means using previously known and established "genres" of narrative plots in order to interpret the present situation and occurrences in line with already established stories. Fitting a situation into a plot within the scope of an overall storyline as a way of making sense of different kinds of situations (and acting accordingly) is nothing unusual. Storylines are commonly used that way in everyday life. Storylines should thus be considered instead to be embodied in social situations, relations, and human experiences, rather than existing as abstract cognitive schemas or story grammars.

An example of how embodied storylines can be used are found in how Martha in Example 3.2 in Chapter 3 deals with a situation that is a bit puzzling for her at the care home where she is living. In the afternoon, Martha and her friend Catherine note that coffee is being prepared by the staff. The assistant nurses accompany Martha, Catherine, and the other residents into the day room, where the coffee is to be served, and give them coffee and cookies. A problem emerges slowly as the ladies are not sure *who* should take care of the arrangements around drinking coffee. Having served the coffee, the assistant nurses withdraw to the kitchen for the day's debriefing, as the evening shift has arrived. Slowly, Martha assumes the status of the hostess, something her stories give testimony to. Innumerable are also her stories about how people had constantly taken advantage of her generosity, both at home and at work, although she had four children to provide for.

These narrative plots occur frequently in the body of material and can be described as variants of one overall storyline that binds together many of Martha's stories. This storyline is based on her being a generous and sharing person throughout her life, to the extent of being taken advantage of, always doing her share, paying her way. This is something that seems essential to the way Martha likes to present herself. In line with these stories, she explicitly presents herself as the hostess in the "here and now," and also complains about being the one that always has to arrange for the coffee.

It is obvious that the storyline Martha uses is fully embodied in several ways. The first way is the immediate *situation*: the persons and objects present, the physical environment, and what is happening. That includes all the aspects of the situation that may function as kinds of affordances for using the storyline. Martha's storytelling has a strong connection to the clues available in the physical surroundings and is also confirmed in, and part of, the ongoing interaction with other participants. Second, the storyline is consistent with Martha's life history; her previous life and experiences, as well as previous storytelling, offer a huge set of storylines that can function as *possible* interpretive frameworks and appropriate manuscripts regarding how to organize action and interaction. Finally, it is also obvious that most of these storylines are not *available* to Martha due to her dementia disorder. Most of the other possible alternative storylines are lost, in the sense that the situation does not evoke these alternative possibilities for her action. Thus, she is limited to using the one storyline that is available to her, which she uses very creatively, at least from her point of view, although the interpretive framework may cause confusion among other participants.

EMBODIMENT AND MEMORY

This chapter has presented the argument that in storytelling a number of different resources are used, specifically "memories" and various semiotic resources. It has been argued that persons with dementia adapt by reorganizing their communication so that they become less dependent on words and can use more nonverbal means like gestures. It has also been suggested that the traditional idea of memory as an "archive" with retrieval of memories that are needed for storytelling is quite problematic. Jens Brockmeier writes that memory as archive implies that memories or representations of events, experiences, or knowledge are *stored* somewhere in the brain and then retrieved when necessary, along with others, through some kind of indexing system (as in old libraries).[39] As early as 1996, memory researcher Daniel Schacter summarized the positions on cognitive and neurocognitive memory research:

> memory is [. . .] composed of a variety of distinct and dissociable processes and systems. Each system depends on a particular constellation of networks in the brain that involve different neural structures, each of which plays a highly specialized role within the system [. . .] [demonstrating how] specific parts of the brain contribute to different memory processes.[40]

In other words, there is no distinct part of the brain that could be called *the memory place*; instead, many different parts of the brain are engaged in producing *memories*. This also implies that all kinds of psychological processes are used in memory processes, from motor processes, to visual imagination, to smell, touch, and verbal aspects; that is, memory processes make use of all kinds of multimodal resources. Furthermore, neurocognitive research shows that the same processes used for engaging with the present are also activated and used when remembering something similar:

> there is no biological correlate that allows us to distinguish between what we traditionally call acts of remembering the past from acts of perceiving the present, whether in a visual, acoustical, or tactile mode. Nor are there any indicators that separate the content of a perception in the here and now from the content

of a perception that we had at some point in the past. For the neuronal circuits involved there is no difference between perceiving, say, a face here and now and having perceived this face a few days or years ago.[41]

Again, a close connection between bodily processes and cognitive processes is suggested. In his well-known work *Remembering*, published in 1932, social psychologist Frederic Bartlett argues that memories are not stored in the brain and then retrieved. Rather, he argues, memories are *constructions*; "in remembering, the subject uses the setting, or scheme, or pattern, and builds up its characteristics afresh to aid whatever response the needs of the moment may demand."[42]

Thus a situation puts demand on a person to make a specific contribution in an ongoing conversation, for instance by telling about what happened last week. The "memory" produced in this situation is constructed from various bits and pieces and is combined into a contribution that makes sense in the situation. This idea of how "memory" and "memories" work allows for an understanding of how persons with dementia can use various aspects of experience as well as of previous tellings in order to construct a "memory," or in order to remember. It also reveals that "memories" of various types come into life in the telling, especially in interaction with other participants. Others can contribute contexts and interpretations that help to give a meaning to "fragmented" memories, either by acknowledging these "memories" or by giving them a biographical context.

NOTES

1. M. Proust, *Remembrance of Things Past*, Volume 1: *Swann's Way: Within a Budding Grove*. The definitive French Pleiade edition, translated by C. K. Scott Moncrieff (London: Pelican, 1922), 48–51.
2. Bolens, 2012.
3. Cf. Herman, 2003, 2010.
4. Goodwin, 2000a; Kendon, 1990.
5. Gallagher, 2005; Gibbs, 2006.
6. Bolens, 2012; Nelson & Fivush, 2004.
7. Gibbs, 2006; Kontos, 2004.
8. Goffman, 1981.
9. Goodwin, 2003, p. 20. Also see, Goodwin, 2004.
10. McNeill, 2005.
11. See Kendon, 1990 and 2004, for further discussions and examples.
12. Gee, 1986.
13. Kendon, 1990.
14. Kendon, 1990.
15. Cf. McNeill, 1992.

16. Cf. McNeill, 2005.
17. Kendon, 2004, p. 15.
18. McNeill, 1992, p. 37.
19. Ibid.
20. Unfortunately, there are few studies of gestures in relation to persons with dementia. See Hubbard et al., 2002; Hydén, 2011; Sandman et al., 1988.
21. Nelson & Fivush, 2004.
22. For examples, see articles by Eleanor Antelius (2009), Pia Kontos (2004), and Jacqueline Kindell and colleagues (2013)
23. See especially *The Phenomenology of Perception* by Maurice Merleau-Ponty (1962) and *The Primacy of Movement* by Maxine Sheets-Johnstone (2011).
24. Streeck, 2013, p. 72.
25. Ibid., p. 73.
26. See Neal Norrick's book about telling the same story, *Conversational Storytelling in Everyday Talk* (2000).
27. Ramanathan, 1997, p. 115.
28. See Wray, 2008.
29. Cf. Linde, 1993; Norrick, 1998.
30. The storytelling endeavors of Martha and her friend Catherine have been the topic of a number of articles written by the present author and colleagues. Professor Linda Örulv originally recorded that material as part of a research project on identity and dementia through a grant to the present author from The Swedish Research Council for Working Life. Over the years, Linda Örulv and I have written about various aspects of the various versions of the story. Recently Professors Christina Samuelsson and Charlotta Plejert have been co-authors of articles. See Hydén & Örulv, 2009, 2010; Hydén, Plejert, Samuelsson, & Örulv, 2013; Örulv & Hydén, 2006.
31. See Elizabeth Holt's article, "Reporting on Talk: The Use of Direct Reported Speech in Conversation" (1996).
32. William Labov, 1972.
33. James Gee, 1986.
34. Labov & Waltzky, 1967/1997.
35. Ramanathan, 1997, p. 115.
36. Turner, 1996.
37. Herman, 2003.
38. Schafer, 1992, p. 29 ff.
39. Jens Brockmeier, 2010.
40. Schacter, 1996, p. 5.
41. Brockmeier, 2010, p. 20.
42. Bartlett, 1932/1995, p. 196.

CHAPTER 7

Selves and Interdependent Identities

1	Nils:	and yes, we've had, previously (.)
2		we've had ehm: (0.8) eh: (0.7)
3		what's it called (.)(looks at his wife)
4		the medication for (0.6)
5		Alzheimer
6		(0.8)
7	Minna:	well Reminyl
8	Nils:	Reminyl yes
9	Minna:	m: m:
10	Nils:	and that we've had ever since the start six (.) years ago
11	I_1:	m:
12	Minna:	m:
13	Nils:	and I've liked Reminyl
14	Minna:	ah:
15	Nils:	I think it has worked well

Who has been taking the medication for Alzheimer's disease? Is it Nils, who is diagnosed with Alzheimer's disease, or is it his wife, Minna, who does not have this diagnosis? At least it is Nils who appreciates the medication.

The subtle shift between the pronouns *we* and *I* in the example is quite interesting. Taken seriously, it reveals that Nils's experience of being ill and taking the drug is part of the couple's joint life, while he might at the same time have an individual experience of the effects of the drug. This shift in pronouns also indicates something about Nils's and Minna's identities in relation to the illness; they may share identities as a *we*, as well as individual *Is*.

As discussed in Chapters 1 and 2, the interest in the relationship between autobiographical stories and identity in persons with dementia has been connected to a re-evaluation of the person with dementia as a person. As researchers have moved beyond the individual with dementia and have begun to involve spousal relationships as well as family relationships, this has implied a need for a reconceptualization of the identity concept, away from a theoretical framework that primarily sees identity in terms of the individual's construction of autobiographical stories. One way to proceed has been to argue that spouses in couples with dementia—as in all other couples—often define themselves in terms of a couplehood, or a *we*, and tend to develop some kind of an identity as a couple. This identity is often expressed in and based on the *joint stories* that couples tell together about themselves.[1]

In line with the argument of this book—that stories are the result of joint endeavors—identity may be seen less as an individual phenomenon, but rather as something that is shared between persons. Instead of taking the individual with dementia as the typical case, it could be assumed that couples in which one spouse is diagnosed with dementia would present a different picture with regard to identity and identity change. Presenting, sustaining, and negotiating a shared identity may be seen as part of a dynamic, complex, and constantly renegotiated relationship between the spouses in the couple, made more complicated by the disease. One source of inspiration for such a broader relational theory about identities is social psychological research on interdependence, as well as research on the role of storytelling as a resource for identity work in family life.[2] In this chapter it will be argued that identities in couples with dementia could be conceptualized in terms of an *interdependent identity*; that is, they can be seen as shared identities, but also as identities that are dependent on the relationship between the spouses.

A theoretical approach to identity, stressing both shared identity and its relationship basis, would imply a focus on the ways the participants organize their interactions in order to deal with the potential problems that may or do emerge in the interaction. Thus the consequences of dementia would be conceptualized less as being an individual problem, but rather as something that is dealt with jointly with other persons in everyday interaction.

SELF AND IDENTITY: CONCEPTUAL ISSUES

In a well-known article on self in chronic illness, sociologist Kathy Charmaz suggested that the self diminishes, crumbles, and ultimately the person will "suffer a loss of self."[3] Although it is not entirely clear what Charmaz meant by "loss of self," the concept has become widespread, especially in research on chronic illnesses. As noted in Chapter 2, much of the research around the self in dementia has focused on whether persons with dementia still have a self or not. Research on how the self changes as the disease progresses is still sparse.[4]

The concept of self (and identity) is one of the perpetually problematic concepts in both philosophy and psychology, as is the idea of a "loss of self." The term *self* is often considered to refer to some kind of entity— for instance, a conceptual structure—residing inside the individual. This is a very problematic conception, often criticized by philosophers and psychologists with a background in phenomenological philosophy, or drawing on Wittgenstein's philosophical heritage.[5] One of the philosophers and psychologists with a background in the Wittgensteinian tradition is psychoanalyst Roy Schafer, who in his book *A New Language for Psychoanalysis* pointed out that "self and identity are not names of identifiable homogeneous or monolithic entities; they are classes of self-representations that exist only in the vocabulary of the observer."[6]

What Schafer suggested was that persons talking about themselves or others have access to a number of ways of describing both themselves and others, drawing on sets of self and other representations. From this perspective, it becomes important to note the many different senses in which "self" words are used to define experience. For example, "I hit myself"; "I hate myself"; "I'm self-conscious"; "I'm self-sufficient"; "I feel like my old self"; "I'm selfish"; "my humiliation was self-inflicted"; and "I couldn't contain myself". Self does not mean exactly the same thing from one of these sentences to the next. It means my body, my personality, my actions, my competence, my continuity, my needs, my agency, and my subjective space. Self is thus a diffuse, multipurpose word. Like the pronouns *I* and *me*, of which it is after all a variant, self is a way of pointing. In other words, it is a way of saying this or that feature of my being. Consequently, one has always to decide, on the basis of the situational and the verbal context in which the word is used at any moment, which aspect of a person is being pointed to; it may, of course, be a comprehensive and complex aspect and it may be *relatively* stable.[7]

In other words, terms like *self, identity, I, you*, and so on, are words that mainly point to or index persons or aspects of persons, as well as various cultural categories and social roles that can be used to describe persons (mother, boss, nurse, smart, beautiful, etc.).

Seen from this perspective, it is not especially meaningful to talk about an actual loss of self. Rather, usage of words like *loss* and *void* should be taken as metaphorical expressions, rather than as words that refer to an actual loss of something or an actual void. Some aspect of a self (i.e., aspects of the person) might be lost due to changes in the brain and are in that sense lost, as in not being there anymore. But the self is not lost or disappeared; it has changed as the person changes. It is better to talk about a reorganization and revision given the new conditions, namely the "new" brain.

An important aspect of self and sense of self is the way persons portray themselves in interaction with others. As social psychologist Erving Goffman argues, persons have a number of different forms and media that are available to them to express and manifest the self, from the way they walk or the pose they strike, to their clothes, manners, style, and so on, all used to present and project a self in interaction.[8] Of particular interest are the possibilities the use of language offers:

- The use of various *categorizations* identifies a person as a father/mother, worker, person with dementia, caregiver, and so on. Categorizations are often culturally and socially loaded and put the categorized person in a wider net of categories and expectations.
- The use of *pronouns* can be very effective in denoting relations between self and other. The use of the pronoun *we* is both inclusive and exclusive, while the use of *I* may set the individual in contrast to others.
- In telling *autobiographical stories*, it becomes possible to construct self as a *character* or figure and to create a contrast between teller and character.

Thus, the self is to be found in all these various non-linguistic as well as language-based forms. Autobiographical stories are especially interesting, as the teller may present him- or herself in many versions. In his book *Retelling a Life*, Roy Schafer writes that a person's "experiential self may be seen as a set of varied narratives that seem to be told by and about a cast of varied selves. And yet, like the dream, which has one dreamer, the entire tale is told by one narrator."[9]

The projection of different selves in a narrative allows the teller to position the experiences of the teller as a five-year-old in contrast to the experiences and values of the teller as an adult. The teller can point to a contrast between the period before a dementia diagnosis to the teller as a person with dementia, and so on. In that way it becomes possible for persons to present themselves in quite creative and innovative ways.

Thus, "the self" is not to be found "inside" the individual's skull, either as a structured cognitive representation or some other kind of object. Rather, the sense of self is connected to the various practices, in particular linguistic ones, that persons use in everyday interaction in order to present and negotiate various aspects of themselves *as persons*.

THE SELF AND CATASTROPHIC REACTIONS

In Chapter 3, the concept of catastrophic reactions was introduced. When a person with acquired brain injuries encounters a situation that is difficult or unknown, the response to this situation may be anxiety and withdrawal from the situation. When the withdrawal includes the abandonment of human relations, some clinicians called this a *disencounter*.

Repeated catastrophic reactions, repeated failures to perform everyday tasks, and the risk of disencounters generally will affect the person's *sense of self*. The self becomes problematic because it is questioned through the person's difficulties with handling and taking part in everyday activities. It also becomes questioned by the fact that the habits and routines—autobiographical stories and storylines (what also could be called "episodic memories") that are possible to tell for a person about him- or herself—that have been central to the self are also disrupted. Some of these habitual resources become unavailable or do not work anymore because they do not reflect the new reality (i.e., they do not make sense). Dementia is thus a *self-involving* disease, because it is quite difficult to define dementia as something that doesn't belong to the self, although the disorder is often experienced as an unwelcome guest, an "it."[10]

A sense of self is important, as it is part of the regulation of the individual's relationship to his or her world as well as to others. A sense of self provides the emotional and practical condition for action and participation—being able to act, manage problems, being successful, knowing how to do things, and so on. Interactionally it has to do with defining and keeping up relationships with others, especially the status as a person that can be counted on in future interactions.

Particularly aspects of the self that have to do with *identity* (being able to do what one always has done), *agency* (actually being able to do things and feel responsible), but also *personhood* (being counted as a full person by oneself and others) become problematic as the disease progresses; that is, *as the conditions of selfhood change, the "self" will change.*

Psychologist Masahiro Nochi pointed out that in persons suffering from traumatic brain injuries, three types of "losses" were involved:

(1) Loss of a clear self-knowledge, who they were and what they could do;
(2) Loss of self by comparison with premorbid self (also involving distress and grief);
(3) Loss of self in the eyes of others and thus the risk of stigma.[11]

Connected to these "losses" are a loss of habits and routines from all the everyday habits that have supported the "self-knowledge," a sense of agency and continuity and thus identity, in the eyes of the person him- or herself, as well as in the eyes of others.

A number of studies about how persons with dementia become aware of their illness give an indication of what persons with dementia experience as areas of loss.[12] Of special importance are experience of *forgetfulness* and *memory problems*, for instance not remembering names, words, and events, as well as "how to do things" like one's morning routines. Often mentioned in interviews is also loss of *competency* and *control* in situations like driving and in various social situations, in particular in conversations (not making sense and making mistakes). A further problem is the experience of fluctuation of symptoms, some days being worse than others. These functional losses are accompanied by feelings of being lost, fear of what is happening and will happen in the near future, feelings of inadequacy, loss and grief, and fear of becoming a burden.

In summary, as cognitive and linguistic functions are challenged, become unreliable, and eventually are lost in the very late phase of dementia, these processes undermine the everyday practices that constitute the sense of a self. These challenges are not just about the various declining cognitive and linguistic resources, but above all are about the challenge of the kind of person one has been; they may thus result in intensive feelings of loss and grief, often causing depression and withdrawal. It is important to note that the challenges and losses are experienced as gradual, in contrast to the losses of persons suffering from the more or less immediate effects of a traumatic brain injury, and as affecting specific cognitive and linguistic functions ("memory") rather than being generalized. The challenges and the eventual and final losses also result in a widening gap between what the persons with dementia used to be able to do and accomplish before the onset of the disease and what they can do as persons with dementia. This emerging and increasing gap has consequences for the persons' identity; they are not who they used to be. The person he or she has become is not identical to the person he or she used to be; the "new" person is often experienced as "alien," as if the person with dementia has no knowledge about the "new" person.

These challenges and changes result in new relationships between the person, his or her body, the world, and other persons. In particular, the person with dementia moves from an experience of being a relatively autonomous individual, to becoming dependent on others in a shrinking world, and with a waning sense of agency. In this respect, the experiences and challenges of the sense of self are fairly similar to other chronic diseases.[13]

What is special with a disorder like dementia that affects the self (and other acquired brain injuries, as well as most psychoses) is that it also *affects the persons' ability to present and negotiate themselves and their identities*, in particular by using language and thus autobiographical storytelling. The challenges and eventual losses of cognitive and linguistic functions are hence part of *a double process*; the losses challenge both the everyday habits of the self, as well as the ability to express and communicate these losses and to revise and reconstruct the sense of self and of identity.

REVISION AND RECONSTRUCTION OF SELF AND IDENTITY

As the brain changes due to the brain disorder, the person will have access to fewer resources, especially those that bridge cognitive and linguistic abilities, particularly categorizations and narrative constructions. As a consequence, the person with dementia will find it difficult to recognize him- or herself. It is a situation where the routines—like all the small autobiographical stories told in various situations—no longer make any sense, or even are difficult to remember and tell. In other words, the self and the stories from before the onset of dementia become *disrupted* and need to be *reconstructed*. Sociologist Michael Bury argued that

> [i]llness, and especially chronic illness, is precisely that kind of experience where the structures of everyday life and the forms of knowledge which underpin them are disrupted. Chronic illness involves a recognition of the worlds of pain and suffering, possibly even death, which is [sic] normally only seen as distant possibilities or the plights of others. In addition, it brings individuals, their families, and their wider social networks face to face with the character of their relationships in stark form, disrupting normal rules of reciprocity and mutual support.[14]

The term *disruption* is related to Kurt Goldstein's concept of catastrophic reactions, but points to the self as a practical problem, rather than something that is lost.[15] Reconstruction implies new grounds for the self and thus a possible revision of the former routines and habits that supported self-representations connected with the life before dementia (or another acquired brain injury). Gareth Williams defines reconstruction as

> [a]n individual's account of the origin of that illness in terms of putative causes [which] can perhaps most profitably be read as an attempt to establish points of reference between body, self, and society and to reconstruct a sense of order from the fragmentation produced by chronic illness.[16]

The concept of reconstruction also suggests that persons with various kinds of acquired brain injuries also actively attempt to adapt their sense of self to the new condition with which the changed or changing brain presents them. This idea is closely related to what psychologist Mark Freeman calls a *rewriting*, or what William Randall and Elisabeth McKim call *restorying* of the life story.[17] This implies going back over old memories and stories, identifying elements that either have been lost and forgotten or never received attention, and re-evaluating these. As a result, it is assumed that the individual's life story will include new elements and connections, but also more coherence, "depth," and wisdom, according to Freeman.[18]

A problem with dementia is its progressive nature, as is the case for many other chronic illnesses. It is not a trauma that then has to be coped with, but rather a long process that involves losses of more cognitive, linguistic, and other bodily resources. Thus for persons with dementia it is not just a question of reconstructing a self and identity. Dementia means living with a changing brain, and it is thus rather about revising and reconstructing a self when the routines and habits that make up the sense of self are constantly in a state of change.

All of Schafer's concepts of self, as well as Bury's and Williams's ideas about disruption and reconstruction, pertain to the single individual. For most people with dementia (or other chronic illnesses), revising and reconstructing identity and a sense of self are a process that involves at least significant others. Many of those routines and habits that are fundamental to the self are part of everyday relational networks that involve other persons, both close relations (spouses and other family members) and caregivers and more peripheral persons. Most routine stories told are part of these relational networks and relate to a *common ground*; other persons expect the person with dementia to tell certain stories and to be familiar with stories told by others, to know things about him- or herself and others, and to remember salient events. This means that a reconstruction and revision of these routines and habits also includes other persons, their expectations, and shared stories and memories (i.e., all the relational routines and habits that make up much of everyday life and are the psychological ground for the participants' senses of self).

INTERDEPENDENCE

It is obvious that individuals living together over longer periods of time will develop a special relationship. Above all, most couples will become more or less dependent on each other, at least in certain areas of their lives, while in other areas they will be quite independent. Certainly, couples differ in terms of their degree of dependency, some valuing independence more, while others will value dependency.[19] Although these differences may exist, most couples develop some areas of mutual dependency, that is, areas where both parties rely on each other for their general well-being.[20] In these areas they have *common interests*, and both of them jointly *control* the interaction. A typical example of an area of mutual dependency would be the intimate aspects of the relationship. When couples are mutually dependent in this way, they are *interdependent*.[21] The term *interdependent* (used in this context) actually goes back to a book published in 1959 by social psychologists John Thibaut and Harold Kelley:

> In any dyad both members are dependent upon the relationship to some degree, so we speak of their being interdependent. This means that each one has some power over the other, which places limits on the extent to which each may with impunity exercise his power over his colleague. The pattern of interdependency which characterizes a relationship also affects the kinds of process agreements the pair must achieve if their relationship is to be maximally satisfactory.[22]

Spouses in a couple are interdependent (and thus have an interdependent relationship) if one spouse is dependent on what the other does (or does not do), and vice versa. Interdependence is not static but varies with the degree of *dependence* between the spouses, the *mutuality* of their dependence, and to what degrees their *interests* coincide.[23] The interdependence may hence be different between couples, but may also shift in degree between spouses over time and various life phases, as well as in different social situations.

Even if interdependent relationships are variable and are just one kind of relationship couples may develop, as they also may do things quite independently of each other, this type of relationship is important, as it is highly related to *mutual commitment* between the spouses.[24] Commitment refers here to the degree to which couples "intend to maintain their marriage"[25] because of their mutual devotion to and satisfaction with each other, and their mutual obligations and investments in the relationship.[26]

Interdependent relationships are also interesting, as they tend to develop not only strong mutual commitment, but also *interdependent cognitions*:

> increasing relationship commitment is accompanied by a restructuring of self-in-relationship mental representations, including tendencies to perceive ourselves less as individuals and more as part of a pluralistic self-and-partner collective. We refer to these collective mental representations of the self-in-relationship as cognitive interdependence.[27]

As spouses develop interdependent relationships characterized by mutual commitment, they also tend to experience and represent themselves in new ways; the borders between the individuals become porous. Consequently, spouses develop mutual interdependent cognitions in which the individuals represent themselves and their relationship cognitively in terms of the other spouse being part of the self, and this self being part of the couple unit. In other words, the individual self will include aspects of the other spouse's self, but this individual self also becomes part of the couple's shared representation of themselves.[28]

It is probably possible to take this idea one step further and argue that spouses develop not only interdependent relationships and cognitions, but also what could be called *interdependent identities*. The individual spouses present themselves not as two independent *I*s with individual and independent identities, but as part of a *we*, with identities that are shared between the spouses and are dependent on mutual recognition. Interdependent identity thus implies that the spouses must *collaborate* around shared identity issues; each individual spouse can only present aspects of his or her identity that the other spouse potentially would support and recognize; that is, the individual spouse's claims about the shared identity are dependent on the other spouse's recognition. A spouse cannot claim to be part of a *we* if the other spouse rejects or questions this claim (with the possible exception of discussions about their present civil status). This often means that identity claims either are accepted or have to be negotiated through extended turns. This also implies that interdependent identities are not absolute, but vary with the degree of the spouses' levels of dependence and the mutuality of their dependence, as well as the degree of covariation of interest.

Interdependent identities can of course be established and negotiated in many ways, but some of the most important resources and sites are probably *joint storytelling* and *joint stories*.[29] Joint stories portray the spouses as belonging together, as sharing experiences and values, as being something more than just two individual persons. Telling joint stories implies that the spouses must position themselves as being knowledgeable about each other and their couplehood. In telling joint stories, spouses must position themselves either *discursively* or *epistemically*, or both. In joint storytelling it is possible to discursively position the individual *I* as part of a collective subject—a *we*—through a certain kind of person-referencing practice.[30] Various pronouns, as well as the use of names, identify persons and, for instance, whether they are individuals or belong to some kind of collectivity. Pronoun use makes it possible for spouses to reference complex relationships between individual *I*s and collective *we*s and for the speaker to position him- or herself in this relational web. The *we* can, for instance, function as an agent, as well as having mental states and attitudes. This kind of positioning is not just about preferring one pronoun over another, but also about committing oneself to another person emotionally and practically, and about a different or enlarged "representation" or sense of self. The individual self has expanded to include the other, and the borders between the two selves become porous.

In joint storytelling, spouses can also position themselves epistemically and act toward the other as if she or he has *knowledge* about certain stories, events, persons, experiences, or values and preferences. This knowledge can be based on the spouses' shared experiences, on what the one spouse told the other, or on inferences about the other spouse. Spouses develop and maintain a *common ground* that consists of their shared experiences and knowledge about themselves as individual persons and about themselves as a pair.[31] When the spouses either do something together or when they tell stories about their individual experiences, they add to their common ground, but they also add their various versions and narrations of stories about their experiences and themselves. These stories—from the first versions to all the retellings and revisions—are probably the most important part of the common ground, and start to be built and grow from the very moment the spouses meet. The stories then form an important part of the common ground of the family.[32]

As spouses share experiences and knowledge, each spouse can safely assume that the other spouse can infer or identify some event, "fact," or previously told story. This means that each spouse, for instance in storytelling situations, can assume that the other spouse knows certain things that do not have to be explained or made explicit. They can be referred to with the help of a hint, as well as when to tell a certain story, to whom, and in what situations. This implies that when one spouse refers to something he or she assumes belongs to their common ground, the other spouse either (tacitly or explicitly) acknowledges the correctness of the assumption—or contests it. Confirming and accepting may strengthen the interdependent relationship, while failing to gain acceptance and confirmation may contribute to a fragmentation of common ground, difficulties in telling joint stories, and hence eventually also an erosion of the relationship.

To summarize, it has been argued that (1) identity can be shared and can be interdependent as part of an interdependent relationship, and (2) interdependent identities have to be interactively negotiated and acknowledged. Consequently, (3) autobiographical stories and storytelling can be seen less as individual expression and more as being shared, and thus as something the spouses can use in their identity work. Finally, (4) the interdependent relationships can vary in terms of dependence, mutuality, and interest, and always entail some kind of recognition.

INTERDEPENDENCE AND DEMENTIA

Of course, spouses in all relationships from time to time face troubles in keeping up their common ground and in positioning themselves as a couple, due to changing social and economic circumstances, aging, and so on. The problems facing couples with dementia have to do with the fact that the person with dementia gradually loses cognitive and linguistic resources, presenting increasing challenges in everyday interaction. As a result, the levels of dependence between the spouses will change and will make the spouse with dementia more dependent on the healthy spouse, while the healthy spouse will increasingly become less dependent on the spouse with dementia as their degree of covariation of interest changes. In everyday interactions, these changes are manifested in the fact that the spouses' common ground starts to fragment as the person with dementia has increasing problems not only in understanding what the healthy spouse refers to, but also in remembering shared events in the past and shared knowledge that is important in storytelling (names of children, date of marriage, etc.). These problems are recurrent and don't go away, but will instead gradually increase as times goes by.

This gradual loss of common ground challenges the interdependent identity as the spouses' shared experiences, knowledge, and previously told versions of stories have become much more difficult to use as a common resource when the spouses tell stories about themselves. The relationship between the spouses will become increasingly asymmetric, as the healthy spouse must take responsibility for their shared identity and life. This change in dependence is affected when the healthy spouse *scaffolds* the storytelling activities in order for the person with dementia to continue as an active participant. Eventually, the healthy spouse must increasingly hold the spouse with dementia in person, as has been suggested by Hilde Lindemann,[33] as the person with dementia loses both cognitive and linguistic resources. This also implies that the healthy spouse eventually must function as a *vicarious voice* when the abilities of the person with dementia to take part in shared identity work are challenged even more as the disease progresses. From the perspective of interdependence, it is also important to point out that the healthy spouse must not only hold the person with dementia in person, but also hold their shared and interdependent identity.

DISCURSIVE POSITIONING

All the spouses in the interviews positioned themselves as part of a *we*, rather than two individual *I*s. The *we* the spouses presented was a relational unit beyond or above the individual *Is*; the individual *Is* were instead considered to be a part of this *we*. This often also implied that the borders between the individuals could be fuzzy in the stories told; instead, it was their unity that was stressed.[34]

In Example 7.1, Martin and Kathy start to tell a story about when and how they met the first time. Both are about 80 years old at the time of the interview, and Kathy has a diagnosis of Alzheimer's dementia. She is fairly fluent linguistically, although she usually has severe problems remembering, especially recent events. She deals with this by telling stories about how it used to be—although without indicating that she is retelling old stories.

Example 7.1.

1	Kathy:	[well] it was probably the first time I met [Martin]
2		[(K's gaze directed at M)] [(K's gaze shifts to the interviewers)]
3		I think it was at my parents' home (0.3)
4		(0.4).hh (0.4) then [he just popped up]. (1.2)
5		[(pats M's hand)]
6		[e and I fell] (1.2) [for his ch<u>a</u>rm]
7		[(looks at M and takes his hand)] [(gazes toward the interviewers)]
8	Martin:	°heh heh°
9		(0.4)
10	Kathy:	he was [so kind and cute]
11	Martin:	[(sniffs) m:] (K lets go of M's hand)
12		(1.5)
13	Kathy:	.hh (0.4) and we've been a couple since then (0.3)
14		(gaze directed at M)
15		ee we have (.) children (0.3) (gaze at the interviewers)
16		who also have (0.2) their own children (1.7)
17		and (0.8).hh yes: (1.2)
18		[I like my Martin]
19		[(takes M's hand in hers)]
20		(1.2)
21	Martin:	.hh THERE [YOU HEAR heh][well] (I was lucky) =
22	I$_1$:	[heh yes:]
23	Kathy:	[he's so sweet]
24	Martin:	=(.) °(m)° (.) love is still blooming [*for us *] (.) =

In Example 7.1, the couple has just received the questions from the interviewer of whether they could tell about the first time they met. After a brief discussion about who should start to tell the story, Kathy begins to tell about the first time she and Martin met. Although it is mainly Kathy who speaks, Martin at several points supports what she says, and he does not object or challenge the story she tells. Rather, it appears that the story is their joint story and he even loudly supports her story (lines 21–24). On lines 1–12, Kathy tells about their first encounter. She constructs this part of the story by using a first-person perspective and sums it up by saying that she and Martin have been a couple since then (line 13). She then shifts from a first-person perspective to telling about them as a couple, and hence starts to use the pronoun *we* ("we have children"; line 15). At the end of the example, Martin comments on the story first by saying that he was lucky, and shifts from the first-person perspective to say that "love is still blooming for us" (lines 21, 24). The transcript also includes some of the nonverbal communication from which it is easy to see that both of them use both gaze and touch as ways to express and display their mutual commitment and affection.

In the example, the couple tells about how they became a couple by shifting between *I* and *we* positions and by positioning themselves as being very close and emotionally committed to each other through their gestures (touch), but also through the direction of their gazes. In this situation they are apparently very close and joined together by the *we*. Whether they have told this story before or not we do not know, although it seems likely they have, at least at some point in their marriage. One problem when one spouse develops dementia is that this common ground is challenged, because the person with dementia will have problems either understanding the meaning of references to common ground, or identifying a reference to some past event or circumstance.

EPISTEMIC IDENTITY CHALLENGES

In the study, one of the recurrent problems the spouses have when they tell their stories is that the spouse with dementia cannot find or identify a name, a date, or sometimes a place. In relationships, names and dates can be very important, and can be part of the fundamental common ground that defines the *we*-relationship. That is the case, for instance, with names of children, the date of their first meeting, and the date of the marriage. Both spouses generally expect the other to remember these dates and names because they are important in defining and commemorating the couple as a relational unit. Thus the spouses have mutual expectations, and it is probably always a bit embarrassing for both spouses if one of them fails to recall a salient date, name, or other fact. Problems with remembering a name or a date are of course something that can be found in all couples, but in couples with dementia it becomes part of everyday life due to the frequency with which it occurs. Generally, it is not possible to improve the ability to remember; instead, the opposite is the normal course, which results in increasing challenges to the couple's common ground.

The following examples are taken from the first interview with a couple that has been married for over 40 years; at the time of the interview they are both in their early seventies. The woman, Ann, received a diagnosis of Alzheimer's disease seven years previously, while her husband (Carl) still is healthy. Ann has problems with finding words, especially more abstract nouns, but also with constructing utterances that include abstractions (although this is not something that hinders her from joking with linguistic expressions). She also has increasing difficulties with identifying events in the past, as well as with dates and names.

Early on in the interview, the couple is asked if they could tell something about when they met for the first time (see Chapter 4). Ann and Carl, like all other interviewees, willingly accept the opportunity and start to tell stories about themselves, not as two individuals, but as a couple. In doing this, Ann and Carl, also like all other interviewees, frequently refer to themselves by using the pronoun *we*. This also implies that they are careful to uphold this *we* by demonstrating their common ground, that is, their shared knowledge of salient names and dates and other aspects of everyday life that they share. In other words, they demonstrate their shared epistemic status.

In telling about this, Ann and Carl also present their family, and one interviewer asks if they have any grandchildren (Example 7.2, line 1). Both of them quickly confirm that they have a grandchild (lines 2, 4, 7, 8). Then Carl turns to Ann and asks her whether she remembers his name (line 9). This question results in quite a long pause and then Ann says a name (line 11) and Carl confirms it is correct (line 12).

Example 7.2.

1	I_1:	do you have grandchildren as well
2	Carl:	a :: [a: ra a: ra]
3	I_1:	[(maybe)]
4	Ann:	[a :: small]
5	I_1:	hm
6	Ann:	[(laugh)]
7	Carl:	[a: one that] soon will be three years
8	Ann:	.hh yes
9	Carl:	m: what's his name then
10		(3.0)

11	Ann:	Julius
12	Carl:	yes :: correct
13	I_1:	m:
14	Carl:	m:
15		(3.0)

It is a bit unclear from the context why Carl asks Ann if she remembers the name of her grandchild. One possible interpretation is that he wants to demonstrate in the interview situation that Ann has what he later calls "memory problems." Another possibility is that he is testing her by asking questions to which she is supposed to know the answers. The rather long pause before Ann answers the question (line 10) at least partly confirms that she has problems finding the name of her grandchild, as she appears to need to "search" for his name. This indicates that she has problems with remembering or identifying knowledge belonging to their common ground, and also that her memory problems are not unknown to them. Instead, Carl's question to Ann can be seen as a preventive way of dealing with the issue; by reframing the situation, he gives Ann a specific task (the name) and then evaluates her answer (a well-known question-answer evaluation sequence). This is a fairly common way for spouses to deal with potential problems—by *scaffolding* the activity. It is something that starts from a concept of the spouses' common interest and reorganizes interaction in such a way that this common interest can be upheld. It is, in other words, a way to protect the *we*-ness of the spouses.

This example illustrates that the spouses continue to use the kind of procedures for common ground that they are familiar with. What happens, though, is that the use of these procedures comes at a cost; joint meaning-making becomes more complicated, labor-intensive, and time-consuming. It also redefines the spouses' interdependent relationship. By engaging in a scaffolding strategy, Carl has to take on much more responsibility for the organization of the storytelling; he has to be proactive and suggest question formats that are possible for Ann to deal with. He has to support her and help her along. This implies that although they are both dependent on each other in order to present themselves as a couple, Ann is becoming more dependent on Carl than he is on her.

DIVERGING INTERESTS

Sometimes spouses do not engage in scaffolding or are unable to pursue the scaffolding process for various reasons. Scaffolding is a process that is filled with potential complications and risks for the healthy spouse as well as the spouse with dementia. The healthy spouse may, for instance, find it difficult to pursue his or her own contributions to the joint activity, being preoccupied with attempts to reach a shared meaning of something already said or done. Both the healthy spouse and the person with dementia may find it too demanding in terms of time and energy to pursue the scaffolding and instead may let it be, thus abandoning the joint activity. The spouses may also have developed different interests, thus finding it difficult to pursue joint activities. This can happen when the healthy spouse finds it very important to be clear on the fact that the diseased person in fact has received a dementia diagnosis. This is something that can be important because it would help the healthy spouse to adapt to a new life situation. The person with dementia, on the other hand, might prefer to play down the diagnosis in order to be able to stress the connection to his or her previous identity and social standing. Thus, in situations involving talk about diagnosis, the two spouses would have different interests that are not always possible to reconcile. Consequently, the interdependent aspects of the spouses' identity are jeopardized and put into question.

Example 7.3 illustrates such a situation, where Beryl and Shaun are given the task by the interviewers to tell jointly about how Shaun received his diagnosis; basically, they are not especially successful in doing so. They are both around 65 years of age and have been married for some 30 years. Shaun was diagnosed with Alzheimer's disease about three years before the interview. He has very few linguistic problems, but he has severe cognitive problems, especially with memory and executive functions. In the joint interview the spouses were questioned about how they started to notice that something was not right with Shaun. Beryl started to tell quite a long story about Shaun losing his way when driving and how they later got in contact with doctors at the local memory clinic. One of the doctors visited them at home and conducted tests and later came back to talk to them about the diagnosis. During Beryl's telling, Shaun started to challenge her description of the past events, saying she got it wrong.

Example 7.3.

1	Beryl:	so they (doctors) decided it was Alzheimer's
2		(3s)
3		and (.) it took a while before he (husband) could say it
4	Shaun:	well I haven't got any diagnosis myself
5	Beryl:	you were there
6	Shaun:	no but I never got the diagnosis
7	Beryl:	(laugh) you were sitting

8		(. . .)
9	Shaun:	well it often goes through my wife
10	Beryl:	but (.) please (.) we were sitting on our chairs in that room (points) (.) when he came back (the doctor) (.) and told this (.) and that's the way it is he said
11	Shaun:	well we don't have any (.) either auditory or written (testimony) (.) it is just rumors (.) or what should we call it (.) tales between us
12	Beryl:	NO/we've got in writing
13	Shaun:	yes yeah but
14	Beryl:	yeah
15	Shaun:	we cannot start to discuss things that might have been said

In this example, the discussion between Beryl and Shaun became quite heated and revolved around memory, remembering what happened and being able to argue for this, and what counts as proof of a correct memory. On line 4, Shaun objects to Beryl's statement that the doctor had informed both of them about the diagnosis, to which Beryl not only retorts that Shaun was present, but also indicates that he was sitting on a specific chair (lines 7, 10). In response to this, Shaun questions whether they have any proof at all, or if it just is something they made up; that is, he takes up a quite radical epistemic position. In the interview this altercation continues and escalates until Shaun actually leaves the interview situation and walks away to his own study, inviting the interviewers to join him (outside the example).

In the example, neither Shaun nor Beryl engages in negotiation about what happened when Shaun received his diagnosis (or even if he received it). Their avoidance negotiations might have to do with the fact that Beryl, in telling about Shaun's diagnosis, turned directly to the interviewers and spoke about Shaun in the third person (line 3) without involving Shaun in the story at that point. So Shaun's protest might be directed against Beryl ascribing him a dementia diagnosis; he also points out (line 9) that he thinks that his wife decides some things without involving him. A consequence of this altercation is that both spouses actively deny and question any common ground having to do with Shaun's diagnosis; there are no negotiations or attempts to create a joint story around what happened. In lines 11, 12, and 15, both of them use the pronoun *we* in arguing about what they actually know. The problem is that they are not able to find and define the ground for this *we*. Consequently, they basically define themselves as two individuals fighting over their common ground, having nothing to hold them together—no *we*. Symbolically, as if to bodily demonstrate this split, Shaun leaves the interview situation and walks away to his own study.

MINIMAL COMMON GROUND

The development of different interests might be one reason that scaffolding and joint storytelling become more difficult in presenting and negotiating shared identity. The continued and increasing erosion of common ground is another reason. As the person with dementia faces severe problems remembering things, the role of the healthy spouse changes from facilitating and supporting participation in joint storytelling to gradually taking over the authorship of the stories, and thus to functioning as a vicarious voice. This is something that started to happen quite frequently in the second and third rounds of interviews with the couples. In Example 7.2, Ann tried to remember the name of her grandchild with support from Carl. One year later, in the second interview, the same kind of problem has become even more pronounced. In Example 7.4, the interviewer asks Ann about what she does during an ordinary day at the day center where spends her weekdays.

Example 7.4.

1	I_1:	what do you do
2	Ann:	(arms crossed, head slightly bowed) (3s)
3		well what I do (arms along both sides)
4		I'm fully occupied the whole day
5		it has to be with things like
6		has connection to what we do (moves left hand in a circular movement)
7	I_1:	mm
8	Ann:	cleaning and
9		well you understand that
10		don't need to explain uh
11	I_1/I_2:	no no mmm
12	Carl:	you don't actually clean do you
13	Ann:	no we don't clean but
14		we want it to be good (moves left hand back and forth horizontally)
15		we can move things if they are in another place (continues left hand horizontal movement)

16		if we think
17		no (also moves right hand horizontally) let's take that instead (puts both hands in her lap)
18		yes
19		that's what we basically do
20	Carl:	no but you have a program (Ann looks at Carl)
21		for the week
22	Ann:	Yes we have
23	Carl:	for the week so you do different things every day
24	Ann:	yes hm yes
25	Carl:	sometimes you sing and you dance and so
26	Ann:	yes that's true
27	Carl:	and you cook some food

Ann starts to tell about her day but has problems finding the right words that would allow her to express in more general terms what they do (lines 2–10). As she has problems finding the words she wants, she makes a lot of gestures supporting her verbal telling (line 6). Then Carl objects to her idea about cleaning (line 12), something that Ann concurs with and uses to continue her narration, again making use of gestures to support her story. Carl points out that they have a program for the week's activities (line 20) and he then takes over some of the telling by detailing the program (lines 23, 25, 27). Carl not only challenges Ann's telling about what she does at the day center, but also takes over the telling of the story by actually adding new elements—something that Ann accepts.

In a sense, Carl takes over Ann's voice by adding story elements that she cannot find or put into a story that Carl and Ann both would recognize as their shared story, hence representing aspects of their shared everyday life. The story elements that Carl adds do not represent his point of view in contrast to Ann's; rather, the elements he adds represent Ann's perspective and experiences, and are part of their common ground, something they both know. Carl is thus scaffolding the storytelling less, but his voice has instead turned into a vicarious voice, filling in those parts of the story that Ann cannot remember and tell on her own.

HOLDING IN IDENTITY

It has been argued that for spouses living together, one important aspect of their identity is their *shared identity*. This means that they position themselves as a *we*, and use shared knowledge, experiences, and stories as resources for presenting and negotiating their identities. This shared identity is *interdependent* in that it is based on their common ground; it presupposes *mutuality*, shared *interests*, and the mutual *recognition* of both spouses. A disease like dementia becomes very problematic for spouses due to the fact that persons with dementia gradually face increasing problems with remembering and using the couple's common ground.

From a theoretical perspective, interdependent identity indicates a shift away from the conventional stress on individual identity and life stories. The point is not that individual identities are nonexistent, but for people living together or for persons with strong commitments to other social units (political, cultural), their identities should be seen as part of, and existing in an interdependent relationship with, one of several *others*. Thus the traditional emphasis on individual memories and stories can also be questioned in favor of shared memories and stories. It also allows for a shift of focus in the field of dementia studies from the loss of stories and memories, to looking at the possibilities for memories and stories being distributed over several individuals, thus making it possible for others to be the keepers and supporters of memories and stories.

From a narrative point of view, the concept of interdependent identities underlines at least two important aspects of autobiographical stories. First, many autobiographical stories are shared in the sense that they belong to both spouses. Both spouses can tell these stories, and the stories reflect their shared (we-) experience rather than their individual experiences. The "shared" concept in this connection is not only about an epistemic relation, that is, both spouses know about and are familiar with the story and the depicted events. It also means that they both recognize each other's importance for the story and the experiences. Second, the concept of interdependent identities also stresses the fact that many of the individual spouse's autobiographical stories are entangled with and in the other spouse's individual stories. In other words, many autobiographical stories have connections with other individual autobiographical stories, some of these connections being established through the repeated conjunct telling of the stories as well as through the connection of experiences. Thus when one person has problems with telling and recognizing autobiographical stories, this will affect the healthy spouse's telling of stories, as some of the worth and meaning are lost when the other spouse cannot recognize them.

Living with a changing brain adds a specific task in the revision and reconstruction of a sense of self. In attempting to compensate for the changes brought about by the disease, the person with dementia has fewer options available. As the number of available resources decline, the person with dementia becomes increasingly dependent on others to keep the self and identity. The philosopher Hilde Lindeman writes that others must *hold* the person with dementia in his or her identity.[35] This implies that others in various ways must support the person with dementia by, for instance, facilitating participation in conversations and storytelling. It also indicates that stable and secure emotional relationships are important in order for the person with dementia and relatives to be able to explore and redefine relations and thus identities.

NOTES

1. Hellström, Nolan, & Lundh, 2005; Molyneaux, Butchard, Simpson, & Murray, 2012; Phinney, 2006; Purves, 2011; Roach, Keady, & Bee, 2014; Robinson, Clare, & Evans, 2005.
2. Kellas, 2005.
3. Charmaz, 1983. Also see her book *Good Days, Bad Days: The Self in Chronic Illness and Time* (1991).
4. Cadell & Clare, 2010.
5. See, for instance, the work of Rom Harré or the work collected in the volume *Oxford Handbook of the Self*, edited by Shaun Gallagher (2011).
6. Schafer, 1976, p. 189.
7. Schafer, 1976, pp. 189–190.
8. See in particular Goffman, 1959 and 1967.
9. Schafer, 1992, p. 26.
10. The distinction between "me" and "not me" illnesses goes back to Eric Cassell's classic article "Disease as an 'It': Concepts of Disease Revealed by Patients' Presentation of Symptoms" (Cassell, 1976). Also see Clare, Goater, & Woods's investigation about representations of dementia among persons with early stage dementia (Clare et al., 2006).
11. Nochi, 1998.
12. See, for instance, Cheston & Bender, 1999; Clare, 2002, 2003; Hellström, 2014; Hellström, Nolan, & Lundh, 2005; Öhman, Josephsson, & Nygård, 2008; Phinney, 2002; Seeley & Miller, 2005.
13. For overviews, see Charmaz, 1983, 1999 and Conrad, 1987.
14. Bury, 1982, p. 169.
15. The concept of disruption and narrative reconstruction was introduced by sociologists Michael Bury and Gareth Williams in 1982 and 1984.
16. Williams, 1984, p. 177.
17. Freeman, 1993; Randall & McKim, 2008.
18. Freeman, 2010.
19. See Gottman, 2011; Rusbult & Van Lange, 2003.
20. Agnew, Van Lange, Rusbult, & Langston, 1998.
21. Rusbult & Van Lange, 1998.
22. Thibaut & Kelley, 1959, p. 124.
23. Rusbult & Van Lange, 2003.
24. Gottman, 2011.
25. Davies, 2011, p. 219.

26. Adams & Jones, 1997.
27. Agnew et al., 1998, p. 939.
28. Aron et al., 1991.
29. Fivush, 2007; Kellas, 2005; Langellier & Peterson, 2004; Tracy & Robles, 2013.
30. Stivers, Enfield & Levinson, 2007; Tracy & Robles, 2013.
31. The concept of common ground as used here is from Herbert Clark, 1996.
32. Berger & Kellner, 1964; Bohanek, Fivush, Zaman, Lepore, Merchant & Duke, 2009; Fivush, 2007; Harris, Keil, Sutton, Barnier & McIlwain, 2011; Kellas, 2005.
33. Lindemann, 2009.
34. Hydén & Nilsson, 2015.
35. Lindemann, 2001, 2009.

CHAPTER 8

Listening with a Third Ear

Dementia has always been and probably always will be a frightening experience. But it can also be so much more. [. . .] I've seen people with dementia as well as those who care for them move through their fears and come to feel fierce pride and overwhelmingly joy, to show compassion and selflessness, and to express bawdy humor and dry wit. I hold out hope that sharing stories of people who succeed in moving through fear and learn to live with stigma, who find meaning in the experience of dementia, might help inspire more people to do the same—to see dementia as more than a death sentence.[1]

These words come from Anne Davis Basting's book *Forget Memory*. She points out something that often is lost in discussions about dementia: dementia is a frightening experience. Alzheimer's disease and other neurodegenerative diseases are fatal, and as they progress they change the persons afflicted with the disease. In this aspect, a dementia diagnosis is similar to many other diagnoses of chronic, degenerative diseases. At the same time, as Basting argues, not only is it necessary to learn to live with dementia, but a life with dementia can be a rewarding life. To her it is important to tell more complicated stories about dementia. Emotional pain and memory "loss" are part of dementia, but so is the ability to learn, and the fact that one's self persists and "social memory remains when individual memory falters."[2] The idea of *social memory* goes back to the French sociologist Maurice Halbwachs, who argued that "if we examine a little more closely how we recollect things, we will surely realize that the greatest number of memories come back to us when our parents, our friends, or other persons recall them to us."[3]

According to this view, memories and stories are less something "stored" inside the individual mind, and more something that is shared among people. Most autobiographical memories are shared memories that involve other people, and in "remembering" and "recollecting" these memories it is the joint efforts of all these people that produce memories.

This also has been the basic argument of this book—with the added idea that it is in the telling of autobiographical stories that "memories" are produced. When one person has access to fewer cognitive and linguistic resources due to dementia, the social organization of the storytelling changes as a consequence.

In this final chapter the consequences of changes in storytelling will be discussed, especially in relation to identity and self, but also in relation to how to understand stories told by persons with dementia, and finally, what limits exist for stories.

ANSWERING JEROME BRUNER

This book started with Jerome Bruner's challenge: if there are no memories, there are no stories, and hence, no self or identity.

> [It] is through narrative that we create and re-create selfhood, that self is a product of our telling and not some essence to be delved for in the recesses of subjectivity. There is now evidence that if we lacked the capacity to make stories about ourselves, there would be no such thing as selfhood.[4]

The arguments in this book began with what is taken for granted in the preceding quotation: what counts as a story. In this book it has been stated that many of the autobiographical stories told by persons with dementia challenge those narrative norms that dictate that autobiographical stories must be coherent and true. This preconception is also connected to the ideal that autobiographical stories should have one teller, who is also the author (and owner) of the story. These normative expectations tend to exclude many of the autobiographical narratives told by persons with dementia. Their stories are often fragmented and repetitive, and thus do not live up to conventional narrative norms and expectations. On the other hand, persons with dementia often tell autobiographical stories much better if they are supported by someone like a spouse, family member, or someone else who is familiar with the person. This implies both a change in narrative expectations as well as in narrative norms. Keeping to the traditional and taken-for-granted narrative norms risks excluding stories without a closer look at them, and thus losing the possibility of discovering something important in and about these stories.

Given more open and perhaps relaxed narrative norms, a central argument in this book has been that persons with dementia in the early and mid-stages are able to tell and use autobiographical stories in order to present and negotiate their identities and selves. Dementia might affect what stories are told—that is, the content of the stories. In line with this argument, persons with dementia can be expected to tell stories about their disease and its effect on their lives; that is, they could be expected to tell illness stories. Of course this can be the case, but what is typical for stories told by persons with dementia is the fact that the storyteller as storyteller is affected by the disease. Some persons can tell autobiographical stories on their own, while others can do it with support, especially from their spouses. Some persons with dementia tell autobiographical stories that leave the listener with a sense of confusion; others repeat the same story over and over again, or never find the words and abandon the story; sometimes gestures become more prominent than words.

Thus the central argument is that persons with dementia are challenged in their storytelling. The challenges that face the person with dementia, as well as the other participants in the storytelling situation, are connected to the fact that the dementia results in fewer available cognitive and linguistic resources for the person with dementia. The neurodegenerative disease slowly destroys the functional systems and networks in the brain that are used in storytelling. Early on, various temporal lobe areas are affected; as the disease progresses, the associative areas that integrate specialized brain areas become affected. The functional systems in the brain are not lost until very late in the disease, but their functionality is compromised. As a consequence, the linguistic and cognitive resources that could be used before the onset of the disease become less available. There is a decrease of available resources as compared to the situation before the diagnosis. As a result of the degenerative processes, the agency of the person with dementia could be characterized as being *bounded*. The concept of *bounded* refers to the fact that compared to the situation before diagnosis, the person with dementia faces increasing constraints in terms of available resources and hence possible contributions and interpretation of others' contributions to the storytelling. This means that the agency of the person with dementia will be bounded in joint activities compared to other participants, and compared to what the person could do before the onset of dementia.

This bounded agency is connected to various attempts to deal with this, and the person with dementia often develops compensatory adaptions both individually and in collaboration with others in order to be able to continue to pursue activities like storytelling. In collaborative situations there is a need to adapt interactionally (in terms of making contributions, what kind of contributions they are, and the content of the contributions) for all participants to the new situation.

In this book it has been suggested that autobiographical storytelling should be seen as a joint activity involving at least two embodied persons situated in a specific social situation, with a relationship that is both defined and revised through the activity. As such, storytelling is part of an activity system, and storytellers make use of the pragmatic aspects of the storytelling situation in order to *tell* a story. In telling stories, both storyteller and listener use a number of functional networks as resources; these include various kinds of memory systems, semiotic systems, and the interactional organization. That is, telling stories is not an activity in which the participants make use of itemized, isolated, abstract knowledge units (lexical meaning, for instance), which then are combined into larger units and finally into stories, following certain processing rules. Instead, everyday, practical experience and knowledge are used and organized functionally.

Telling autobiographical stories, as well as listening to those stories, is not about mapping some kind of abstract amodal knowledge onto linguistic and discursive structures. It is much more about transforming various kinds of experiences—motor experiences, as well as images and linguistic experiences—through the use of shared semiotic resources into a story that is performed and perceived multimodally by the participants. Storytelling is thus an activity that engages many aspects of the body. Hence, telling and listening to an autobiographical story are not about adding together different bodily channels (talk plus gestures plus eye movements, etc.). Rather, it is about *distributing* experiences through many different bodily systems and semiotic resources.

It also has been argued that persons with dementia are challenged by connecting singular and specific events into larger coherent discursive units, making these events part of a temporally evolving series of events. Even in persons with dementia who still can use linguistic resources, it was found that longer autobiographical stories tend to be parsed into small units centered on specific events. The storyteller then has severe problems ordering these events temporally and connecting them in terms of a temporal progression. As a result, the story from a listener's perspective becomes jumbled, and most events are told repeatedly. Further, it also has been argued that persons with dementia actually have autobiographical memories, although they have problems using linguistic means for communicating these memories. That is, autobiographical memories of autobiographical events or event fragments seem to exist in an embodied state, and as the person's ability to use linguistic means is challenged, he or she reverts to the use of other semiotic resources and use of the body to physically enact and perform memories of past events and activities.

IDENTITY AND SELF

Persons with dementia thus do not lose their ability to tell autobiographical stories—although they tell stories that do not live up to the taken-for-granted narrative norms, either in terms of the discursive organization of the story or in terms of the idea that author, animator, and principal in autobiographical stories must be identical. This is an argument against a loss of identity and self, as Jerome Bruner has argued. But it is also an argument against the idea that both identity and self remain more or less unaffected in persons with dementia, which can be attributed to Steven Sabat and Rom Harré in their articles about the self in dementia.[5] The storytelling abilities are affected by dementia, so the autobiographical stories change as a result. Telling stories in new ways can be expected to result in new ways of experiencing self and others, in particular the relationship between self, other, and the world.

As far as can be understood from everyday clinical and research practice, persons with dementia do not lose their subjectivity, that is, the ability to experience the world from a first-person perspective. But it is evident that dementia involves different, constantly evolving and changing, and for the individual, new ways of experiencing the world. These new ways of being in the world are the result of fewer cognitive and linguistic resources being available to the individual. As a result, subjectivity and self are reorganized in order to adapt to less usable resources and to everyday life situations that become more and more restricted. In terms of the relationship between autobiographical stories and identity and self, there are three issues that can be put forward as contributing to a change in identity and self.

First, as *the agency* of the person with dementia changes and becomes more bounded, the person becomes more dependent on others in the actual telling of autobiographical stories. In social psychological terms, this could be conceptualized as a change in the position of the person with dementia in the joint activity of storytelling. Most persons with dementia often go from having had what can be called a central position in joint activities to occupying a peripheral position. That is, the person with dementia before the onset of the dementia in most cases shared equal interactional responsibility with other participants in joint activities; the storytelling participants both initiated roughly the same number of new topics and probably shared discursive space equally. As a consequence of dementia, there is a shift in interactional responsibility, and the person with dementia will have a more peripheral position in terms of actions like taking initiatives and introducing new topics in storytelling.

Second, the changing brain implies a restructuring of the cognitive and semiotic *resources* used to tell autobiographical stories and to express and communicate identity. There is a shift between verbal and other semiotic resources, especially bodily enactments. This implies that the discursive organization of autobiographical stories will be affected, often including nonverbal substitutions, repetitions, and becoming more fragmented. As "memories," both of events and previously told versions of stories, become less reliable and often difficult to identity, there will be a change in the common ground between the person with dementia and significant others. What were previously shared experiences and knowledge become over time more unilateral.

Third, there is a shift in the *narrative voice*. In autobiographical storytelling, the teller is generally believed to be the one who "owns" the experiences and is responsible for the story. Although this identity is questionable, as especially Elinor Ochs and Lisa Capps have pointed out,[6] dementia still implies that the person with dementia over time will be less able to both animate and author stories. As the dementia progresses and the person with dementia can only make minimal communicative contributions, the person with dementia will also be less considered to be the principal of the story. Thus it will be others who tell those autobiographical stories that the person with dementia used to tell; they will tell stories *about* the person with dementia, rather than together *with* the person with dementia. Ultimately, the person with dementia will thus be the subject or protagonist of the story, but not the animator, author, or principal.

The shifts in agency, resource use, and voice all contribute to changes in identity and sense of self. As the *power* of the person with dementia to present different versions of events, as well as self, diminishes over time, this of course results in a less faceted identity. There will be a tendency for certain aspects of identity to dominate over others, as these aspects are more readily available (as was argued with a number of examples in Chapter 6). The person will also have less power to *negotiate* identity and self, and thus will become more dependent on those stories that are available, or those that are told by others. The *unique voice* of the person with dementia also becomes less pronounced. Autobiographical stories often imply a specific unique animation, that is, a special physical voice and way of telling. As this unique voice falters, something of what is typical of the teller will be lost in the telling of autobiographical stories.

Especially the bounded agency and reorganization of the cognitive resources imply a change in the relationship between the person with dementia and significant others. In particular, aspects of interdependent identities will be lost as the person with dementia faces troubles identifying events and stories. The healthy spouse—or other family member—will be the one who must unilaterally keep and sustain the shared experiences and memories.

Thus, the premorbid identity and self change through the dementia, not once, but constantly, as the modes of being in the world change, from being a person like most others, to a person that has a different kind of agency, but also experiences the world differently in terms of perception of time, space, sounds, colors, and so on, and who is increasingly challenged in communicating stories.

CONSEQUENCES

This approach to storytelling has certain consequences for understanding storytelling in dementia; it becomes possible to understand why persons with dementia are generally quite good at telling (or at least trying to tell) about specific events or episodes. That is, they can tell about something specific happening, with a beginning and an end—in contrast to longer and more elaborated discursive structures encompassing many different events. At the same time, storytellers with dementia often have some problems with adding further information about these events, that is, in rendering detailed descriptions. They also generally have severe problems nesting specific events together into larger, more complex, and conventionally coherent stories. It also becomes understandable why persons with dementia may have problems with finding words or more complex linguistic and discursive structures, while at the same time they seem to retain the ability to envision, remember, and communicate an event using other semiotic resources than spoken language.

Approaching storytelling as an embodied activity makes it possible to understand some of the ways in which disease and storytelling may be connected. Often storytelling and stories involving illness are portrayed to be about illness and the experience of illness. An embodied approach to storytelling suggests, rather, that changes in the body and especially the brain have effects on the ability to both tell and perceive stories. They may make way for other semiotic resources than spoken language, and may put a stronger emphasis on the performance of storytelling, rather than on the text.

Two more specific consequences of the changes in storytelling will be discussed: how to understand and listen to stories told by persons with dementia, and what the limits of storytelling are.

THE "BRICOLEUR" AND THE "THIRD EAR"

One conclusion from the research and arguments presented in this book is that persons with dementia tend be creative storytellers, finding new semiotic resources in order to continue as participants in storytelling activities and thus sustain both their personhood and their sense of self and identity. One way to conceptualize persons with dementia as storytellers is to say that they are "bricoleurs":

> In its old sense the verb "bricoler" applied to ball games and billiards, to hunting, shooting, and riding. It was, however, always used with reference to some extraneous movement: a ball rebounding, a dog straying, or a horse swerving from its direct course to avoid an obstacle. And in our own time the "bricoleur" is still someone who works with his hands and uses devious means compared to those of a craftsman. The characteristic feature of mythical thought is that it expresses itself by means of a heterogeneous repertoire which, even if extensive, is nevertheless limited. It has to use this repertoire, however, whatever the task in hand because it has nothing else at its disposal.[7]

This quotation is from the French anthropologist Claude Levi-Strauss, when he discusses the differences between the Western conception of scientific reasoning and what he calls "mythical" thinking. Western scientific thought is characterized by rationality based on abstract logical principles, and "mythical" thought is based on "what is at hand," solving tasks and problems pragmatically. Similarly, the telling and understanding of storytelling is often based on the notion that the "construction" and telling of stories is a cognitive linear process. Thus there is little room for the creative use of language, from the use of previous stories as a template for new stories, to metaphors and similes, as well as gestures and bodily enactment. Both body and language are, in this sense, resources and tools "at hand," and the storyteller is a "bricoleur" who makes use of the available resources. Leaving the actual, physical body, as well as creative use of language, out of the analysis and understanding of stories thus becomes especially problematic in research with persons with dementia (or other kinds of acquired brain injuries).

Understanding a "bricoleur" telling stories, of course, puts special demands on the other participants, especially as both tellers and listeners are guided by narrative norms in telling and listening to stories. Literary scholar Suzanne Fleischman once wrote that narrative norms are "a set of shared conventions and assumptions about what constitutes a well-formed story" that are internalized by speakers.[8] Although Suzanne Fleischman as a literary historian primarily wrote about written texts, the same is true for conversational storytelling because this is also a social (and cultural) practice based on the telling of a story in such a way that others can take part in this event and understand what is going on, as well as understand the story. And like all social practices, conversational storytelling is guided by often implicit and embodied norms that help the participants by guiding them in how to produce a story so that it will be recognized as a certain kind of story, how to organize the performance, as well as enhancing listening and understanding the story, and how to evaluate both the storytelling event and the story. Thus all participants have certain expectations about the organization of the story, and of how the story should be told. These norms are learned by the participants from an early age and will result in most people not only becoming very versatile storytellers, but also becoming able to appreciate a wide variety of stories, told by different people, in different contexts.[9]

The normative expectations help the listener to build an interpretation of the emerging story, of how to understand events up to the present point of the story. This process—as narratologist Wolfgang Iser once pointed out—is a hypothesis-testing process in which the listener tests, revises, and checks interpretations of the story.[10] In conversational storytelling, the listening participants constantly check their understanding of the story so far against the teller by nodding or assessing the story to that point, thus giving the teller a feedback in order to construct a shared understanding of the story. The norms help the teller to tell the story in such a way that it can be expected that the listener will understand what is said and thus understand the emerging story. A special category of listeners consists of researchers and other hearers of stories, for instance clinicians. They are all guided by the same everyday narrative norms as most others.

A problem is that these narrative norms often tend to exclude creative use of communicative resources—that is, the way "bricoleurs" tell stories. These stories do not live up to the generally assumed story norms; they rarely have a precise beginning, middle, and end. They are not organized around a progressive temporal axis, nor do they respect the primacy of the spoken, verbal language over other semiotic resources like gestures, or the norm of telling only "true" autobiographical stories.

The "bricoleur" stories challenge received everyday narrative norms and thus defy ordinary ways of listening and understanding stories. As such, this could easily result in a situation that is often described as a "communicative breakdown" in the literature. That is, the participants cannot establish a shared understanding and meaning, and thus one or both of the participants threaten to withdraw from the ongoing activity. This would risk resulting in yet another "disencounter." One way around such a relational defeat would be for the participants, especially the healthy participants, to engage in the meaning-making process in a way that allows new possibilities of meaning. Maybe another metaphor, this time from a psychoanalyst, could help conceptualize this possibility.

The Austrian-American psychoanalyst Theodor Reik published a book in 1948 called *Listening with a Third Ear*.[11] One of the ideas he pursued in the book had to do with how he thought clinical psychoanalysts should listen to their patients. He argued that the established idea about listening to patients was to focus on what today would be called the verbal utterances of the patients—that is, the words. Reik pointed out that the "verbal message" actually constituted only a minor part of the resources the analyst used in constructing an understanding of the meaning of the stories told by the patient. Other extremely important resources had to do with the embodied communication—the way the patients made use of their bodies, voices, gestures, the rhythm and prosody—as well as the timing in telling a story. Thus, in constructing meaning the "conjecturing analyst"

> does not concern himself [*sic*] first and foremost with the logical proof of his idea, and often pursues contradictory trains of thought. He has an open mind and does not shrink from yielding himself, by way of experiment, to a train of thought that seems senseless and absurd. [. . .] He must learn to listen "with the third ear."[12]

According to Reik, it is thus less important to adhere to the traditional communicative norms having to do with coherence and truth than to "a train of thought that seems senseless and absurd." The "senseless and absurd" could even perhaps be seen as poetic, rather than just without meaning. In other words, it is important sometimes to engage in mutual meaning-making by listening and understanding in new and often surprising ways, especially in order to find out what could be salvaged beyond the pure verbal utterance. Although people engaging in storytelling with persons with dementia rarely are psychoanalysts, Reik's advice is still interesting.

In Chapter 2, Richard Cheston was quoted as arguing that listeners must engage with the "poetical, the metaphorical aspects of language," rather than with language's "truthfulness."[13] In a similar way, Alison Phinney has argued that the Alzheimer's symptom story is "inherently and fundamentally unknowable and untellable" and that "meaning is in the telling itself"; listeners are called to bear witness to the suffering when meanings cannot be told.[14] Both Cheston and Phinney argue that it is the "poetic" possibilities in the stories that are told by persons with dementia that matter. It could be added that participants need to go even further than the possibilities of "poetic" meaning, beyond the words spoken, to embrace the possibilities that are found in the bodily resources and especially in the embodied meaning. Engaging with the possibilities of embodied meaning implies finding parallel, embodied experiences that would allow a possible construction of meaning. Furthermore, it is important to remember that the various levels of meanings in a story are not found or uncovered; they are co-constructed by the participants. It means that meanings must be negotiated and always open for the possibility that the participants settle for some kind of meaning, rather than trying to establish the correct, established, or expected meaning.

THE LIMITS OF STORIES

Although this book has championed autobiographical storytelling, it is important to acknowledge the limits of stories, especially in relation to persons with dementia. Most of the persons with dementia in this book have been in what generally is known as the mid-stage of dementia; they can use at least some of their linguistic and cognitive resources, and most of them live at home. As the dementia progresses, persons will have fewer and fewer linguistic and cognitive resources at hand, and thus engaging in storytelling becomes not only difficult but also threatens to become yet another disappointment and "disencounter." Entering the last phase of dementia means that both significant others and caregivers will have to take on even more of the responsibility of the interaction and scaffold it in such a way that even the faintest sign from the person with dementia will be allowed to be taken as a token of acknowledgment. The voice of the person with dementia will inevitably give way to the vicarious voices of significant others and caregivers. Autobiographical stories are told with the physical voice of the other, while hopefully retaining the perspective and thus the voice of the person with dementia.

Vicarious voices always create a delicate situation: Whose voice is heard in the vicarious storytelling? There is always the risk that the stories told by family members or staff are their stories, rather than the stories of the person with dementia. This is particularly pertinent in relation to life story work (LSW). Constructing life story books may be important to staff as a way to get to know the person "beyond" the diagnosis. But these stories are not necessarily the story the person with dementia would like to tell or stick to. One obvious reason for this is that the person with dementia is engaging with a progressive disease that changes his or her brain and thus life, leaving few if any stones unturned. Sticking to a story about the healthy person always risks leaving no room for reflection and especially for the emotions that are connected to the changing life—and ultimately, death.

Finally, it is important to accept that autobiographical stories are not necessarily the only way for a person to present and negotiate her or his identity and self. As argued in the early chapters, anthropologists like Pia Kontos have forcefully argued that subjectivity and self are embodied and can be expressed and communicated in many ways besides the telling of stories, especially in bodily skills like knitting or singing or dancing. And ultimately, what is storytelling about, if not expressing, establishing, and negotiating the self?

NOTES

1. Anne Basting, *Forget Memory* (2009), p. 4.
2. Ibid., p. 156.
3. Halbwachs, 1992, p. 38.
4. Bruner, 2002, pp. 85–86.
5. Sabat & Harré, 1992, 1994.
6. Ochs & Capps, 2001.
7. Levi-Strauss, 1966, p. 19.
8. Suzanne Fleischman, 1990, p. 263. The quotation is from Phelan, 1994.
9. A classical account about the beginning of this process is the book *Narratives from the Crib* (Nelson, 1989).
10. Iser, 1978.
11. This was the American title. The English edition was *The Inner Experience of a Psychoanalyst* (1948).
12. Reik, 1949, pp. 223, 144.
13. Cheston, 1996, p. 398.
14. Phinney, 2002, p. 340.

REFERENCES

Adams, J. K., & Jones, W. H. (1997). The conceptualization of marital commitment: An integrative analysis. *Journal of Personality and Social Psychology, 72,* 1177–1196.

Agnew, C. R., Van Lange, P. A. M., Rusbult, C. E., & Langston, C. A. (1998). Cognitive interdependence: Commitment and the mental representation of close relationships. *Journal of Personality and Social Psychology, 74,* 939–954.

Andrews, M., Squire, C., & Tamboukou, M. (Eds.). (2014). *Doing narrative research* (2nd ed.). London: Sage.

Angus, J., & Bowen, S. (2011). "Quiet please, there's a lady on stage": Centering the person with dementia in life story narrative. *Journal of Aging Studies, 25,* 110–117.

Arbib, M. (2011). *How the brain got language: The mirror system hypothesis.* New York: Oxford University Press.

Aron, A., Aron, E. N., Tudor, M., & Nelson, G. (1991). Close relationships as including other in the self. *Journal of Personality and Social Psychology, 60,* 241–253.

Bäckman, L., & Dixon, R. A. (1992). Psychological Compensation: A Theoretical Framework. *Psychological Bulletin, 112,* 259–283.

Bakhtin, M. (1984). *Problems of Dostoevsky's poetics.* Minneapolis: University of Minnesota Press.

Baldwin, C., & Capstick, A. (Eds.). (2007). *Tom Kitwood on dementia: A reader and critical commentary.* New York: McGraw-Hill Education.

Ballenger, J. F. (2006). *Self, senility, and Alzheimer's disease in modern America.* Baltimore, MD: Johns Hopkins University Press.

Bamberg, M. (1997). Positioning between structure and performance. *Journal of Narrative and Life History, 7,* 335–342.

Barnes, D. E., & Yaffe, K. (2011). The projected effect of risk factor reduction on Alzheimer's disease prevalence. *Lancet Neurology, 10,* 819–828.

Barnier, A. J., Sutton, J., Harris, C. B., & Wilson, B. A. (2008). A conceptual and empirical framework for the social distribution of cognition: The case of memory. *Cognitive Systems Research, 9,* 33–51.

Barrett, L. (2011). *Beyond the brain: How body and environment shape animal and human minds.* Princeton, NJ: Princeton University Press.

Barthes, R. (1975). Introduction to the Structual Analysis of Narratives. *New Literary History, 6,* 237–272.

Bartlett, F. C. (1995). *Remembering: A study in experimental and social psychology.* Cambridge: Cambridge University Press.

Bartlett, R., & O'Connor, D. (2010). *Broadening the dementia debate: Toward social citizenship*. Bristol: Policy Press.

Basting, A. D. (2009). *Forget memory: Creating better lives for people with dementia*. Baltimore, MD: Johns Hopkins University Press.

Berger, P. L., & Kellner, H. (1964). Marriage and the construction of reality. *Diogenes*, 46, 1–14.

Berrios, G. E. (1990). Alzheimer's disease: A conceptual history. *International Journal of Geriatric Psychiatry*, 5, 355–365.

Bohanek, J. G., Fivush, R., Zaman, W., Lepore, C. E., Merchant, C., & Duke, M. P. (2009). Narrative interaction in family dinnertime conversations. *Merrill-Palmer Quarterly*, 55, 488–515.

Bohling, H. R. (1991). Communication with Alzheimer's patients: An analysis of caregiver listening patterns. *International Journal of Aging and Human Development*, 33, 249–267.

Bolens, G. (2012). *The style of gestures: Embodiment and cognition in literary narrative*. Baltimore, MD: Johns Hopkins University Press.

Booth, W. C. (1983). *The rhetoric of fiction* (2nd ed.). Chicago: University of Chicago Press.

Bowles, S., & Gintis, H. (2011). *A cooperative species: Human reciprocity and its evolution*. Princeton, NJ: Princeton University Press.

Braak, H., & Braak, E. (1991). Neuropathological stageing of Alzheimer-related changes. *Acta Neuropathologica*, 82, 230–259.

Braak, H., & Braak, E. (1995). Staging of Alzheimer's disease-related neurofibrillary changes. *Neurobiology of Aging*, 16, 271–284.

Bratman, M. E. (1992). Shared cooperative activity. *The Philosophical Review*, 101, 327–341.

Bratman, M. E. (1993). Shared intention. *Ethics*, 104, 97–113.

Brockmeier, J. (2000). Autobiographical time. *Narrative Inquiry*, 10, 51–73.

Brockmeier, J. (2010). After the archive: Remapping memory. *Culture and Psychology*, 16, 5–35.

Brockmeier, J. (2013). Afterword: The monkey wrenches of narrative. In M. Andrews, C. Squire & M. Tamboukou (Eds.), *Doing narrative research* (2nd ed., pp. 261–270). London: Sage.

Brockmeier, J. (2015). *Beyond the archive. Memory, narrative, and the autobiographical process*. New York: Oxford University Press.

Brockmeier, J., & Carbaugh, D. (Eds.). (2001). *Narrative and identity: Studies in autobiography, self and culture*. Amsterdam: John Benjamins.

Bruner, J. (1985). *Child's talk: Learning to use language*. New York: W. W. Norton.

Bruner, J. (1987). Life as narrative. *Social Research*, 54, 11–32.

Bruner, J. (2001). Self-making and world-making. In J. Brockmeier & D. Carbaugh (Eds.), *Narrative and identity: Studies in autobiography, self and culture* (pp. 25–38). Amsterdam: John Benjamins.

Bruner, J. (2002). *Making Stories. Law, Literature, Life*. New York: Farrar, Straus and Giroux.

Buchanan, K., & Middleton, D. (1995). Voices of experience: Talk, identity and membership in reminiscence groups. *Ageing and Society*, 15, 457–491.

Bury, M. (1982). Chronic illness as biographical disruption. *Sociology of Health and Illness*, 4, 167–182.

Carlsson, E., Paterson, B. L., Scott-Findlay, S., Ehnfors, M., & Ehrenberg, A. (2007). Methodological issues in interviews involving people with communication impairments after acquired brain damage. *Qualitative Health Research, 17,* 1361–1371.

Caron, W., Hepburn, K. W., Luptak, M., Grant, L., Ostwald, S., & Keenan, J. M. (1999). Expanding the Discourse of Care: Family Constructed Biographies of Nursing Home Residents. *Families, Systems, & Health, 17,* 323–335.

Capps, L., & Ochs, E. (1995). Out of Place: Narrative Insights Into Agoraphobia. *Discourse Processes, 19,* 407–439.

Cassell, E. J. (1976). Disease as an "it": Concepts of disease revealed by patients' presentation of symptoms. *Social Science and Medicine, 10,* 143–146.

Chafe, W. (1994). *Discourse, consciousness, and time: The flow and displacement of conscious experience in speaking and writing.* Chicago: University of Chicago Press.

Charmaz, K. (1983). Loss of self: A fundamental form of suffering in the chronically ill. *Sociology of Health and Illness, 5,* 168–197.

Charmaz, K. (1991). *Good days, bad days: The self in chronic illness and time.* New Brunswick, NJ: Rutgers University Press.

Charmaz, K. (1999). Stories of suffering: Subjective tales and research narratives. *Qualitative Health Research, 9,* 362–382.

Cheston, R. (1996). Stories and metaphors: Talking about the past in a psychotherapy group for people with dementia. *Ageing and Society, 16,* 576–602.

Cheston, R., & Bender, M. (1999). Brains, minds and selves: Changing conceptions of the losses involved in dementia. *British Journal of Medical Psychology, 72,* 203–216.

Cheston, R., & Bender, M. (2003). *Understanding dementia: The man with the worried eyes.* London: Jessica Kingsley Publishers.

Christensen, K, Thinggaard, M., Oksuzyan, A., Steenstrup, T., Andersen-Ranberg, K., Jeune, B., . . . Vaupel, J. W. (2013). Physical and cognitive functioning of people older than 90 years: A comparison of two Danish cohorts born 10 years apart. *Lancet, 382,* 1507–1513.

Clare, L. (2002). We'll fight it as long as we can: Coping with the onset of Alzheimer's disease. *Aging & Mental Health, 6,* 139–148.

Clare, L. (2003). Managing threats to self: Awareness in early stage Alzheimer's disease. *Social Science and Medicine, 57,* 1017–1029.

Clare, L. (2008). *Neuropsychological rehabilitation and people with dementia.* Hove: Psychology Press.

Clare, L. (2010). Awareness in people with severe dementia: Review and integration. *Aging & Mental Health, 14,* 20–32.

Clare, L., Goater, T., & Woods, B. (2006). Illness representations in early-stage dementia: A preliminary investigation. *International Journal of Geriatric Psychiatry, 21,* 761–767.

Clark, A. (2006). Soft selves and ecological control. In D. Spurrett, D. J. Ross, H. Koncaid, & L. Stephens (Eds.), *Distributed cognition and the will* (pp. 101–122). Cambridge, MA: MIT Press.

Clark, A. (2008). *Supersizing the mind: Embodiment, action, and cognitive extension.* New York: Oxford University Press.

Clark, H. H. (1996). *Using language.* New York: Cambridge University Press.

Clark, H. H., & Schaefer, E. F. (1987). Collaborating on contributions to conversations. *Language and Cognitive Processes, 2,* 19–41.

Clark, H. H., & Schaefer, E. F. (1989). Contributing to discourse. *Cognitive Science, 13,* 259–294.

Cohen, L. (1995). Toward an anthropology of senility: Anger, weakness, and Alzheimer's in Banaras, India. *Medical Anthropology Quarterly, 9*, 314–334.

Cohen, L. (1998). *No aging in India: Alzheimer's, the bad family, and other modern things.* Berkeley: University of California Press.

Cohen-Mansfield, J., Golander, H., & Arnheim, G. (2000). Self-identity in older persons suffering from dementia: Preliminary results. *Social Science and Medicine, 51*, 381–394.

Cohen-Mansfield, J., Parpura-Gilla, A., & Golander, H. (2006). Utilization of self-identity roles for designing interventions for persons with dementia. *Journal of Gerontology, 61B*, 202–212.

Conrad, P. (1987). The experience of illness: Recent and new directions. *Research in the Sociology of Health Care, 6*, 1–31.

Cotrell, V., & Schulz, R. (1993). The perspective of the patient with Alzheimer's disease: A neglected dimension of dementia research. *The Gerontologist, 33*, 205–211.

Daviglus, M. L., Bell, C. C., Berrettini, W., Bowen, P. E., Connolly, E. S. Jr., Cox, N. J., . . . Trevisan, M. (2010). National Institutes of Health State-of-the-Science Conference statement: Preventing Alzheimer disease and cognitive decline. *Annals of Internal Medicine, 153*, 176–181.

Daviglus, M. L., Plassman, B. L., Pirzada, A., Bell, C. C., Bowen, P. E., Burke, J. R., . . . Williams, J. W. (2011). Risk factors and preventive interventions for Alzheimer's disease. *Archives of Neurology, 68*, 1185–1190.

Davies, J. C. (2011). Preserving the "us identity" through marriage commitment while living with early-stage dementia. *Dementia: The International Journal of Social Research and Practice, 10*, 217–234.

DeBaggio, T. (2003). *Losing my mind.* New York: Free Press.

Dixon, R. A., Garrett, D. D., & Bäckman, L. (2008). Principles of compensation in cognitive neuroscience and neurorehabilitation. In D. T. Stuss, G. Winocur, & I. H. Robertson (Eds.), *Cognitive Neurorehabilitation. Evidence and Application* (Second ed., pp. 22–38). New York: Cambridge University Press.

Downs, M. (1997). The emergence of the person in dementia research. *Ageing and Society, 17*, 597–607.

Eakin, P. J. (2001). Breaking rules: The consequences of self-narration. *Biography, 24*, 113–127.

Enfield, N. J., & Levinson, S. C. (Eds.). (2006). *Roots of human sociality: Culture, cognition and interaction.* Oxford: Berg.

Estroff, S. E. (1995). Whose story is it anyway? Authority, voice and responsibility in narratives of chronic illness. In S. K. Toombs, D. Barnard, & R. A. Carson (Eds.), *Chronic illness: From experience to policy* (pp. 77–102). Bloomington: Indiana University Press.

Feil, N., & de Klerk-Rubin, V. (2012). *The validation breakthrough* (3rd ed.). Baltimore, MD: Health Profession Press.

Fivush, R. (2007). Remembering and reminiscing: How individual lives are constructed in family narratives. *Memory Studies, 1*, 45–54.

Fleischman, S. (1990). *Tense and narrativity: From medieval performance to modern fiction.* Austin: University of Texas Press.

Fontana, A., & Smith, R. W. (1989). Alzheimer's disease victims: The "unbecoming" of self and the normalization of competence. *Sociological Perspectives, 32*, 35–46.

Frank, A. W. (2014). *The wounded storyteller: Body, illness, and ethics* (2nd ed.). Chicago: University of Chicago Press.

Fratiglioni, L., & Wang, H-U. (2007). Brain reserve hypothesis in dementia. *Journal of Alzheimer's Disease, 12*, 11–22.

Freed, P. (2002). Meeting of the minds: Ego reintegration after traumatic brain injury. *Bulletin of the Menninger Clinic, 66*, 61–78.

Freeman, M. (1993). *Rewriting the self: History, memory, narrative*. London: Routledge.

Freeman, M. (2010). *Hindsight: The promise and peril of looking backward*. New York: Oxford University Press.

Gallagher, S. (2005). *How the Body Shapes the Mind*. Oxford: Oxford University Press.

Gallagher, S. (Ed.). (2011). *The Oxford handbook of the self*. Oxford: Oxford University Press.

Gallagher-Thompson, D., Dal Canto, P. G., Jacob, T., & Thompson, L. W. (2001). A Comparison of Marital Interaction Patterns Between Couples in Which the Husband Does or Does Not Have Alzheimer's Disease. *Journals of Gerontoloy: Social Sciences, 56B*, S140–S150.

Gee, J. P. (1986). Units in the production of narrative discourse. *Discourse Processes, 9*, 391–422.

Gibbs, R. W. (2006). *Embodiment and cognitive science*. New York: Cambridge University Press.

Gilbert, M. (1990). Walking Together: A Paradigmatic Social Phenomenon. *Midwest Studies in Philosophy, xv*, 1–14.

Gillespie, A., & Zittoun, T. (2010). Using resources: Conceptualizing the mediation and reflective use of tools and signs. *Culture and Psychology, 16*, 37–62.

Gleason, P. (1983). Identifying identity: A semantic history. *Journal of American History, 69*, 910–931.

Goffman, E. (1959). *The presentation of self in everyday life*. New York: Anchor Books.

Goffman, E. (1967). *Interaction ritual: Essays on face-to-face behavior*. New York: Doubleday.

Goffman, E. (1974). *Frame analysis: An essay on the organization of experience*. Cambridge, MA: Harvard University Press.

Goffman, E. (1981). *Forms of talk*. Philadelphia: University of Pennsylvania Press.

Goldstein, K. (1948). *Language and language disturbances: Aphasic symptom complexes and their significance for medicine and theory of language*. New York: Grune and Stratton.

Goldstein, K. (1997). *The organism*. Cambridge: Zone Books.

Goodwin, C. (1981). *Conversational organization: Interaction between speakers and hearers*. New York: Academic Press.

Goodwin, C. (2003). Conversational frameworks for the accomplishment of meaning in aphasia. In C. Goodwin (Ed.), *Conversation and brain damage* (pp. 90–116). Oxford: Oxford University Press.

Goodwin, C. (2004). A competent speaker who can't speak: The social life of aphasia. *Journal of Linguistic Anthropology, 14*, 151–170.

Gottman, J. M. (2011). *The science of trust: Emotional attunement for couples*. New York: W. W. Norton.

Greenwood, P. M., & Parasuraman, R. (2012). *Nurturing the older brain and mind*. Cambridge, MA: MIT Press.

Grice, P. (1975). Logic and conversation. In P. Cole & J. Morgan (Eds.), *Syntax and semantic*, vol 3: *Speech acts* (pp. 41–58). New York: Academic Press.

Gubrium, J. F. (1986). The social preservation of mind: The Alzheimer's disease experience. *Symbolic Interaction, 9*, 37–51.

Gubrium, J. F. (1988). Incommunicables and poetic documentation in the Alzheimer's disease experience. *Semiotica, 72*, 235–253.

Halbwachs, M. (1992). *On collective memory* (Edited and translated by L. A. Coser). Chicago: University of Chicago Press.

Hamilton, H. E. (1994). *Conversations with an Alzheimer's patient: An interactional sociolinguistic study*. New York: Cambridge University Press.

Hamilton, H. E. (1996). Intratextuality, intertextuality, and the construction of identity as patient in Alzheimer's disease. *Text, 16*, 61–90.

Hamilton, H. E. (2008). Narrative as snapshot: Glimpses into the past in Alzheimer's discourse. *Narrative Inquiry, 18*, 53–82.

Hardy, B. (1968). Towards a poetics of fiction. *Novel, 2*, 5–14.

Harris, C. B., Keil, P. G., Sutton, J., Barnier, A. J., & McIlwain, D. J. F. (2011). We remember, we forget: Collaborative remembering in older couples. *Discourse Processes, 48*, 267–303.

Hedman, R., Hansebo, G., Ternstedt, B. M., Hellström, I., & Norberg, A. (2013). How people with Alzheimer's disease express their sense of self: Analysis using Rom Harré's theory of selfhood. *Dementia, 12*, 713–733.

Hedman, R., Hellström, I., Ternstedt, B. M., Hansebo, G., & Norberg, A. (2014). Social positioning by people with Alzheimer's disease in a support group. *Journal of Aging Studies, 28*, 11–21.

Hellström, I. (2014). "I'm his wife not his carer!" Dignity and couplehood in dementia. In Hydén, L-C., Brockmeier, J., & Lindemann, H. (Eds.), *Beyond loss: Dementia, identity, personhood*. New York: Oxford University Press.

Hellström, I., Nolan, M., & Lundh, U. (2005). We do things together: A case study of couplehood in dementia. *Dementia, 4*, 7–22.

Hellström, I., Nolan, M., & Lundh, U. (2007). Sustaining couplehood': Spousesstrategies for living positively with dementia. *Dementia, 6*, 383–409.

Hepburn, K. W., Caron, W., Luptak, M., Ostwald, S., Grant, L., & Keenan, J. M. (1997). The Family Stories Workshop: Stories for Those Who Cannot Remember. *The Gerontologist, 37*, 827–832.

Herman, D. (Ed.). (2003). *Narrative theory and cognitive sciences*. Stanford, CA: CSLI Publications.

Herman, D. (2010). Word-image/utterance-gesture: Case studies in multimodal storytelling. In R. Page (Ed.), *New perspectives on narrative and multimodality* (pp. 78–98). New York: Routledge.

Herman, D. (2013). Approaches to narrative worldmaking. In M. Andrews, C. Squire, & M. Tamboukou (Eds.), *Doing narrative research* (2nd ed., pp. 176–196). London: Sage.

Herman, J. L. (1992). *Trauma and recovery*. New York: Basic Books.

Herskovits, E. (1995). Struggling over Subjectivity: Debates about the 'Self' and Alzheimer's Disease. *Medical Anthropology Quarterly, 9*, 146–164.

Holst, G., Edberg, A-K., & Hallberg, I. R. (1999). Nurses' narrations and reflections about caring for patients with severe dementia as revealed in systematic clinical supervision sessions. *Journal of Aging Studies, 13*, 89–107.

Holt, E. (1996). Reporting on talk: The use of direct reported speech in conversation. *Research on Language and Social Interaction, 29*, 219–245.

Hubbard, G., Cook, A., Tester, S., & Downs, M. (2002). Beyond words: Older people with dementia using and interpreting nonverbal behaviour. *Social Science and Medicine, 16*, 155–167.

Hughes, J. C., Louw, S. J., & Sabat, S. R. (Eds.). (2006). *Dementia: Mind, meaning, and the person*. New York: Oxford University Press.

Hutchins, E. (1995). *Cognition in the wild*. Cambridge, MA: MIT Press.

Hydén, L. C. (1997). Illness and narrative. *Sociology of Health and Illness, 19*, 48–69.

Hydén, L. C. (2011). Non-verbal vocalizations, dementia and social interaction. *Communication and Medicine, 8*, 135–144.

Hydén, L. C., & Brockmeier, J. (Eds.). (2008). *Health, culture and illness: Broken narratives*. New York: Routledge.

Hydén, L. C., & Nilsson, E. (2015). Couples with dementia: Positioning the "we." *Dementia, 14*, 716–733.

Hydén, L. C., & Örulv, L. (2009). Narrative and identity in Alzheimer's disease: A case study. *Journal of Aging Studies, 23*, 205–214.

Hydén, L. C., Plejert, C., Samuelsson, C., & Örulv, L. (2013). Feedback and common ground in conversational storytelling involving people with Alzheimer's disease. *Journal of Interactional Research in Communication Disorders, 4*, 211–247.

Iser, W. (1978). *The act of reading: A theory of aesthetic response*. Baltimore, MD: Johns Hopkins University Press.

Jacyna, L. S. (2000). *Lost words: Narratives of language and the brain*. Princeton: Princeton University Press.

Jeannerod, M. (2006). *Motor cognition: What actions tell the self*. New York: Oxford University Press.

Keady, J., Ashcroft-Simpson, S., Halligan, K., & Williams, S. (2007). Admiral nursing and the family care of a parent with dementia: Using autobiographical narrative as grounding for negotiated clinical practice and decision-making. *Scandinavian Journal of Caring Science, 21*, 345–353.

Keady, J., & Nolan, M. (1994). Younger onset dementia: Developing a longitudinal model as the basis for a research agenda and as a guide to interventions with sufferers and carers. *Journal of Advanced Nursing, 19*, 659–669.

Kellas, J. K. (2005). Family ties: Communicating identity through jointly told family stories. *Communication Monographs, 72*, 365–389.

Kempler, D., & Goral, M. (2008). Language and dementia: Neuropsychological aspects. *Annual Review of Applied Linguistics, 28*, 73–90.

Kendon, A. (1990). *Conducting interaction: Patterns of behavior in focused encounters*. New York: Cambridge University Press.

Kendon, A. (2004). *Gesture: Visible action as utterance*. New York: Cambridge University Press.

Kerby, P. (1991). *Narrative and the self*. Bloomington: Indiana University Press.

Kindell, J., Burrow, S., Wilkinson, R., & Keady, J. (2014). Life story resources in dementia care: A review. *Quality in Ageing and Older Adults, 15*, 151–161.

Kindell, J., Sage, K., Keady, J., & Wilkinson, R. (2013). Adapting to conversation with semantic dementia: Using enactment as a compensatory strategy in everyday social interaction. *International Journal of Language & Communication Disorders, 48*, 497–507.

Kintsch, W., & van Dijk, T. (1978). Toward a model of text comprehension and production. *Psychological Review, 85*, 363–394.

Kirsh, D. (1995). The intelligent use of space. *Artificial Intelligence, 73*, 31–68.

Kitwood, T. (1990). The dialectics of dementia: With particular reference to Alzheimer's disease. *Ageing & Society, 10*, 177–196.

Kitwood, T. (1996). A dialectical framework for dementia. In R. T. Woods (Ed.), *Handbook of clinical psychology of ageing* (pp. 267–282). London: John Wiley & Sons.

Kitwood, T. (1997). *Dementia reconsidered: The person comes first*. Philadelphia: Open University Press.

Kleinman, A. (1988). *The illness narratives: Suffering, healing, and the human condition*. New York: Basic Books.

Kontos, P. C. (2004). Ethnographic reflections on selfhood, embodiment and Alzheimers disease. *Ageing & Society, 24*, 829–849.

Kontos, P. C. (2005). Embodied selfhood in Alzheimers disease: Rethinking person-centred care. *Dementia, 4*, 553–570.

Labov, W. (1972). The transformation of experience in narrative syntax. In W. Labov, *Language in the inner city* (pp. 354–405). Philadelphia: University of Pennsylvania Press.

Labov, W., & Waletzky, J. (1967/1997). Narrative analysis: Oral versions of personal experience. *Journal of Narrative and Life History, 7*, 3–38.

Langellier, K. M., & Peterson, E. E. (2004). *Storytelling in daily life: Performing narrative*. Philadelphia: Temple University Press.

Lave, J., & Wenger, E. (1991). *Situated learning: Legitimate peripheral participation*. New York: Cambridge University Press.

Lee, J. (2003). *Just love me: My life turned upside-down by Alzheimer's*. West Lafayette, IN: Purdue University Press.

Lejeune, P. (1989). *On autobiography*. Minneapolis: University of Minnesota Press.

Levinson, S. C. (1992). Activity types and language. In P. Drew & J. Heritage (Eds.), *Talk at work. Interaction in institutional settings* (pp. 66–100). Cambridge: Cambridge University Press.

Levi-Strauss, C. (1966). *The savage mind*. Chicago: University of Chicago Press.

Lezak, M. D., Howieson, D. B., Bigler, E. D., & Tranel, D. (2012). *Neuropsychological assessment* (5th ed.). New York: Oxford University Press.

Liebing, A., & Cohen, L. (Eds.). (2006). *Thinking about dementia: Culture, loss, and the anthropology of senility*. New Brunswick, NJ: Rutgers University Press.

Linde, C. (1993). *Life stories; The creation of coherence*. New York: Oxford University Press.

Lindemann Nelson, H. (2001). *Damaged identities, narrative repair*. Ithaca, NY: Cornell University Press.

Lindemann, H. (2009). Holding one another (well, wrongly, clumsily) in a time of dementia. *Metaphilosophy, 40*, 416–424.

Lindemann, H. (2014a). Second nature and the tragedy of Alzheimer's. In L. C. Hydén, H. Lindemann, & J. Brockmeier (Eds.), *Beyond loss: Dementia, identity, personhood* (pp. 11–23). New York: Oxford University Press.

Lindemann, H. (2014b). *Holding and letting go: The social practice of personal identities*. New York: Oxford University Press.

Lobo, A., Saz, P., Marcos, G., et al., and the ZARADEMP Workgroup. Prevalence of dementia in a southern European population in two different time periods: The ZARADEMP project. (2007). *Acta Psychiatrica Scandinavica, 116*, 299–307.

Lock, M. (2013). *The Alzheimer conundrum: Entanglements of dementia and aging*. Princeton, NJ: Princeton University Press.

Luria, A. R. (1970). Traumatic Aphasia. Its Syndromes, Psychology and Treatment. The Hague: Mouton.

Luria, A. R. (1973). *The working brain: An introduction to neuropsychology*. Harmondsworth: Allen Lane, Penguin Press.

Luria, A. R. (1980). *Higher cortical functions in man* (2nd ed.). New York: Basic Books.

Lysaker, P. H., & Lysaker, J. T. (2006). A typology of narrative impoverishment in schizophrenia: Implications for understanding the processes of establishing and sustaining dialogue in individual psychotherapy. *Counselling Psychology Quarterly*, *19*, 57–68.

Mandelbaum, J. (1987). Couples sharing stories. *Communication Quarterly* (Spring), 144–171.

Mar, R. A. (2004). The neuropsychology of narrative: Story comprehension, story production and their interrelation. *Neuropsychologia*, *42*, 1414–1434.

Matthews, E. (2006). Dementia and the identity of the person. In J. C. Hughes, S. J. Louw, & S. R. Sabat (Eds.), *Dementia: Mind, meaning, and the person* (pp. 163–177). Oxford: Oxford University Press.

Matthews, F. E., Arthur, A., Barnes, L. E., Bond, J., Jagger, C., Robinson, L., & Brayne, C. (2013). A two-decade comparison of prevalence of dementia in individuals aged 65 years and older from three geographical areas of England: Results of the Cognitive Function and Ageing Study I and II. *Lancet*, *382*, 1405–1412.

Maurer, K., & Maurer, U. (2003). *Alzheimer: The life of a physician and the career of a disease*. New York: Columbia University Press.

Maurer, K., Volk, S., & Gerbaldo, H. (1997). Auguste D. and Alzheimer's disease. *Lancet*, *349*, 1546–1549.

McAdams, D. (2006). The problem of narrative coherence. *Journal of Constructivist Psychology*, *19*, 109–125.

McAdams, D. P. (2006). *The redemptive self: Stories Americans live by*. New York: Oxford University Press.

McAdams, D. P., Josselson, R., & Lieblich, A. (Eds.). (2001). *Turns in the road: Narrative studies of lives in transition*. Washington, DC: APA.

McGowin, D. F. (1994). *Living in the labyrinth*. New York: Delacorte Press.

McKeown, J., Clarke, A., & Repper, J. (2006). Life story work in health and social care: systematic literature review. *Journal of Advanced Nursing*, *55*, 237–247.

McNeill, D. (1992). *Hand and mind: What gestures reveal about thought*. Chicago: University of Chicago Press.

McNeill, D. (2005). *Gesture and thought*. Chicago: University of Chicago Press.

Medved, M. (2014). Everyday dramas: Comparing life with dementia and acquired brain injury. In L. C. Hydén, H. Lindemann, & J. Brockmeier (Eds.), *Beyond loss: Dementia, identity, personhood* (pp. 91–106). New York: Oxford University Press.

Mentis, M., Briggs-Whittaker, J., & Gramigna, G. D. (1995). Discourse topic management in senile dementia of the Alzheimer's type. *Journal of Speech and Hearing Research*, *38*, 1054–1066.

Merleau-Ponty, M. (1962). *Phenomenology of perception*. London: Routledge & Kegan Paul.

Merleau-Ponty, M. (1963). *The structure of behavior*. Boston: Beacon Press.

Mikesell, L. (2009). Conversational Practices of a Frontotemporal Dementia Patient and His Interlocutors. *Research on Language and Social Interaction*, *42*, 135–162.

Mills, M. A. (1997). Narrative Identity and Dementia: A Study of Emotion and Narrative in Older People with Dementia. *Ageing and Society*, *17*, 673–698.

Milroy, L., & Perkins, L. (1992). Repair strategies in aphasic dialogue: Towards a collaborative model. *Clinical Linguistics and Phonetics*, *6*, 27–40.

Mishler, E. G. (1990). Validation in inquiry-guided research: The roles of examplars in narrative studies. *Harvard Educational Review*, *60*, 415–442.

Mishler, E. G. (1999). *Storylines: Crafts artists' narratives of identity*. Cambridge, MA: Harvard University Press.

Molyneaux, V. J., Butchard, S., Simpson, J., & Murray, C. (2012). The co-construction of couplehood in dementia. *Dementia, 11*, 483–502.

Müller, N., & Guendouzi, J. A. (2005). Order and disorder in conversation: Encounters with dementia of the Alzheimers type. *Clinical Linguistics and Phonetics, 19*, 393–404.

Müller, N., & Mok, Z. (2013). "Getting to know you": Situated and distributed cognitive effort in dementia. In N. Müller & Z. Mok (Eds.), *Dialogue and dementia: Cognitive and communicative resources for engagement* (pp. 61–86). New York: Psychology Press.

Nelson, K. (Ed.). (1989). *Narratives from the crib*. Cambridge, MA: Harvard University Press.

Nelson, K., & Fivush, R. (2004). The emergence of autobiographical memory: A social cultural developmental theory. *Psychological Review, 111*, 486–511.

Nochi, M. (1998). "Loss of self" in the narratives of people with traumatic brain injuries: A qualitative analysis. *Social Science and Medicine, 46*, 869–878.

Norrick, N. R. (1998). Retelling stories in spontaneous conversation. *Discourse Processes, 25*, 75–97.

Norrick, N. R. (2000). *Conversational narrative. Storytelling in everyday talk*. Amsterdam: John Benjamins.

Obler, L. K., & Gjerlow, K. (1999). *Language and the brain*. New York: Cambridge University Press.

Ochs, E., & Capps, L. (2001). *Living narrative: Creating lives in everyday storytelling*. Cambridge, MA: Harvard University Press.

O'Connor, D., Phinney, A., Smith, A., Small, J. A., Purves, B., Perry, J., . . . Beattie, L. (2007). Personhood in dementia care: Developing a research agenda for broadening the vision. *Dementia, 6*, 121–142.

Öhman, A., Josephsson, S., & Nygård, L. (2008). Awareness through interaction in everyday occupations: Experiences of people with Alzheimers disease. *Scandinavian Journal of Occupational Therapy, 15*, 43–51.

Orange, J. B., Lubinski, R. B., & Higginbotham, D. J. (1996). Conversational repair by individuals with dementia of the Alzheimer's type. *Journal of Speech and Hearing Research, 39*, 881–895.

Örulv, L. (2010). Placing the place, and placing oneself within it: (Dis)orientation and (dis)continuity in dementia. *Dementia, 9*, 21–44.

Örulv, L., & Hydén, L. C. (2006). Confabulation: Sense-making, self-making and world-making in dementia. *Discourse Studies, 8*, 647–673.

Page, S., & Fletcher, T. (2006). Auguste D. One hundred years on: "The person" not "the case." *Dementia, 5*, 571–583.

Panksepp, J. (2005). *Affective neuroscience: The foundations of human and animal emotions*. New York: Oxford University Press.

Perkins, L., Whitworth, A., & Lesser, R. (1998). Conversing in dementia: A conversation analytic approach. *Journal of Neurolinguistics, 11*, 33–53.

Perkins, M. (2007). *Pragmatic impairment*. Cambridge: Cambridge University Press.

Phelan, J. (1994). Self-help for narratee and narrative audience: How "I"—and "You"—read "How." *Style, 28*, 350–366.

Phinney, A. (2002). Fluctuating awareness and the breakdown of the illness narrative in dementia. *Dementia, 1*, 329–344.

Phinney, A. (2006). Family strategies for supporting involvement in meaningful activity by persons with dementia. *Journal of Family Nursing, 12*, 80–101.

Phoenix, C., Smith, B., & Sparkes, A. C. (2010). Narrative analysis in aging studies: A typology for consideration. *Journal of Aging Studies, 24*, 1–11.

Pratt, M. L. (1977). *Toward a speech act theory of literary discourse*. Bloomington: Indiana University Press.

Proust, M, (1922). *Remembrance of Things Past*, Volume 1: *Swann's Way: Within a Budding Grove*. The definitive French Pleiade edition, translated by C. K. Scott Moncrieff. London: Pelican.

Purves, B. (2011). Exploring positioning in Alzheimer Disease through analyses of family talk. *Dementia, 10*, 35–58.

Qiu, C., von Strauss, E., Bäckman, L., Winblad, B., & Fratiglioni, L. (2013). Twenty-year changes in dementia occurrence suggest decreasing incidence in central Stockholm, Sweden. *Neurology, 80*, 1888–94.

Quaeghebeur, L., & Reynaert, P. (2010). Does the need for linguistic expression constitute a problem to be solved? *Phenomenology and Cognitive Science, 9*, 15–36.

Ramanathan, V. (1995). Narrative well-formedness in Alzheimer's discourse: An interactional examination across settings. *Journal of Pragmatics, 23*, 395–419.

Ramanathan, V. (1997). *Alzheimer discourse: Some sociolinguistic dimensions*. Mahwah, NJ: Lawrence Erlbaum.

Ramanathan, V. (2009). Scripting selves, stalling last shadows: (Auto)biographical writing of Alzheimer patients and their caregivers. *Critical Inquiry in Language Studies, 6*, 292–314.

Randall, W. L., & McKim, A. E. (2004). Towards a Poetics of Aging: The Links Between Literature and Life. *Narrative Inquiry, 14*, 235–260.

Randall, W. L., & McKim, A. E. (2008). *Reading our lives: The poetics of growing old*. New York: Oxford University Press.

Reik, T. (1949). *The inner experience of a psychoanalyst*. London: George Allen & Unwin.

Roach, P., Keady, J., & Bee, P. (2014). "Familyhood" and young-onset dementia: Using narrative and biography to understand longitudinal adjustment to diagnosis. In L. C. Hydén, H. Lindemann, & J. Brockmeier (Eds.), *Beyond loss: Dementia, identity, personhood* (pp. 173–190). New York: Oxford University Press.

Richerson, P. J., & Boyd, R. (2005). *Not by genes alone: How culture transformed human evolution*. Chicago: University of Chicago Press.

Ripich, D., Vertes, D., Whitehouse, P., Fulton, S., & Ekelman, B. (1991). Turn-taking and speech act patterns in the discourse of senile dementia of the Alzheimer's type patients. *Brain and Language, 40*, 330–343.

Rizzalotti, G., & Sinigaglia, C. (2008). *Mirrors in the brain: How our minds share actions and emotions*. Oxford: Oxford University Press.

Robinson, L., Clare, L., & Evans, K. (2005). Making sense of dementia and adjusting to loss: Psychological reactions to a diagnosis of dementia in couples. *Aging & Mental Health, 9*, 337–347.

Rogoff, B. (1998). Cognition as a collaborative process. In D. Kuhn & R. S. Siegler (Eds.), *Handbook of child psychology*, Vol. 2: *Cognition, perception, and language* (pp. 679–744). New York: John Wiley & Sons.

Rusbult, C. E., & Van Lange, P. A. M. (2003). Interdependence, interaction, and relationships. *Annual Review of Psychology, 54*, 351–375.

Sabat, S. R. (1991). Facilitating conversation via indirect repair: A case study of Alzheimer's disease. *Georgetown Journal of Languages and Linguistics, 2*, 284–296.

Sabat, S. R. (2001). *Experience of Alzheimer's Disease: Life through a tangled veil.* Oxford: Blackwell.

Sabat, S. R., & Harré, R. (1992). The construction and deconstruction of self in Alzheimer's disease. *Ageing and Society, 12,* 443–461.

Sabat, S. R., & Harré, R. (1994). The Alzheimer's disease sufferer as a semiotic subject. *Philosophy, Psychology, Psychiatry, 1,* 145–160.

Sacks, O. (1985). *The man who mistook his wife for a hat.* London: Duckworth.

Salas, C. E. (2012). Surviving catastrophic reaction after brain injury: The use of self-regulation and self–other regulation. *Neuropsychoanalysis, 14,* 77–92.

Samuelsson, C., & Hydén, L. C. (2011). Intonational Patterns of Non-verbal Vocalizations in People with Dementia. *American Journal of Alzheimer's Disease and Other Dementias, 26,* 563–572.

Sandman, P. O., Norberg, A., & Adolfsson, R. (1988). Verbal communication and behaviour during meals in five institutionalized patients with Alzheimer-type dementia. *Journal of Advanced Nursing, 13,* 571–578.

Schacter, D. L. (1996). *Searching for memory: The brain, the mind, and the past.* New York: Basic Books.

Schafer, R. (1976). *A new language for psychoanalysis.* New Haven, CT: Yale University Press.

Schafer, R. (1983). *The Analytic Attitude.* New York: Basic Books.

Schafer, R. (1992). *Retelling a life. Narration and dialogue in psychoanalysis.* New York: Basic Books.

Schegloff, E. A., Jefferson, G., & Sacks, H. (1977). The preference for self-correction in the organization of repair in conversation. *Language, 53,* 361–382.

Schiffrin, D. (1996). Narrative as self-portrait: Sociolinguistic constructions of identity. *Language in Society, 25,* 167–203.

Schrijvers, E. M., Verhaaren, B. F., Koudstaal, P. J., Hofman, A., Ikram, M. A., & Breteler, M. M. (2012). Is dementia incidence declining? Trends in dementia incidence since 1990 in the Rotterdam Study. *Neurology, 78,* 1456–63.

Schutz, A. (1962). On multiple realities. In A. Schutz (Ed.), *Collected papers,* vol I. (pp. 207–259). The Hague: Martinus Nijhoff.

Seeley, W. W., & Miller, B. L. (2005). Disorders of the self in dementia. In T. E. Feinberg & J. P. Keenan (Eds.), *The lost self: Pathologies of the brain and identity* (pp. 147–165). New York: Oxford University Press.

Shay, J. (1995). *Achilles in Vietnam: Combat trauma and the undoing of character.* New York: Scribner.

Sheets-Johnstone, M. (2011). *The primacy of movement* (2nd expanded ed.). Amsterdam: John Benjamins.

Slobin, D. (1996). From "thought and language" to "thinking for speaking." In J. J. Gumperz & S. C. Levinson (Eds.), *Rethinking linguistic relativity* (pp. 70–96). New York: Cambridge University Press.

Small, J. A., Geldart, K., Gutman, G., & Scott, M. A. C. (1998). The discourse of self in dementia. *Aging and Society, 18,* 291–316.

Small, J. A., Gutman, G., & Hillhouse, S. M. B. (2003). Effectiveness of Communication Strategies Used by Caregivers of Persons With Alzheimers Disease During Activities of Daily Living. *Journal of Speech, Language and Hearing Research, 46,* 353–367.

Smith, B. H. (1981). Narrative versions, narrative theories. In W. J. T. Mitchell (Ed.), *On narrative* (pp. 209–232). Chicago: University of Chicago Press.

Staske, S. A. (1998). The normalization of problematic emotion in conversations between close relational partners: Interpersonal emotion work. *Symbolic Interaction*, *21*, 59–86.

Stern, Y. (2002). What is cognitive reserve? Theory and research application of the reserve concept. *Journal of the International Neuropsychological Society*, *8*, 448–460.

Stivers, T., Enfield, N. J., & Levinson, S. C. (2007). Person reference in interaction. In N. J. Enfield & T. Stivers (Eds.), *Person reference in interaction* (pp. 1–20). New York: Cambdrige University Press.

Streeck, J. (2013). Interaction and the living body. *Journal of Pragmatics*, *46*, 69–90.

Suddendorf, T., & Corballis, M. C. (2007). The evolution of foresight: What is mental time travel, and is it unique to humans? *Behavioral and Brain Sciences*, *30*, 299–351.

Sugiyama, M. S. (2001). Narrative theory and function: Why evolution matters. *Philosophy and Literature*, *25*, 233–250.

Susswein, N., & Racine, T. P. (2008). Sharing mental states: Casual and definitional issues in intersubjectivity. In J. Zlatev, T. P. Racine, C. Sinha, & E. Itkonen (Eds.), *The shared mind: Perspectives on intersubjectivity* (pp. 141–162). Boston: John Benjamins.

Sweeting, H., & Gilhooly, M. (1997). Dementia and the phenomenon of social death. *Sociology of Health and Illness*, *19*, 93–117.

Thelen, E. (2000). Grounded in the world: Developmental origins of the embodied mind. *Infancy*, *1*, 3–28.

Thibaut, J. W., & Kelley, H. H. (1959). *The social psychology of groups*. New York: John Wiley & Sons.

Tomasello, M. (2014). *A natural history of human thinking*. Cambridge, MA: Harvard University Press.

Tomasello, M., Carpenter, M., Call, J., Behne, T., & Moll, H. (2005). Understanding and sharing intentions: The origins of cultural cognition. *Behavioral and Brain Sciences*, *28*, 675–735.

Tracy, K., & Robles, J. S. (2013). *Everyday talk: Building and reflecting identities*. New York: Guilford Publications.

Traphagan, J. (1998). Localizing senility: Illness and agency among older Japanese. *Journal of Cross-Cultural Gerontology*, *13*, 81–98.

Turner, M. (1996). *The literary mind: The origins of thought and language*. New York: Oxford University Press.

Usita, P. M., Hyman, I. E., & Herman, K. C. (1998). Narrative intentions: Listening to life stories in Alzheimers disease. *Journal of Aging Studies*, *12*, 185–198.

Valenzuela, M. J., & Sachdev, P. S. (2006). Brain reserve and dementia: A systematic review. *Psychological Medicine*, *36*, 441–454.

Vygotsky, L. S. (1987). Thinking and speech. In R. W. Rieber & A. S. Carton (Eds.), *The collected works of L. S. Vygotsky* (Vol. 1, pp. 39–285). New York: Plenum Press.

Walton, K. L. (1990). *Mimesis as make-believe: On the foundations of the representational arts*. Cambridge, MA: Harvard University Press.

Watson, C. M., Chenery, H. J., & Carter, M. S. (1999). Analysis of trouble and repair in the natural conversations of people with dementia of the Alzheimers type. *Aphasiology*, *13*, 195–218.

Wertsch, J. (1985). *Vygotsky and the social formation of mind*. Cambridge, MA: Harvard University Press.

Whitehouse, P., Maurer, K., & Ballenger, J. F. (Eds.). (2000). *Concepts of Alzheimer's disease: Biological, clinical, and cultural perspectives*. Baltimore, MD: Johns Hopkins University Press.

WHO (2013). *Dementia: A public health priority*. WHO.

Williams, G. (1984). The genesis of chronic illness: Narrative re-construction. *Sociology of Health and Illness, 6,* 175–200.

Wood, D., Bruner, J., & Ross, G. (1976). The role of tutoring in problem solving. *Journal of Child Psychology and Psychiatry, 17,* 89–100.

Wray, A. (2008). *Formulaic language: Pushing the boundaries*. Oxford: Oxford University Press.

Young, K. (1987). *Taleworlds and storyrealms: The phenomenology of narrative*. Dordrecht: Martinius Nijhoff Publishers.

Young, K., & Saver, J. L. (2001). The neurology of narrative. *Substance: A Review of Theory and Literary Criticism, 30*(1/2), 72–84.

INDEX

activity frames, for joint activity, 135
aging
  and memory loss, 31–32
  and restorying, 4
Alzheimer, Alois
  brain injuries and behavior, 66
  patient encounter, 29–30, 34
Alzheimer's disease
  challenges for conversational
    storytelling, 65–66
  identification of, 30–31
  living with changes in brain, 66–73
  memoirs of, 53–54
  and narrative abilities, 43–45
  neurodegenerative process of, 58–60
  self-presentation and stigma of, 13, 14
animator, as voice in story, 108–109,
    112, 127
anxiety, in reaction to changes in the
    brain, 74–75
arrested narration, 41
authorial voice, and narrative, 108–109,
    112, 127
autobiographical life stories
  based on previous tellings, 157–158
  fragments and repetitions
    in, 157–167
  layered or laminated nature of, 93–94,
    103–104
  multimodal resources for, 63–66,
    117–120, 198
  narrative and identity, 15
  positioning self and story,
    103–106, 113
  progression of, 88–90
  restructured resources for, 200

and self and identity, 47–49, 101–102,
    199–201
social organization of, 195–196
teller as character in, 174
units of, 163b
averted gaze, as sign of catastrophic
    reaction, 75–76

Bäckmann, Lars, 78
Bakhtin, Michail, concept of "voice" in
    stories, 108
Ballenger, Jesse, 31
Bamberg, Michael, 103, 104
barren narratives, 41
Barthes, Roland, 2–3
Bartlett, Frederic, 168
Basting, Anne Davis, 195
biography
  and authorial voice, 108
  and life-story work, 48
  and social psychological theory of
    dementia, 36
Booth, Wayne, 45
bounded storytellers, people with
    dementia as, 9, 81, 197
brain
  brain injuries and behavior, 67, 83–84
  dementia and injuries to,
    53–55, 58–60
  functional perspective on, 55–58, 60
  living with changes, 66–73, 178
  losses involved with traumatic injury,
    175–176
  neurodegenerative vs. vascular
    disorders, 58–60
  role in storytelling, 60–63

brain, reactions to changes in, 73–83
  catastrophic *vs.* ordered
    reactions, 73–75
  collaborative compensatory
    adaptation, 80–81
  compensatory adaptations,
    77–78, 83–84
  cultural aspects of compensatory
    adaptation, 81–83
  gaze, as sign of catastrophic
    reaction, 75–76
  reconceptualizing
    compensation, 78–80
  withdrawal, as sign of catastrophic
    reaction, 76–77
bricoleurs, storytellers with dementia as,
    202–205
Broca, Paul, 66
Brockmeier, Jens
  defining stories, 91
  identity and narrative, 14
  retrieving stored memories, 167
broken stories
  characteristics of, 4–6
  and dementia, 40–43
Bruner, Jerome
  memories, self, and identity, 5, 196
  narrative scaffolding, 107, 124
  and personhood in dementia, 5, 8
Buchanan, Kevin, 48
Bury, Michael, 177

cacophonous story, 41
Capps, Lisa, 100, 106
catastrophic reactions
  and the self, 175–177
  signs of, 75–77
  vs. ordered reactions, 73–75
categorizations, and self-identity, 174
Chafe, Wallace, 96
chaos narratives, 42
Charmaz, Kathy, 172–173
Cheston, Richard, 47–48, 204–205
chronic illness, and self-identity,
    172–173, 176
Clark, Herbert
  collaborative activities, 98, 122
  storytelling in conversation, 99
Clarke, Amanda, 48
co-constructed stories, 106–107, 113, 145

cognitive resources
  and collaborative compensatory
    adaptation, 80
  and conversational storytelling,
    131, 197
  restructuring of, 200
  use of in joint activities, 21
cognitive styles, and storytelling, 94
Cohen, Lawrence, 82
collaboration
  collaborative compensatory
    adaptation, 80–81, 122–124
  commitment and support in, 121–122,
    139–140
  couples living with dementia, 138–140
  and entangled relations, 113–114
  organizing and reorganizing, 122–124
  scaffolding in storytelling, 26, 107,
    124–126
  in storytelling, 18–22, 22*f*, 47–48,
    50, 89–90
  vicarious voice in storytelling, 110–112,
    127, 182, 190, 200, 205–206
collaborative compensation
  dimensions of conversational stories,
    126–127
  and family storytelling, 115–117
  interactional patterns in, 127–130
  and joint activities, 120–122
  repair of conversations, 130–135
  use of scaffolding and gestures,
    117–120, 124–126
collaborative compensatory adaptation,
    80–81, 122–124
commitment and support, in
    collaborative activities, 121–122,
    139–140
common ground
  challenges to maintaining in
    dementia, 184–186, 188–189
  establishing, 99
  minimum required for interdependent
    identity, 189–190, 191
  for storytelling, 178, 181, 182,
    189–190, 200
communicative disabilities, and repairing
    conversations, 137–138
compensatory adaptations, 197–198
  collaboration in, 80–81, 122–124
  cultural aspects of, 81–83

planning for, 144–145
reconceptualizing
    compensation, 78–80
in response to changes in the
    brain, 77–78
compensatory strategies, in dementia
    and storytelling, 50
confabulation, and living with changes in
    brain, 69–73
contributions, nature of in collaborative
    compensation, 122
conversational repair, 78–79,
    130–135, 138
conversational storytelling, 99–101
    and cognitive and physical
        disabilities, 131
    dimensions of, 100, 126–127
    enactment in, 153–156
    incomplete turns in, 131–132
    indicating acceptance during, 98
    and meaning-making, 91–92
    progression of, 88–90
    reducing distractions, 136
    use of paraphrasing, 133
cooperation, and functional brain
    systems, 55
cortical networks, and functional brain
    systems, 56–57, 60, 62–63
co-tellership, and collaborative
    compensation, 126
Cotrell, Victoria, 7
couples
    discursive positioning, 182–184
    diverging interests and
        interdependent identity, 186–189
    epistemic challenges to
        interdependent identity, 184–185
    interactional roles in storytelling,
        127–130
    interdependence and dementia, 182
    interdependent identities, 171–172,
        178–181
    and joint storytelling, 180–181
    and living with dementia, 138–140
creativity
    and living with changes in
        brain, 69–73
    in storytelling, 202–205
cultural aspects of compensatory
    adaptation, 81–83

DeBaggio, Thomas, 53–54
dementia
    and cognitive processing, 61
    couples living with, 138–140
    cultural variation in social
        consequences of, 82–83
    etiology of, 33–34, 81–82
    historical use of term, 30–31
    and interdependent identity, 182
    and living with a changing brain,
        66–73, 178
    losses associated with, 34–35, 176–177
    medical vs. social concept of, 25
    neurodegenerative vs. vascular
        disorders, 58–60
    as neurological disorder, 31–32
    perspectives on identity and, 9–12
    progressive injuries to brain,
        53–55, 58–60
    public health issues, 32–34
    regaining personhood in, 6–9
    and self-identity, 34–39, 172–174
    as self-involving disease, 175
    self-presentation and stigma of, 13, 14
    social and relational approach
        to, 11–12
    social psychological theory of, 36–37
    and use of language, 39
dementia, and storytelling
    bounded storytellers, people with
        dementia as, 9, 81, 197
    brain injuries and behavior, 68
    challenges for storytelling, 2, 65–66
    characteristics of, 201–202
    embodied gestures, 153–156
    and embodiment of memory, 145–149
    and identity, 2–6, 199–201
    illness narratives, 18
    inquiry-guided approach to, 22–24
    and linguistic resources, 149, 197
    maintaining narrative norms, 102
    multimodal bodily engagement,
        143–144
    progression of stories, 88–90
    relevancy of, 5–6
    and repairing conversations, 137–138
    shifts in resources, agency, and voice,
        199–200
    and stages of dementia, 6
    stories and dementia, 43–47

dementia, and storytelling (*cont.*)
  use of fragments and repetitions,
    157–167
  using gestures with words, 150–152
  using open *vs.* closed questions, 136
  vicarious voices, 110–112, 127, 182,
    190, 200, 205–206
demographic factors in development of
    dementia, 33–34, 81–82
denarration, 42
depression, and symptoms of
    dementia, 60
*Diagnostic and Statistical Manual of
    Mental Disorders (DSM-5)*, 32
direct *vs.* indirect repair of
    conversations, 131
discursive positioning, couples and,
    182–184
disease
  associated memory loss, 31–32
  dementia as self-involving disease, 175
  illness narratives, construction
    of, 16–18
  narrative as illness, 41
  self-presentation and stigma of, 13, 14
disorganization, feelings of, 74–75
disruption, of everyday routines and
    habits, 74–75
distractions, reducing for
    conversation, 136
Dixon, Roger, 78
dysnarration, 41–42

Eakin, Paul, 102
economic factors in development of
    dementia, 33–34, 81–82
Ehrlich, Jonathan, 44, 45
embeddedness, and conversational
    stories, 100, 126–127
embodied communication,
    observing, 204
embodied memories, and gestures,
    149–157
  and autobiographical stories, 198–199
  embodied gestures, 153–156
  gestures and words, 150–152
  Kendon's continuum, 149–150
  from story world to conversational
    realm, 156–157
embodied storytelling

hands and eyes, 148
  the voice, 147
embodiment of memory
  components of, 143–145
  as conversational resource, 145,
    146–149
  expressions of embodied memory, 206
  physiology of, 167–168
  and storytelling in dementia, 63,
    145–149
  and use of language, 38–39
emotional support, in collaborative
    compensation, 136
enactment, in conversational stories,
    153–156
entangled stories
  and everyday narrative norms,
    113–114
  and meaning-making, 49–50, 91–92
epistemic relationships, and co-
    constructed stories, 106, 113,
    180–181
Essay on Human Understanding
    (Locke), 9–10
etiology of dementia, 33–34
eyes, and embodied storytelling, 148

factors in development of dementia,
    33–34, 81–82
families
  couples living with dementia, 138–140
  family storytelling and collaborative
    compensation, 115–117
  sharing of autobiographical
    stories, 15
fiction
  concept of unreliable narrator in, 45
  expectations of, 92–93
Fleischman, Suzanne, 203
Fontana, Andrea, 35
Forget Memory (Basting), 195
fragments and repetitions, use of,
    157–167
  in established narratives, 157–162
  existing stories as recognizable
    formats, 165–167
  themes, stanzas, lines, 162–165
Frank, Arthur, 17, 42
Freed, Paula, 77
frontotemporal lobe dementia, 59

Garrett, Douglas, 78
gaze, as sign of catastrophic
    reaction, 75–76
Gee, James, 97, 162, 164
gestures, and embodied memories,
    149–157
    and autobiographical stories, 198–199
    embodied gestures, 153–156
    gestures and words, 150–152
    Kendon's continuum, 149–150
    from story world to conversational
        realm, 156–157
gestures, substitution for words, 117–120
Gilbert, Margaret, 121
Goffman, Erving
    concept of "voice" in stories, 108
    layers in storytelling, 93
    self and identity, 12–13, 174
    storytelling face-to-face, 146
Goldstein, Kurt
    catastrophic reactions, 177
    reactions to changes in the brain,
        67–68, 74, 76
Goodwin, Charles, 146
Goral, Mira, 44–45

habits and routines
    compensatory adaptation of, 77–78
    disruption of, 74–75, 83–84
Halbwachs, Maurice, 195
Hamilton, Heidi, 45–46
hands, and embodied storytelling, 148
Hardy, Barbara, 3
Harré, Rom, 37–38
hereditary factors in dementia, 33–34
Herman, David, 93, 165
Herskovits, Elizabeth, 35

idea units, in storytelling, 96–98
identity
    couples and interdependent identities,
        171–172
    epistemic challenges to, 184–186
    importance of narrative for, 14–16
    interdependent identity, 26–27
    perspectives on dementia and, 9–12
    relationship to memory and story, 10f
    and shared storytelling, 6
identity and self
    and autobiographical stories, 199–201

and catastrophic reactions, 175–177
concept of, 12–14
conceptual issues, 172–174
couples and discursive positioning,
    182–184
and dementia, 2–6, 34–39
epistemic challenges to identity,
    184–186
holding individuals in identity,
    190–192
interdependent identity, 178–181, 182
layering of, 93–94, 103–104
revision and reconstruction of,
    177–178
and traumatic brain injury, 175–176
illness narratives
    proposed typology of, 42
    storytelling and, 16–18
Illness Narratives (Kleinman), 17
imagination, human brain and use of, 56
India, interpretation of dementia
    symptoms in, 82
indirect vs. direct repair of
    conversations, 131
inquiry-guided approach, to dementia
    and storytelling, 22–24
interactional roles in storytelling
    couples and, 127–130
    interactive repair of
        conversations, 138
    overcoming problems with,
        122–124, 130
    and sociocultural tradition, 20
interdependent identity, 26–27,
    178–181
    couples and, 171–172
    and dementia, 182
    and discursive positioning, 182–184
    and diverging interests, 186–189
    epistemic challenges to, 184–186
    holding individuals in identity,
        190–192
    minimal common ground for,
        189–190, 191
interpretive resources, storytelling with
    limited, 165–167

James, William, concept of self, 12
Japan, interpretation of dementia
    symptoms in, 82

joint activity
  co-constructed stories, 106–107, 113
  and collaborative compensation,
    120–122
  commitment required for, 139–140
  compensatory adaptations in, 80
  effect of diverging interests, 186–189
  families and autobiographical
    storytelling, 15
  and interactional roles in storytelling,
    20, 127–130
  and joint problem-solving, 138
  model for joint storytelling, 96–99
  overcoming interactional troubles in,
    122–124, 130
  providing framework for, 135
  repair of conversations, 130–135
  and the sociocultural tradition, 18–21
  storytelling as, 22f, 180–181, 198
  using individual resources in, 20–22
  using scaffolding to construct, 136
  vicarious voice in storytelling, 110–
    112, 127, 182, 190, 200, 205–206

Kelley, Harold, 179
Kempler, Daniel, 44–45
Kendon, Adam, 149–150
Kirby, Paul, 14
Kirsh, David, 79
Kitwood, Tom
  concept of personhood, 7–8
  relational approach to dementia, 11
  social psychological theory of
    dementia, 35–37
Kleinman, Arthur, 17
Kontos, Pia, 38–39, 63

Labov, William, 100
language
  and functional brain systems, 56, 60
  use of by persons with dementia, 39
Lejeune, Philippe, 102
Levinson, Stephen, 120
Levi-Strauss, Claude, 202
life stories, and narrative and identity, 15
life story work
  definition of, 48
  limits of, 205–206
  storytelling as tool in, 4
Linde, Charlotte, 101

Lindemann, Hilde, 8, 192
linearity, and conversational stories, 100,
  126–127
lines, in story repetitions and fragments,
  162–165
linguistic resources
  and use of gestures in storytelling, 149
  use of in joint activities, 21
Listening with a Third Ear (Reik), 204
Locke, John, 9–10
loss, concept of in dementia, 34–35
Luria, Aleksander, 56–58, 67
Lysaker, Paul and John, 41

Making Stories (Bruner), 5
Mandelbaum, Jenny, 107
manipulation of tools, and functional
  brain systems, 55–56
Matthews, Eric
  concept of embodiment, 38–39
  levels of individuality, 8
  narrative and identity, 16
McKeown, Jane, 48
McKim, Elizabeth, 40
Mead, George Herbert
  concept of self, 12
  identity and self as social objects, 13
meaning-making, and entangled stories,
  49–50, 91–92
Medved, Maria, 59
memoirs of Alzheimer's disease, 53–54
memory
  and aging, 31–32
  embodiment of, 198–199, 226
  and epistemic challenges to identity,
    184–185
  loss *vs.* inability to recount, 63
  multimodal memories and
    storytelling, 62, 63–66, 117–120,
    143–144, 198
  relationship with identity and story,
    10, 10f
  retrieval and production of, 167–168
  social *vs.* individual memory, 195
  and use of story fragments and
    repetition, 164–165
Merleau-Ponty, Maurice
  brain injuries and behavior, 67
  embodiment, concept of, 38
Middleton, David, 48

Mills, Marie, 47
Mishler, Elliot, 12
monological stories, 41
moral stance, and conversational stories,
    100, 126–127
multimodal memories
    and collaborative compensation,
        117–120
    and storytelling, 62, 63–66,
        143–144, 198

narrative
    and broken stories, 40–43
    dysnarration, 41–42
    fragments and repetitions of, 157–167
    illness narratives, 16–18, 42
    importance for identity, 14–16
    narrative voice, 200
    narrative worldmaking, 92–96,
        156–157
    organization of oral narratives,
        162–165, 163b
    self-identity in, 174
    significance in human history, 2–3
    and unreliable narrator, 45
    widening study of, 3
"Narrative Analysis: Oral Versions of
    Personal Experience" (Labov &
    Waletzky), 100
narrative environment
    and family storytelling, 116
    restoring, 48–49
narrative norms, 90–91
    in autobiographical stories, 102
    confronting, 196–197, 203–204
    in conversational stories, 112–113
narrative scaffolding
    as collaborative activity, 26
    and collaborative compensation,
        124–126
    and couples, 138–140
    and redistributing activities and
        responsibilities, 107
neurodegenerative disorders
    living with changes in brain, 66–73
    vs. vascular disorders, 58–60
neurological disorder
    and availability of narrative resources,
        41–42, 62
    dementia as a, 31–32

New Language for Psychoanalysis, A
    (Schafer), 173
Nochi, Masahiro, 175–176

Ochs, Elinor, 100, 106
Organism, The (Goldstein), 67–68

paraphrasing, and repair of
    conversations, 133
Perkins, Michael
    compensatory adaptations, 77
    repetitive questions in conversation,
        136–137
    stories and dementia, 43
personal agency, and storytelling, 199
philosophy, and approaching dementia
    and storytelling, 12
Phinney, Alison
    entangled stories and
        meaning-making, 49
    stories and self-identity, 5
    unknowable and untellable stories,
        204–205
physical disabilities, and conversational
    storytelling, 131
policy issues, and dementia, 32–34
Presentation of Self in Everyday Life, The
    (Goffman), 12–13
primary self, concept of, 37
principal voice, as narrative concept,
    108–109, 127
progressive aphasia, 59
pronouns, and self-identity, 174
psychology, and approaching dementia
    and storytelling, 12
public health issues and
    dementia, 32–34

questions, using open vs. closed, 136
quest narratives, 42

Ramanathan, Vai, 45–47, 88
Randall, William
    family storytelling and narrative
        environment, 116
    restoring narrative
        environment, 48–49
    stories and self-identity, 40
reality in storytelling, multiple
    realities, 93–96

reconstruction of self and identity,
177–178
Reik, Theodor, 204
relational approach to dementia, 11–12
Remembering (Bartlett), 168
reminiscence, using autobiographical
stories for, 48–49
repair of conversations
anticipating, 135–136
in cases of communicative disabilities,
137–138
and collaborative compensation,
130–135
and compensatory adaptation, 78–79
identifying need for, 137
interactive repair, 138
repetitions and fragments, use of,
157–167
as established narratives, 157–162
existing stories as recognizable
formats, 165–167
themes, stanzas, lines, 162–165
resourcefulness, in storytelling, 202–205
resources, use of in joint activities, 20–21
restitution narratives, 42
restorying, and aging, 4
Retelling a Life (Schafer), 174
revision of self and identity, 177–178
Rhetoric of Fiction, The (Booth), 45
routines and habits
compensatory adaptation of, 77–78
disruption of, 74–75, 83–84

Sabat, Steven, 37–38
Sacks, Oliver, narrative as illness, 41
Salas, Christian, 77
Saver, Jeffrey, 41
scaffolding
and co-constructed stories, 107, 113
and collaboration in storytelling, 26,
117–120
and diverging interests, 186–189
and indirect repair of conversations,
131, 135
open *vs.* closed questions, 136
overcoming problems with interaction,
124–126
planning for, 135–136, 144–145
types of, 135–138
Schacter, Daniel, 167

Schafer, Roy, self and identity, 12,
173, 174
Schiffrin, Deborah, 101–102
schizophrenia, broken stories in, 41
Schultz, Richard, 7
Schütz, Alfred, 93–94
*Self, Senility, and Alzheimer's Disease in
Modern America* (Ballenger), 31
self and identity
and autobiographical stories, 199–201
and catastrophic reactions, 175–177
concept of, 12–14
conceptual issues, 172–174
couples and discursive positioning,
182–184
and dementia, 34–39
epistemic challenges to identity,
184–186
holding individuals in identity,
190–192
interdependent identity, 178–181, 182
layering of, 93–94, 103–104
revision and reconstruction of,
177–178
and traumatic brain injury, 175–176
self-identity
maintaining, 101–102, 157–158
media for projecting, 174
self-making
as collaborative exercise, 73
positioning self and story,
103–106, 113
self-repair of conversations, 130
semantic dementia, 59
semiotic resources
and autobiographical storytelling,
63–66, 157–158
and collaborative compensatory
adaptation, 80
diminishment of and story
enactment, 153–156
restructuring of, 200
use of in joint activities, 21
semiotic signs, and embodiment of
memory, 146–149
sense-making, as collaborative
exercise, 73
Slobin, Dan, 63
Smith, Barbara Hernnstein, 91
Smith, Ronald, 35

social approach to dementia, 11–12
social consequences of dementia,
    cultural variation in, 82–83
social factors in development of
    dementia, 33–34, 81–82
social isolation, in reaction to changes in
    the brain, 77
social memory, 195
social objects, identity and self as, 13, 15
social psychological theory of dementia,
    36–37, 54–55
social sciences, and approaching
    dementia and storytelling, 12
social self, concept of, 37
sociocultural tradition, and joint
    activity, 18–21
stanzas, in story repetitions and
    fragments, 162–165
stories
    basic theoretical structure of, 61
    co-constructed stories, 106–107,
        113, 145
    couples and joint stories, 180–181
    defining, 91–92
    limits of, 205–206
    positioning self and story,
        103–106, 113
    teller as character in, 174
    units of, 163b
stories, entangled stories
    and everyday narrative norms, 113–114
    and meaning-making, 49–50, 91–92
storytelling
    and care contexts, 4
    and cognitive styles, 94
    collaboration in, 18–22, 89–90,
        113–114
    common ground for, 99, 178, 181, 182,
        189–190, 200
    conversational storytelling, 99–101
    creativity and resourcefulness in,
        202–205
    effect of dementia on, 61
    as embodied activity, 201
    existing stories as recognizable
        formats, 165–167
    family storytelling and collaborative
        compensation, 115–117
    fictional storytelling, expectations
        of, 92–93

and functional brain systems,
    55–58, 62–63
illness narratives, 16–18
joint storytelling, 22f, 198
joint storytelling, couples and,
    180–181
joint storytelling, model for, 96–99
laminated or layered nature of, 93–94
with limited interpretive resources,
    165–167
multimodal resources for, 62,
    117–120, 198
multiple realities in, 93–96
narrative norms in, 26, 90–91,
    112–113
positioning self and story,
    103–106, 113
realms of, 93–96, 94f, 105–106,
    156–157
and regaining personhood, 6–9
relationship to memory and identity,
    10, 10f
relevancy of in dementia, 5–6
role of brain in, 60–63
shared storytelling and identity, 1, 2, 6
as socially distributed ability, 107
social organization of, 195–196
"thinking for speaking," 63–66
varieties of, 6, 9
vicarious voices in, 110–112, 127, 182,
    190, 200, 205–206
voices in, 107–112, 127
storytelling, and dementia
    bounded storytellers, people with
        dementia as, 9, 81, 197
    brain injuries and behavior, 68
    broken stories, 4–6, 40–43
    challenges for storytelling, 2, 4, 65–66
    characteristics of, 201–202
    embodied gestures, 153–156
    embodied memories, 145–149
    fragments and repetitions, 157–167
    gestures with words, 150–152
    identity and self, 199–201
    inquiry-guided approach to, 22–24
    intersecting academic traditions, 12
    and linguistic resources, 149, 197
    maintaining narrative norms, 102
    multimodal bodily engagement,
        143–144

storytelling, and dementia (*cont.*)
 open *vs.* closed questions, 136
 progression of stories, 88–90
 and repairing conversations, 137–138
 shifts in resources, agency, and voice, 199–200
 stories and dementia, 43–47
Streeck, Jürgen, 153
support and commitment, in collaborative activities, 121–122, 139–140

tellership, and conversational stories, 100, 126–127
themes, in story repetitions and fragments, 162–165
Thibaut, John, 179
tools, human brain and use of, 55–56
Turner, Mark, 165

uncontrolled narration, 41–42
undernarration, 42
unreliable narrator, concept of, 45

vascular disorders, *vs.* neurodegenerative disorders, 58–60
voice
 concept of in storytelling, 107–112, 127
 and embodied storytelling, 147
 vicarious voice in storytelling, 110–112, 127, 182, 190, 200, 205–206
Vygotsky, Lev, 18, 56–57

Waletzky, Joshua, 100
Williams, Gareth, 16, 177–178
withdrawal, as sign of catastrophic reaction, 76–77
worldmaking, in narratives
 gestures and, 156–157
 positioning self and story, 103–106, 113
 story world model, 92–96
Wounded Storyteller, The (Frank), 17

Young, Kay, 41